Praise for Danny Wallace and *Join Me!*

"One of the funniest stories you will ever read." —*Daily Mail* (London)

"Extremely enjoyable... one cannot help wondering whether he has stumbled over the future of spirituality." —*The Daily Telegraph* (London)

"Hilarious and brilliant." —*The Bookseller* magazine (UK)

"[Wallace is] a very funny man." —Stephen Fry, actor and comedian

"*Join Me!* is the kind of book I love: effortlessly funny, painfully accurate and entertaining to the very end. Brilliant."
—Mike Gayle, author of *My Legendary Girlfriend* and *Mr. Commitment*

"If [Danny Wallace] doesn't make you join, he will almost certainly make you laugh." —Rebecca Dickinson, *The Big Issue* (UK)

Danny Wallace is an award-winning comedy producer and journalist who was recently appointed head of new comedy development for the BBC. He lives in London.

Visit www.joinme.info

suits
HE LEADE
IN U
US

JOIN ME!

DANNY WALLACE

A PLUME BOOK

PLUME
Published by the Penguin Group
Penguin Group (USA) Inc., 375 Hudson Street, New York,
New York 10014, U.S.A.
Penguin Books Ltd, 80 Strand, London WC2R 0RL, England
Penguin Books Australia Ltd, 250 Camberwell Road,
Camberwell, Victoria 3124, Australia
Penguin Books Canada Ltd, 10 Alcorn Avenue, Toronto,
Ontario, Canada M4V 3B2
Penguin Books India (P) Ltd, 11 Community Centre, Panchsheel Park,
New Delhi—110 017, India
Penguin Books (N.Z.) Ltd, Cnr Rosedale and Airborne Roads, Albany,
Auckland 1310, New Zealand
Penguin Books (South Africa) (Pty) Ltd, 24 Sturdee Avenue, Rosebank,
Johannesburg 2196, South Africa

Penguin Books Ltd, Registered Offices: 80 Strand, London WC2R 0RL, England

Published by Plume, a member of Penguin Group (USA) Inc.
First published in Great Britain in different form by Ebury Press.

First Plume Printing, March 2004
10 9 8 7 6 5 4 3 2 1

Photographs by Danny Wallace, Bob Glanville and Sarah Hogan

 REGISTERED TRADEMARK—MARCA REGISTRADA

CIP data is available.

ISBN 0-452-28501-1

Printed in the United States of America

This is for my grandma, Irma Breitenmoser.
And, of course, for Gallus.

Never doubt that a small group of thoughtful, committed citizens can change the world.

Indeed, it's the only thing that ever has.

—Margaret Mead

WANTED:
AMERICANS

I require Americans just like you to Join Me!

Joining Me is easy! Simply send
one passport-sized photograph to . . .

Join Me, P.O. Box 33561,
London, E3 2YW, England

And that's that!

So Join Me! Do it! Join Me now!
And together we will tidy up the Americas!

www.joinmeusa.com

PROLOGUE

Hello there. My name's Danny. And I've been thinking a lot about Americans lately.

Americans like you.

You see, over here, in Britain, you see rather a lot of Americans. Sometimes you notice them in shops, or on buses, speaking in their American voices and saying their American things. You see them on TV and in films, too, in all their different American shapes and American sizes.

There are big ones, small ones, white ones, black ones. There are tall ones, short ones, fat ones, thin ones. There's even a gay one.

And I like them.

You're friendly, you Americans, and you often come up with some quite unusual words and phrases, which I like to make a note of as I wander around what I believe you sometimes term "the jolly old London."

And you're right; London *is* jolly. Especially *now*. Especially for *me*. Because I've been doing my best to *make* London jolly. And not just London—lots of places. And not just me—lots of people. Lots of people who I hope, over the next few hundred pages or so, you'll want to get to know. Lots of people, in fact, who I hope you'll want to *join*.

Because I need you.

I should explain. This was never supposed to be a book. It was meant to be a bit of fun. A piece of random whimsy. It turned out to be something far bigger—something which would affect thousands of lives, in hundreds of places, right across the world, bringing me new friends, a little bit of heartache, and a whole heap of satisfaction. Something which would, in fact, become . . . well . . . important, somehow.

So important, in fact, that this week, with no real planning whatsoever, I spent several thousand dollars that I don't really have.

And right now, I am on a plane. A plane heading for America. My next stop on what has become an international quest. A global mission. A nice way to spend an afternoon.

In three hours, I will be landing in New York.

And in New York, I will be meeting a man.

I don't know much about this man. Only his name, his address, what he looks like, and that he responded to the rather pricey advert I placed in this week's *Village Voice* newspaper.

He knows far less about me. He doesn't know my name. He doesn't know my face. And he certainly doesn't know that late last night I decided to buy a ticket to America, that early this morning I boarded a plane, and that soon I will be in a yellow taxi burning through Manhattan, toward the apartment block in which I hope and plan and pray I'll find him.

Because that man is my first American joinee.

I am his Leader.

And this is where my American adventure will begin.

My name is Danny Wallace. I am a cult leader. I need your help. And the next three hundred pages will tell you why . . .

Danny Wallace
Somewhere over the Atlantic
Fall 2003

Joinee Jonesy

CHAPTER · 1

> 1. *In the beginning was the Word.*
> 2. *And the word was There.*

There is a man who lives in Camden, North London, who once made me very happy.

He'd written me a letter.

This is what it said:

To whom it may concern,

As requested, here is my passport photo. I have also troubled myself to include our local Indian restaurant menu, and can recommend the Chicken Dansak if you're ever in the area and feeling hungry. I look forward to hearing about the next step in our endeavors.

Cheers, *Christian Jones*
London NW1

I'd opened it immediately and excitedly, and then read it over and over again. I found it one of the most incredible letters I'd ever received. Why? Because it was a reply to my advert. The advert I'd placed on a whim. And it contained a passport photo of Christian, smiling. Smiling at me, the bloke he'd joined.

"Wow," I'd said to myself. "Someone actually did it . . ."

I was overawed. I had my first joinee. A new best friend, of sorts. I mean . . . imagine it. From now on, whatever happened, I would always have this; I would always have Christian Jones of London NW1. Even if no one else ever deemed me worthy of joining in the future . . . even if no one in the entire world ever wanted to accept my offer again . . . Chris Jones was mine, and mine alone. My friend. My mate. My cheeky-faced pal.

Granted, we hadn't actually *met* yet, and if it came down to it and the whole world treated me with disinterest and scorn, why would he feel any different? But I had a hunch Jonesy wouldn't desert me. We'd come this far, me and him, and besides, I was already calling him "Jonesy."

• • •

I should probably explain.

You see, like all good books, this one takes place just after the death of an old Swiss man. And, like all good books—modern classics, you might say—this one unwittingly began life in spring, on a farm, in a village, in a Switzerland sprinkled with sunlight and dew.

It's early afternoon, and the old Swiss man is tired.

He's not as young as he used to be—because he's old—and the farm he once ran with tireless efficiency has got the better of him, as it does every day now. He hasn't many animals, nor many crops, but he still tries to clean out the cowshed and find fresh hay for the goats and keep up with the weeds, which never seem to tire as he does, the weedy green bastards. He is ninety.

His wife died some years before, leaving the old man to cook himself some lonely and basic meals of potato and ham, and it's some time after lunch, when the day is already nine hours old for him, that he decides to head back to the untidy wooden house to take his afternoon rest. There are still things to do, but they can wait, they can wait, because he must rest, he must rest.

He washes his face and hands with one of the lavender soaps his wife had collected but rarely used, lies on his bed, closes his eyes and exhales. The sun is draped around the room, sneaking through the dark slats of the window, dousing the place in muted amber. The only sound is the distant clank of a dozen cow bells on the hillside, and the whistley wheeze of this old, tired man.

He falls into the deepest of sleeps, the last one he'll ever need, the last he'll ever be given.

And the old Swiss man pops his old Swiss clogs.

If indeed the Swiss have clogs. I don't know. I'm only half-Swiss. And it's not even my best half. I'm still at home in London, probably playing on my PlayStation, or staring at my feet, unaware that any of this has even happened.

I soon would be.

And how.

• • •

I studied the menu Chris had enclosed with his letter. "The Madras Valley . . . 123 Castlehaven Road, northwest London." It looked great. Maybe I was romanticizing it slightly because of the mood I was in, but I don't think that any restaurant has ever seemed so appealing as the Madras Valley did at that moment.

"We are proud of our chefs and our management," it read. "We are proud that you the customer choose us to satisfy your appetite." Well, that was lovely. They hadn't needed to write that, but they'd done it anyway. What a great world my joinee lived in. A friendly world, where restaurants are proud of themselves, and you get a free bottle of Coke with every takeaway order over £15.

And this sealed it for me: "Our chef has twenty years experience as a chef." Oh, Jonesy knew his stuff when it came to restaurants, all right. He was a man of taste. A man of quality. A man I knew I should know.

I imagined our shared future. I imagined our summers in the park, drinking cool beers and kicking a battered old football around, laughing like ladies in the afternoon sun. I imagined us marrying twins, and living next door to each other, and going halves on a caravan we'd take to the Lake District twice a year. I imagined growing old with him, maybe by now having to share just the one twin wife, trading in the caravan for a timeshare on the coast . . . and you know what? Life would be good. Life would be great. Because Jonesy would be there.

"Who is that a picture of and why are you staring at it?" said Hanne, my girlfriend, suddenly there, interrupting my dreams of what might be. She was drying her hair and smelled of coconuts.

"It's Jonesy," I said.

"Who is Jonesy?" she said, moving closer to take a look. "And why are you grinning like that?"

"I can't help it," I said. "He makes me happy. Look at his face!"

I held Jonesy's picture up. Hanne didn't react. I pointed at it with my finger, as if that would somehow help. Hanne looked at Jonesy, and then looked at me in the way I imagine some people get looked at after treading on a kitten.

"Right," she said, unsurely. "And why does he make you happy?"

"He just does," I said, tucking the photo into my shirt pocket. "He's got a happy face."

"You know who have happy faces? Simpletons."

I made a point of ignoring this unnecessary slight against my new friend by merely grinning at her, but suddenly felt as if I were proving her point for her.

"Anyway, why do you have a picture of this man?" she asked.

I decided to try and subtly change the subject.

"Shall we go out now?"

It's as subtle as I get under pressure.

"Where?" said Hanne.

"I don't know. I have absolutely no idea where we could go or what we could do once we got there."

I left a pause long enough for me to fake having an idea.

"How about we go to northwest London for a meal at a quality restaurant?"

• • •

I realize, now, that I haven't really given you ample explanation as to what this whole "joining" business is all about. Well, like those who have joined me, you'll just have to trust me for a bit. At least you know what my name is. You know I'm a bloke. You know my girlfriend sometimes smells of coconuts. You've probably guessed I live in London, given that I was about to head off to a restaurant there. And you know I was excited.

I could scarcely contain myself, in fact. I was about to visit a restaurant recommended to me by the first person ever to have joined me. The first person to have sent his passport photo in, and, consequently, the first to have committed himself to my cause. My grand quest. My very important mission.

What cause? What quest? What mission? I'm still not telling you. Not yet.

But I had to hand it to him: he'd acted bravely. After all, as you're beginning to understand, I'd given precious little away. He'd simply seen, in that week's copy of *Loot,* a tiny, boxed, small ad, saying:

JOIN ME

Send one passport-sized photo to . . .

And then my address. That was all. All I'd written. All he had to go on. And yet he'd done it. Done it without knowing who he was joining, or what he was joining, or *why* he was joining, or even what "joining" meant. Truth is, at this stage, even I wasn't bothered about any of that stuff. I was just overjoyed that he'd joined.

I'll be honest: I instantly wanted to meet him. But what would we talk about? How would I introduce myself? Would I just say "Oh, hello Christian Jones, my name's Danny, and you agreed to Join Me without really knowing who or what or why you were joining . . . Fancy a curry?" He'd scream and run away, and it's better to have no joinees at all than one who thinks you're probably about to try and get off with him.

But anyway, I wasn't going to actually *meet* Christian Jones. Not tonight. That'd be crazy. Creepy, even. No, I was simply going to take my girlfriend to a local curryhouse for a local curry. The fact that it was *Chris's* local curryhouse and not mine was by the by.

I grabbed my coat. We were off.

Well, I grabbed my coat, waited the best part of an hour for Hanne to choose between one pair of black trousers and another virtually identical pair, had a cup of tea, approved the trousers, and *then* we were off.

• • •

Now, all this talk of restaurants, tea and black trousers may all *sound* very exciting, but rest assured, my life wasn't always this enthralling.

Two weeks earlier, in fact, I was bored.

I'd been bored for a while, but this one day in particular was actually a day I found especially boring. That's not to say it had been uneventful—far from it. Already, today, I'd stubbed my toe and burnt an egg. So I think you'll agree, it was all happening, round my way.

And I'm not even usually someone who gets bored. I'm a go-getter, a jet-setter, a heavy-petter. I know what I want out of life, and by gracious, I know how to get it. But what I want out of life is usually a nice cup of tea and a biscuit, and how to get it involves nothing more than a short stroll to the kitchen, so I'm not sure if that really counts alongside the achievements of others.

But please don't start thinking this is because I'm lazy. I'm not. I can find plenty of ways to fill my days. Plenty of ways that I find completely entertaining and important and vital, but which my friends and acquaintances—and probably *their* friends and acquaintances—find rather . . . well . . . pointless. But then, that's half the point. Why commit yourself to a life of entirely admirable research? Why dedicate yourself completely and utterly to the pursuit of things that might actually make a difference? Yeah, yeah . . . it's *useful* and *worthy* and *useful*. But when's *useful* ever been *fun?*

So these days, I seemed to be doing a lot of sitting down. A lot of glancing about. A lot of wondering whether or not I should be doing something else. Something more important. Something for which someone would actually pay me some money. In an ideal world, of course, I'd be a NASA engineer, already being rather adept at just sitting on a chair, staring into space.

I used to work for the BBC, an organization guaranteed to impress elderly relatives, but had found myself hankering after the good old days, when I'd had no real responsibilities, no one asked me about budgets or to look at a spreadsheet, and, most importantly, when I could sit about for hours in my pants. I'd agreed to work on one more program—a lighthearted documentary about the merits of astrology—and then I would return to my previous life for a while. I'd managed to convince a few friends who work on magazines to throw some reviews my way, so I could spend my days watching films, playing videogames and scratching.

Although that implies that I have friends on magazines dedicated to scratching, and I would like to stress at this point that I do not.

Hanne hadn't been particularly happy with my move away from the BBC. She'd liked me working there. She'd liked the fact that—despite no one really knowing what one is or what one does—she could call me a "producer." She'd liked having lunch in the BBC canteen, and drinking in the BBC bar, and getting ten percent off BBC mugs and pencil cases. Plus, it was all a lot more respectable than telling people your boyfriend just sits at home in his pants, scratching, which is something she did actually once tell someone. But while I'd imagined my days working at home would be the perfect tonic to the drudgery of office life . . . well . . . things could actually get a little dull. Even with me around.

The problem was, I'd only recently moved into my flat, having come out of a happy flatshare with my good friend Dave. We'd been flatmates first of all in Harrow-on-the-Hill, and then in the East End of London, where we'd got up to all sorts of mischief and japes. But since the day we'd decided that our flatmate days were over, I'd had rather a lot of time on my hands. There was something about having a flatmate which made it all right to do nothing. To just sit there, commenting on the world, observing it go by. Chatting there, with him, was only one step away from being an intellectual, in my opinion. In fact, it may even have been one step *up* from being an intellectual. We got a lot done. Put the world to rights. Solved a lot of very difficult problems, over cups of tea and cans of Stella. It is my considered opinion that if, say, a celebrated intellectual such as Samuel Pepys had had a flatmate, he'd have gotten a lot more done, and perhaps his so-called diaries might be a little more helpful to modern man than they are.

Now, fair enough, many of the conversations I enjoyed with Dave revolved around what you civilians might term "the trivial" . . . but to us, the trivial was to be celebrated. Dissected. Discussed. It was a good way to live, and I missed it sometimes. Like today, for example. Sitting alone, telly off, with Dave an entire East End mile away from me, probably doing precisely the same thing as I was. I stood up and walked to the corner of the room, picked up the phone, and dialed his number. He wasn't in. I made a cup of tea. I rang him again. He still wasn't in. This was odd. *I* was in. Why would *he* be out?

I wandered aimlessly around my flat, from window to window, peering out from time to time to take in my East London view. The railway line that ferries commuters from Liverpool Street Station to their homes in deepest, darkest Essex. The bus garage, which, late each night, welcomes all the number eights that've been driving from Bow to Oxford Circus and back again all day, and lets them rest until very early the next morning. The council high-rises, lined up in a neat row, with their dodgy hallway lights that blink, twitch and stutter. In the distance, Canary Wharf and the Millennium Dome. Closer, the corner shop. A magpie nest in a tree. A bloke on a bike. Some lampposts. A dog. A fence. A car. A van. A bin.

Christ, I was bored.

And then the phone rang. I looked at it. It could only be Dave.

It wasn't. It was my mum, and she was close to tears.

That afternoon, one of our family had died. Not someone I'd been particularly close to—the fact that I had to strain to remember if we'd ever actually met pointed to that—but someone whose presence had always been felt. My great-uncle. A farmer by the name of Gallus Breitenmoser.

He'd passed away that afternoon, in his sleep, in his bed, on his farm, in his village, in his clogs, which he'd popped.

I'm not certain about that last bit. I suppose I added it for some kind of vague comic effect, but the truth is, it wasn't that kind of day any more. My mum's voice cracked with emotion on the other end of the line. I hadn't known Gallus too well—I'd grown up in Britain, after all—but the sound of my mum's voice, as flat and down as ever I'd heard it, was enough to trigger a real sadness in me. It was a day I'd remember for that. But it was also a day I'd come to remember as one that would affect my life in a thousand different ways.

Ways that would confuse me, bewilder me, make me happy, sad and proud. Ways that I still can't fully comprehend or appreciate. Ways that changed my world.

Yep. This day, this dull and boring day . . . this is the day it all began . . .

Gallus Breitenmoser (1912 – 2002)

CHAPTER · 2

6. *It came to pass that Daniel entered the land of the Swittish, wherein were gathered a multitude of his elders and kinsmen.*
7. *And they lifted up their voice with instruments of musick, with cymbals, psalteries, and with harps.*
8. *And it was a day of gladness and feasting, and a good day.*

"So, Daniel," said my auntie. "What are you doing with yourself these days?"

I thought long and hard about how to answer her. Probably *too* long and hard, because she wandered off and started talking to someone else.

I was in the small Swiss town of Mosnang, an hour and a half out of Zurich, and it was ten minutes after Gallus Breitenmoser's funeral. In those ten minutes I had been asked by nearly every member of my family what it was I was up to, and struggled each time to answer them adequately. In the old days, I'd been able to just mutter something under my breath, and so long as they'd heard the letters "B," "B" and "C," all was well with the world. Now, though, I didn't really know what I was doing with myself. I'd lost my sense of purpose. My sense of direction in life.

I broke away from the crowd and wandered around Mosnang for a while—an achingly Swiss town, with vast wooden houses, dozens of green-slatted shutters and elaborately painted facades, scattered across daisy-covered hills, and surrounded by happy cows and goats. The kind of town you'd have drawn when you were a kid, and had only the slightest grasp of basic town planning. Past the houses and cows, the mountains in the background made every view from every angle a timeless picture postcard in itself. Nothing ever changed too much here. This could have been any year, any era. I stood and stared for a while. It was just past noon and the sun was shining, the air was warm, and an insect was trying to mate with my face.

I decided I shouldn't worry too much about what I was doing with my life. I mean, look at this place. It was beautiful. Sure, I'd had to lose a great-uncle to see it, but that's what life is all about: give and take.

Gallus had been lucky to see this kind of thing every day of his life, smoking his pipe as he sat on the hillsides. I'm sure *he* hadn't worried about where he was going or what he was doing. He was, by all accounts, a deeply happy man. Content with his lot. Satisfied. I knew I needed to be more like Gallus. Just slightly less farm-based, and, crucially, considerably more alive.

I made it back to the church in time to meet my family for lunch. We sat on a long table, on the lawn outside the local tavern, on wooden benches that creaked with every burst of laughter. There were fourteen of us in all; not a bad turnout for the old fella, though many of us, I suspected, may have seen the funeral as a handy excuse for a family get-together.

I was placed between my grandma and one of my great-aunts.

"So, Daniel," said my great-aunt, who despite pushing ninety took up English lessons only two years ago. "What do you do now with you?"

I thought long and hard about how to answer her, hoping that she too would lose interest and maybe start eating her baguette, or something, but she wasn't budging. Great-aunts rarely do. That's why you can never get a seat at an old people's home.

"Oh, you know, keeping myself busy with this and that," I said. "But I'm really enjoying it."

This seemed to satisfy her, and she tucked into her baguette.

"And how is Hanne?" asked my grandma.

"She's great," I said.

And she was. Hanne and I had been going out for over three years.

We'd met at university, and discovered an uncanny amount of things in common. She was two years below me, for example, and the first night she invited me back to her university room I was somewhat surprised to find that it was the same room I had occupied two years earlier. We chose to interpret that one-in-eight-hundred chance as fate, and had been together ever since. It was a happy relationship. I was prepared to forgive her slight Norwegian quirks, she was prepared to forgive my entire personality.

The family ate, and laughed, and reminisced. My uncle Rico got his guitar out and sang a song. My cousins clapped along. Everyone—apart from me—told stories about Gallus; Gallus the ladies' man, Gallus the adventurer, Gallus the clown . . . and I was fascinated by what I heard. Fascinated by one thing in particular. The one thing people kept mentioning, but not elaborating on. Much of the talk was in Swiss German, a language I only barely understand, so that may have been part of the problem, but what I picked up sounded rather interesting. It seems Gallus hadn't always been the happy and satisfied man I'd thought he was. And at one point I was sure I'd heard the German word for "commune" thrown in, followed by intense laughter. I tried to ask questions, tried to get a word in, but they were laughing too hard, the conversation was moving too quickly, and soon everyone was talking about different, unrelated things.

"Grandma," I whispered. "What was all that about Gallus and communes?"

Grandma laughed.

"Nothing, nothing. We were just remembering. Just a silly idea of his . . ."

"Of whose?"

"Of Gallus's. Just a silly idea. He could be a silly man. Silly."

I wanted to know more but it was time for coffee, and my grandma stood up to pour. Whenever I was a kid and with the family, they'd all opt for coffee after a meal, while I would still be drinking my Coke. My grandma would, *absolutely without exception,* mistake my Coke for coffee and proceed to top it up with milk. For years I thought that was how you were supposed to drink it, despite the tears and retching.

Later in the afternoon, we visited Gallus's somewhat dilapidated farmhouse to take one last look around. Most of his possessions had been packed away and stored by now, a dark and dour process my grandma had taken care of, but there remained a few odds and ends. We were ordered to take a souvenir each. I felt guilty. I'd hardly known the man. I elected to leave the others to pick something that would genuinely mean something to them, and I took a walk around the garden for a while.

"Daniel!" called my grandma. It was time to take something.

What was left was spread around the old wooden dining table Gallus had made himself back in the '60s, from wood he'd collected in the forest near the house. It was scratched and marked from years of use, battered from being at the center of family gatherings since the day it was made. I looked at the few things that were scattered across it, and picked up a pipe and some letters.

I popped the pipe into my mouth to try it on for size.

"Yes!" said my grandma. "It looks good!"

"Maybe I'll give it to Hanne."

"Yes!" said my grandma, again. To be honest, I don't think she'd understood me there. But we were alone now, and her full attention was mine. So I asked her again.

"Grandma, what kind of silly idea?"

"Idea?"

"Gallus. What kind of silly idea did Gallus have?"

"Ah . . ." she chuckled. "Long time ago."

"What do you talk about?" asked one my cousins, suddenly there.

"Lara, what's all this about Gallus and communes?" I asked.

"You don't know this?" she said, in disbelief.

And then she proceeded to tell me.

• • •

I arrived back at Heathrow to be surprised by Hanne.

"I thought I'd come and collect you. You've been to a funeral, after all. And also, I wanted to see if you'd brought me a present."

"Here you go," I said, pulling out the first thing I found in my pocket.

Hanne looked at it. "You have brought me a pipe," she said, matter-of-factly.

"I thought it would suit you," I said. "You know I've always fancied girls who smoke pipes."

We hugged and found the Heathrow Express together. I'd only been gone three days, but I'd missed her, and was pleased to be back in her company. We headed into London, where we had a drink and then found a restaurant in Chinatown.

What my cousin Lara had told me was still on my mind, though.

"If I said the word 'commune' to you," I said as Hanne dropped her chopsticks for the fourth time, "what would you think?"

" 'Commune'? Like, hippies and stuff? Or mad people, like cults?" she said. "Why? Are you going to live on a commune?"

"Not me. Gallus. Well, not now he isn't. But once."

"Your great-uncle? Really?"

Yes. Really. It appears that in the '40s, in the months after he'd spent his days lying on the ground with his friends on the Swiss borders, rifles aimed toward Austria and the Nazis, Gallus had become disillusioned with the small-town way of life. He'd made a few petty enemies in the town—a town of only a thousand or so—thanks to his big opinions and his big ideas. Those who ran the town looked upon him as a bit of a loose cannon, a bit of a troublemaker. Gallus wasn't happy there. But he didn't want to move to Zurich or one of the other big cities . . . they were too *zinvoll* for him. And then, one day in June, he decided he'd had enough.

"So he decided to start a commune?" said Hanne, surprised. "What a nutter!"

I didn't think he was a nutter. I thought he was a visionary. I had an amazing newfound respect for the great-uncle I'd never really known. And anyway, it wasn't really a "commune," in the strictest sense of the word, was it? He'd simply wanted to live alongside like-minded people. He had some land through various family connections, and decided he could start a large-scale farm, provided enough people joined him in the venture.

"How many people did he want?" said Hanne, smiling.

"One hundred or so," I said. "Which is actually very ambitious. I mean, he had a lot of land, but there were only a thousand people in the whole town in the first place."

"One hundred," said Hanne, shaking her head. "How many did he get?"

"Well . . . three," I said.

Hanne laughed. There was no need for that. I'm sure badgering people to join you in starting something new like that can't be all that easy. All credit to him for trying.

"He wanted one hundred and he got three," Hanne giggled. "That's not exactly a community—that's more of a houseshare!"

Hanne was starting to annoy me now.

"Well, *I* think it was very brave of him. And I'm sad that he gave up."

I was. Genuinely. That spark of passion could have gone so far. But Gallus, demoralized by a lack of interest, and, I suspect, somewhat bullied by his wife, had given up about a week after having the idea. Ten years later he sold the land. With the money he made he gave up the shop he'd been running and bought the farm he lived on until he died.

And that was that. He'd been mocked in the town, and even now, sixty years later, my grandma couldn't talk about Gallus's efforts to get people to join him without having a little granny-chuckle.

"I'm glad you don't take after him," said Hanne, finishing her wine.

I wasn't glad. Gallus had found precisely the kind of direction in life I wished I had. He'd made a decision, and he'd followed through. Not for long, but for a bit, and that was more than I was doing. I was sad that he hadn't gone all the way with his idea. I was sad that he hadn't found his hundred people. I couldn't help but feel he'd given up too early, that he'd caved in under whatever pressures he was under, that he should have given it another week, at least.

"How do you mean you're glad I don't take after him?" I said.

"Well . . . you're more sensible. Apart from ditching your job and sitting at home all day, at least. You wouldn't do what he did."

"Why wouldn't I?"

"Well, because for one thing, you don't have a farm."

"I've got my own flat," I said, slightly too defensively.

"And you'd invite one hundred people to live there with you, would you?"

"Well . . . no. But I don't think that's the important thing. I think Gallus wanted to link with people. He wanted to connect with people who thought like he did, rather than with the other people in the town."

"No, Gallus wanted to live on a big farm with all his pals and probably do ritual sacrifices and make everyone wear orange."

"It wasn't a cult. He wasn't starting a cult."

Hanne was winding me up and she was enjoying it. "I think he was. I think your great-uncle Gallus wanted to be a cult leader."

"It wasn't a cult. It was . . . a collective."

"Of three people."

"Plus Gallus."

Hanne laughed.

And then I realized how ludicrous our conversation was, and I laughed too.

• • •

But the next day, when Hanne had left my flat bright and early for work, I lay in bed thinking about Gallus. How must he have felt when he only got three people to say they'd believe in his idea? In him? Was he embarrassed? Humiliated? Had he taken it in good faith? Had he only done it to prove a point? To let the other people in the town know how strongly he felt? Or had he genuinely wanted to make a go of it?

A hundred people. I started to think about it. If I had a farm, who'd come and live on it with me? Not just *say* they would, but actually *do* it? Well . . . no one, clearly. My friends live largely in rented accommodation, where they have central heating and their own rooms, and don't have to worry about mucking out cowsheds or strangling chickens. They wouldn't join me. No one would. I shouldn't feel too downhearted about it; no one joins *anything* any more, apart from the gym, and even then that's only for show. If you're me.

I got up and jumped into the shower. Well, I got up, walked to the bathroom, and *then* jumped into the shower. I don't want you thinking I've got a shower within leaping distance of my bed, or that I sleep on the toilet. That'd be crazy. But Gallus continued to dominate my thoughts. It was stupid, and it was silly, but I still felt sorry for him. I felt guilty that Hanne had laughed at him, guilty that his actions had still caused such amusement at his own funeral, guilty that no one had wanted to join him.

What if I could make that up to him? What if I could get him his hundred people? The world's a different place now. People are more open-minded. And there are more than a thousand of them. It was a stupid idea, and I put it out of my mind immediately.

And then it popped back in.

Who'd join me? And why? Hanne had been right last night—I don't even have a farm for them all to live on. But what if *I'd* been right too? What if it *wasn't* about living on a farm? What if it was just about connecting with people? What if it was about faith in the unknown? What if was about getting people to trust in something they had no idea about?

I was now standing in the shower staring at the ceiling. I hadn't even really noticed that I was beginning to run out of hot water. Because I was lost in the possibilities.

What was I really saying here? Was I saying that I could get people to join me for no apparent reason? That I could get one hundred people to agree to let me lead them to a better way of life, without telling them what that better way of life was—without even knowing myself what that better way of life was? And, furthermore, get them to take me seriously while I was doing it?

No. Surely not.

I got out of the shower, dried myself, brushed my teeth. I wandered into the kitchen and made myself a cup of tea, and tried to forget about it.

Anyway, how would I know they were serious, these so-called "joinees"? Anyone can say yes. I'd need some indication that they were serious. They'd need to prove themselves to me somehow.

I got a piece of paper. I wrote on it. I phoned the London small ads newspaper *Loot,* and I read it out.

Three days later my small ad was printed.

JOIN ME

Send one passport-sized photo to . . .

Join Me. Two words that summed up perfectly what I wanted people to do. Join Me. Not to live on a farm in a village in Switzerland with me. Not to all dress in orange and learn chants and bang a bongo and kidnap and brainwash our family members with me. Not to do *anything* with me, really.

Just to Join Me.

I was just interested to see whether people would. And if nothing else, the small ad was a late, personal tribute to my great-uncle Gallus, to show him that at least *I* believed in what he'd tried to do. It was just a gesture, in many ways.

And then I forgot about it.

But a few days later, somewhere in Camden, northwest London, a man named Christian Jones was studying that small ad over breakfast. He read it, and read it, and didn't understand it. He was intrigued. He acted on a whim. He replied.

And with his reply was his passport photo. The one thing I'd asked for, so that I'd know he wasn't just someone who says "yes" to things. To know that he's someone who *does* things. That small amount of hassle, effort and expense—the same amount that would have put off so many other people who'd seen that ad and read those words—told me I'd found someone like me. Like Gallus. A do-er. A joinee. My first.

Had I told Hanne what I'd done, and who'd written back, I dare say that this would be the final chapter of the book, and you would have asked for your money back. I would have stopped there and then, red-faced and suitably chastened. I would have shoved the picture of Christian Jones in a drawer somewhere and put it all down to a moment of light-headed madness. I would have given up, just as Gallus had done.

But I didn't tell her. And I wasn't going to. Not now. Not yet. Not when I was starting to have fun.

And now, I think, you're up to speed.

So . . . as I was saying . . . we were on our way to the Madras Valley, in northwest London . . .

WELCOME TO

TANDOORI
TAKE AWAY

FREE HOME DELIVERY
on orders over £10

123 CASTLEHAVEN ROAD
LONDON NW1 8SJ
OFF PRINCE OF WALES ROAD
www.curry2go.cc

Open 7 Days a week
5.00pm to 11.30pm

Tel: 020 7482 6460
020 7482 6463

10% Discount on orders over £8.00
(Cash, Collection only)

Best Quality Indian Food

ONLY ONE OFFER PER ORDER

FREE BOTTLE OF COKE
FOR ORDERS OVER £15

We are proud of our chefs and our management. We are proud that you the customer choose us to satisfy your appetite.

Our chef has 20 years experience as a chef in Bombay and has introduced New dishes to this existing menu.

CHAPTER · 3

10. *Hanne took great indignation, and her face did gather blackness.*

11. *So Daniel fell on his face and offered tithes of grain.*

12. *And there was a calm.*

Hanne and I stepped onto the tube.

"Are you sure I'm going to like this place?" she asked.

"Yes. I read about it somewhere. The chef has twenty years experience as a chef," I said, remembering what the leaflet had said. I made a face like she should be impressed, but apparently she found the notion of a chef having experience of being a chef rather less impressive than I did.

"And where is it?"

"NW1," I said theatrically. I was excited.

"Oh, God. It'll take a while to get there, then. Is it worth it? Why don't we get a Chinese? We could get a bottle of wine and rent a video too."

"Nah, it won't take too long to get there. We'll be home by eleven. Sooner, if we eat fast and skip the starter and dessert and don't have any coffee or mints or too much wine."

"I can't wait," she said, rather more flatly than I think she meant to, but I shared her basic excitement. This was a restaurant recommended to me by my first ever joinee, after all. A joinee who had not only gone out of his way to send me his photo, but had even thought to enclose a menu from his favourite restaurant as well—just in case I was ever in the area and feeling peckish. Wow. This was a wonderful world, all right, and it was all thanks to people like Joinee Jones. Hey—see how nice that sounded? Joinee Jones. Lovely.

"What are you smiling about now?" said Hanne.

"I'm just . . . y'know. Enjoying the ride."

"Yes," said Hanne. "I know how much you love these filthy, deafening tube trains you have in this country."

I looked Hanne in the eye.

"Answer me honestly," I said. "Are you being sarcastic?"

"Yes," she said.

"No curry for you, then."

"Curry?"

Ah. It was at this point that I suddenly remembered that Hanne doesn't like curry—it disagrees with her.

"Yes, curry," I said. "You like curry don't you?"

"No! It disagrees with me!"

Sorry, it was actually at *this* point. But in my defense, I'd like to point out that it's precisely *because* Hanne doesn't like curry that I forgot that Hanne doesn't like curry. Because she doesn't like it, we never eat it together, so, naturally, the conversation about her not liking what we're not eating very rarely crops up. So what I'm essentially saying is, this was all *her* fault.

"This is all your fault, Danny."

Women lack logic, don't they?

"I'm sure they do other things," I said. "Every curryhouse does chicken and chips. You like chicken and chips, don't you? Come on, let's go to the Madras Valley. There'll be candles and everything. Look, we're already at King's Cross, we're only a few stops away. I'm paying."

Hanne looked annoyed but agreed.

"You've got to learn to remember facts like that, Dan," she muttered. "How come you can remember facts about helicopters and lions, but you can't remember I don't like curry?"

It's because helicopters and lions are interesting.

Ten minutes later we were walking past the pushers and tramps of Camden Town tube station.

"We should have booked a table," said Hanne, as we wandered down Chalk Farm Road. "I hate turning up somewhere and not getting a seat. It's embarrassing."

"It'll be fine," I said. "Trust me. It's a Saturday. Who goes out on Saturdays? That's so '90s . . ."

Hanne smiled, and we held hands as we crossed the road and made our way up Castlehaven Road.

"Quite a quiet road to have a restaurant on," she said, and she was right, but that just made it all the nicer as far as I was concerned. This was clearly going to be a classy joint . . . a lovely restaurant on a lovely street; a wide, tree-lined street in the heart of Camden.

I began to lose confidence, however, when I actually spotted the Madras Valley.

"Is that it?" said Hanne, her grip on my hand loosening. "Is that where you're taking me?"

"Er . . . I'm not sure . . ."

"It says the Madras Valley. That's what you said earlier. I can't believe this is the place. Why did you take me here?"

"Maybe there are two of them on this street," I said, my eyes feverishly scanning the street for some place, any place with even just a whiff of romantic candlelit dining on show . . .

"This isn't a restaurant, Danny."

I could have lied, but really, all the evidence she needed was now right in front of her. I tried anyway.

"Yes it is."

She stared at me.

"No. It. Is. Not."

She was right. It was a small room with strip lighting and a few randomly placed plants. A scrawny boy in a baseball cap sat in a red plastic chair, tapping his knee. There was a yellowing photo of a curry on one of the walls. A curry that was clearly made and photographed in the '70s. If there was one thing that wouldn't make things better right now, it was buying Hanne a thirty-year-old curry.

"This is a takeaway," said Hanne. "Very bloody romantic. A bloody takeaway."

"Well . . . yes . . . but I *said* we were getting a takeaway, didn't I?"

"No, Danny, you didn't. You said we were going to a restaurant. You said there'd be candles."

"We've got candles at home."

"Yes, and we've got a phone at home. We could have called this place and told them to deliver."

"But we wouldn't have done that, would we?"

"Why on earth not?"

"Because *you* don't like curry."

I was pleased with myself. I *was* learning to remember facts like that. I'd probably lost a great fact about a helicopter to make way for it, but hey—relationships are all about sacrifice.

"But *Jesus,* Danny! Why take me to a takeaway on the other side of London? You travel to *restaurants*—not takeaways! And you know I don't like Indian food! You did this purely because you knew I wouldn't let you order it in for us!"

"It's not my fault."

"Oh. Well, whose fault is it?"

Hmm. This was tricky. It's not as if I could really tell her, now, is it? I didn't think that explaining that a complete stranger who'd responded to a whimsical small ad I'd placed in a local newspaper had recommended the Madras Valley to me would really absolve me of all blame. It might even make me seem *sillier* to her—we've already established that women lack logic.

"Well, I'm getting the Chicken Dansak," I said, confidently, remembering Chris's recommendation. "Let's get you that chicken and chips, yeah?"

Except, of course, that they didn't sell chicken and chips.

Or egg and chips.

Or *anything* and chips.

Or chips.

To her credit, Hanne munched her way through the small box of boiled rice I bought her without doing me any actual physical harm whatsoever, and I got away with a mere stony silence as we sat on the tube train home, twenty minutes later.

"Why don't we grab a quick drink, or something?" I tried.

"Yes," said Hanne. "Why don't we? We could go right the way across London to find some fancy bar you've heard about and then find out it's a vending machine in a leisure center."

At Euston, she wordlessly got her things together and prepared to get off the train. Apparently she wouldn't be staying at mine that night. I went for a kiss but missed, and she stepped off the train, turning round just long enough to throw me a withering glance and say "*And* you made me wear the wrong trousers," before the doors closed. The withering glance made way for the back of her head and she walked off. Oops.

I reached into my shirt pocket and brought out the picture of Christian Jones. I instantly forgave him when I saw that smile. It wasn't really his fault. And he'd been right about the Dansak. If only Hanne liked curry . . . I'm sure she'd have appreciated the advice. I stared at Joinee Jones's big, grinning face and grinned back.

This man was special. He was surely a sign. And the excellent curry I'd had at his recommendation was a sign, as well. The fact that Hanne was now a bit angry with me . . . well, that was probably a sign too, but I was willing to let that one go for now.

Because all the evidence pointed to the fact that I could make this work. For Gallus, and for me. I could, theoretically, get more people like Jonesy to sign up. More people who'd want nothing more than to recommend restaurants, or send me cheerful passport photos . . . more people, in short, to Join Me. I didn't know what I'd do with them once they had, but that didn't matter, because I was sure that whatever it was I was doing was A Good Thing. It felt right. Despite the fact that I was now going home alone.

I looked forward to the future, and my next ninety-nine Joinee Joneses.

I put the photo away, leaned back in my seat, realized I'd missed my stop, swore a little too loudly and then waited forty minutes to get a train that would take me safely home.

The evening may not have gone quite to plan, but I was certain that things were about to change.

And they were.

• • •

We were in the Horse & Groom on Great Portland Street. Ian put his pint down on the table and raised an eyebrow.

"So what you're essentially saying is, you're starting a cult."

"No, not at all. Let's not start calling it a cult. If anything it's a . . ."

I struggled to find the right word. Cult was definitely not it. Cult had negative connotations. Cult implied suicide pacts, and space travel and odd chanting. No, this wasn't a cult. What had I called it before?

"It's a collective."

I let the word hang in the air. Yes. A collective. That's what this was. I looked around the pub, proudly, like I'd just answered the hardest question in a pub quiz, but no one had heard me.

"A collective of two people," said Ian. "You, and this Jones bloke. And this is all because your great-uncle decided it'd be a laugh sixty years ago? What does Hanne think?"

Ian's a radio presenter, and has an annoying knack of getting straight to the point.

"There's no need for Hanne to be involved," I said. "So don't tell her please. Not yet. You know what she's like about things like this."

"Particularly when you promise to take her to a fancy restaurant and it turns out to be some dodgy Indian takeaway. This could get out of hand, Danny. You don't want to annoy her too much. Remember what happened last time?"

And he had a point. Maybe I should explain exactly why telling Hanne what I was up to wouldn't be the wisest thing in the world to do. Hanne has, in the three years we've been going out, put up with rather a lot from me. One time, because I was bored, I'd decided that I wanted to see if I could go a whole week without once introducing myself to people I met. That failed on the first day, when Hanne had taken me to a party and everyone thought I was extremely rude. I had to pretend to be a mute at one point.

Another time, it fell to me to plan our holiday. She'd wanted to go somewhere "different but familiar." I felt this was a challenge. I started to think about where we could go that would be different but familiar. We were at my parents' house in Bath at the time, and I realized that whichever town Bath was twinned with would be quite different but at the same time fundamentally familiar. And then I discovered that Bath was twinned with *lots* of different towns. And those towns, in turn, were twinned with lots of different towns themselves. So in one busy afternoon, I planned a route around the world. I proudly showed it to Hanne.

"This is what we'll do," I said. "All these towns should really be very similar to Bath, but they'll be quite different, too. From Bath, we go to its twin town, Braunschweig, in Germany. Then we get on a train and go to one of *its* twins, Nimes, in France. After that, we head for Preston, in north England, which will be nice. Now, that's also twinned with Almelo in Holland, and once we've seen that, we'll jump on a plane and fly to Danishle, in Turkey. Then it's Frankfurt, before heading to its second twin, Milan, before finishing the holiday off with a night in Birmingham."

Hanne just looked at me. "But I want to go to Barbados."

Despite my extensive notes, maps and pleading, we went to Barbados. A few months later, I'd told Hanne I was still quite keen on playing this game of twin town dominoes. She told me in no uncertain terms what she'd do to me if I did. And yes, Milan *is* twinned with Birmingham.

Then there was the bet I'd had with my old flatmate, Dave, a year or two previously. It was a macho, booze-fuelled challenge involving tracking down and photographing dozens of men with the same name as him, which had dominated six months of our lives, sent us around the world, and very nearly cost me my relationship with Hanne. To be honest, there's a longer story there, which could almost be a book in itself. But things had got so bad at one point that Hanne had actually left me, and gone back to Norway. That scared me. I promised her that things would change from that moment on, and to be honest, they had. I'd stopped indulging myself in what she called "stupid boy-projects."

But I could feel myself starting to be pulled into that world again . . .

"I'm telling you, Dan, it's not worth it. Hanne will kill you. You know what she always says—"

" 'If you're going to be spontaneous, at least plan it properly,' yes.

But I'm not going to take this so seriously, Ian. It's just a little something to keep me occupied. And remember, it's for Gallus, not me. Anyway, no one else is going to join me, are they? I'm sure I'll get two more at most, just like Gallus, and then I'll give up. I mean, I actually want a hundred, but how's that going to happen?"

"Well, all you'd have to do is walk down Oxford Street one afternoon, I'm sure you'd get loads of people to say they'd join you."

Ah, I'd thought of that. Ian was right. Sure, I'd be able to just wander down a crowded shopping street, and sure, all the nutters would *say* they'd join me. But they wouldn't count. It's all very well *saying* . . . but I want *do*-ing. Joinee Jones had passed the first test of Join Me. He'd sent me his passport photo. He'd shown he was serious. That's all I needed; I wouldn't ask for ten percent of people's earnings, or for their first-born child, or that they all wear the same turquoise shellsuit as me. I wouldn't ask them to believe that the world is run by twelve-foot lizards, or that one day a vast celestial force will arrive to take us away on a comet, or that Elvis is dead.

I would just ask them to trust me enough to send me a photo. Just as Jonesy had done, the only man with the nerve to have joined me. God, he was brilliant.

"But what I don't understand," said Ian, "is why this bloke has agreed to join you in the first place. Given that he's no idea what it is, why would he do it?"

"I don't know. I don't care. All I care is that he's joined. Maybe he's done it because he's got a sense of adventure. Maybe he's missing something in his life and he thinks this is it. Maybe he just likes joining things. I don't know. It's interesting."

"He probably thought it was a lonely hearts ad. Maybe he's going to try and kiss you when you meet."

"I'm sure he won't do that."

"You mean you *are* going to meet him? Really?"

I thought about it. I suppose I'd just thought it was natural that we should meet at some point. If only to discuss where we were going to find a couple of twins to marry.

"I think I'd like to meet him, yes. I want to meet my joinee. Wouldn't you?"

"You're like that bloke you were telling me about that time."

I cast my mind back. Surely if I'd told Ian about a bloke once in the past I'd remember it?

"Could you be more specific at all?"

"You know. Moon man. That American fella."

"Dennis Hope? I'd forgotten about him. I'm nothing like him."

"You bloody are," said Ian.

"I'm bloody not. And don't knock him. He's a visionary. Like Gallus."

"You're *all* odd, the lot of you. But hey—at least I can say I know a cult leader now."

E-mail

To: Dennis M. Hope, President of the Galactic Government
From: Danny Wallace

Dear Dennis,
I hope you don't mind me writing to you out of the blue like this. I'm e-mailing you from London, and was hoping I could get your advice.

I have been interested in your organization since I heard someone talking about it on a bus a year or two ago.

I think it's great that you own the moon.

And it's great that, in the 23 years since you claimed ownership of Earth's nearest neighbor, the UN, Russia and the USA have all respected your claim and left you be. That's one space race you won fair and square!

I was reminded of you recently while talking to a friend about the funeral of my great-uncle.

Like you, my great-uncle had new ideas for society. Like you, he wanted people to join him in beginning something new, somewhere new. Like you, he wanted to make things better. He inspired me.

He had a quest, of sorts, one he never finished. He gave up. Well, I want to complete his quest for him. To find good, dedicated people who my great-uncle Gallus would have approved of, and ask them to Join Me.

I know that you are planning to take your people to the moon at some stage, and that you are currently looking into the practicalities of space travel. I'm not sure if I can really afford to do that with the people I hope will join me; I've no land like you, and my flat is barely big enough for me, let alone 100 others.

What I'm essentially saying is . . . is what I'm doing stupid? Should I quit now? One person—a complete stranger—has already joined me. I don't want to let him, or anyone else, down.

Please advise.

All the best,
Danny Wallace
London

E-mail

To: Danny Wallace
From: Dennis M. Hope, President of the Galactic Government

Dear Danny:

Greetings from the Lunar Embassy and the Galactic Government.

I think you are the type of individual that understands the concept of "following the little voice inside."

Your story is intriguing and relevant to what we are doing even if it has nothing to do with space or space travel.

You have found a spark of passion albeit originally from your great-uncle.

Remember this: If Albert Einstein had not understood the interests of the other mathematicians of his time he would never have been inspired to combine all the theories into one "General Theory of Relativity."

The source or journey to our passion is really unimportant.

The important part is to follow the path you feel is laid out for you. If you ever find yourself near Lake Tahoe, feel free to drop by.

Good luck, Danny.

Dennis M. Hope
President—The Galactic Government
AKA—"The Head Cheese"
www.lunarembassy.com

P.S. If I were you, I would meet with the person who has joined you.

Joinee Cobbett

CHAPTER · 4

1. *In the year one thousand nine hundred seventy and six was born to the family of Jones a son; and his name was Christian.*
2. *And he was to become the First.*

Dennis M. Hope—aka "The Head Cheese"—was a very wise man indeed. He'd been right when he'd said I should meet the person who'd joined me. I suppose I'd just been slightly nervous of being rejected or branded odd. Slightly nervous of losing my first joinee and then having to start again from scratch. But hey—this is probably what Gallus went through, and if he'd given up at this stage he'd never have got his second and third joinees.

And so I had posted a letter to Chris, heartily congratulating him on his decision to join me, explaining that I wasn't a nutter, and asking him if he fancied a pint. I enclosed my e-mail address, and a day later he replied. He was up for meeting!

We would meet local to him, back in Camden, at the World's End pub, at seven o'clock, on Tuesday night.

Before I knew it, I was there. I've always liked Camden, despite its slightly seedy feel, something it perfected in the Victorian era when it was a *fantastic* place—if you liked slums and filth. The gentrification of the last twenty years has done a lot to change that, but for me, cleaning a few buildings up is a nice effort, but if you can't stop mad-eyed men offering me crack every ten minutes, I start to forget to look out for the freshly painted windowsills.

• • •

Christian Glenn Jones was born seven months before me, in April 1976, in Kendal, Cumbria.

"It's famous for mint cake," he said flatly.

I was about to say the same thing, but with more enthusiasm.

"It's always the first thing people say when they hear the word Kendal."

I bit my lip. I tried to think of something else Kendal-related to say to impress him.

"Yes. I've eaten some of that."

It wasn't really good enough, but at least it was my own unique spin on the whole Kendal mint cake thing. Christian ignored it.

"I guess you can't blame people for that. I mean, I lived there for eighteen years and it's the only thing *I* know about the place."

"Really? There's nothing else?"

"Nothing. Well, nothing interesting. I mean, K Shoes come from there. That's where they get the 'K' from Kendal. Because that begins with a 'K,' too."

I tried to look impressed, but I could tell it wasn't working.

"And I suppose there's the River Kent, which when it's raining is the fastest-flowing river in England."

"I'll have to check that out," I said, attempting to give the impression that the very next chance I got I'd be up in Kendal with an umbrella and a stopwatch.

We both took a sip of our pints and put them back on the table, in near perfect symmetry. And then we said nothing for about ten or twenty seconds.

Finally, Chris decided to speak. He'd been building up to something.

"So . . . er . . . Danny . . . this 'Join Me' thing . . ."

"Yes?" I replied brightly.

"Well . . . I'll be honest with you. I have absolutely no idea what it is."

He smiled apologetically, as if it was somehow his fault.

"That's okay, don't worry about it."

"None whatsoever, I mean."

"It's fine!"

I flashed him a reassuring, slightly over-the-top, really-doesn't-matter smile. The type you'd flash at a very important dinner guest who'd just poured red wine over your poodle the night before Crufts.

"No, you see, what I mean is, I don't know what I've joined. I just responded to that ad for a bit of fun. I hope I'm not wasting your time, because what I'm basically trying to say is . . . what the hell *is* Join Me?"

Oh.

I hadn't been expecting that.

What was I going to say?

It sounds strange now that I think about it, but I really hadn't been expecting Chris to be quite so inquisitive. I'd been focused on discovering who *he* was, what *he* liked doing, why *he'd* joined . . . I'd forgotten he might possibly have a few questions of his own.

The fact of the matter was, I didn't know the answer to his question. What the hell *was* Join Me?

"Er . . . well . . . what do *you* think it is?" I tried, looking as mysterious and confident as I could, hoping to give the impression I knew exactly where I was going with this.

"Well, I don't know. Some kind of sinister cult?"

He started to laugh, but I cut him off.

"It's not a cult," I said, raising my finger. "It's a collective."

"A collective of what, though?"

"Er, you know . . . of people."

"Right," he said, considering my answer. He nodded to himself and took another sip of his pint. I sat back, relieved, hoping that was the end of the grilling.

"And how many people are in this collective?" continued Chris, annoyingly. He wasn't giving up. This man was the Columbo of Camden.

"Well, numbers aren't important at this stage, it's early days for the collective, and—"

"But, y'know . . . how many to date?"

"Um . . . what, in total?"

"Yes."

"Well . . ." I took a deep breath. "Two."

I watched, worried, while Chris did the math.

"Two," he said, matter-of-factly. "Right."

I suppose it must have been a bit odd for him. He'd responded to an advert saying Join Me, and that's just what he'd done. Joined Me. Me and No One Else. He was now in a "collective" of precisely two people. I could have called it a "partnership," but he might have thought I had other ideas in mind.

I could tell he didn't quite know how to react. I could tell this because he'd gone all quiet and was avoiding my eye, and he'd muttered the words, "I don't quite know how to react to that." I'd essentially just told him he was in the world's most pathetic club. We were two grown men, strangers twenty minutes earlier, and now the only two members of some kind of apparently utterly pointless organization.

What must I have seemed like to this man? A loner, reduced to advertising for friends in *Loot*. A man who, until Chris had stumbled into it, was the *only* member of *his own* club.

I looked up at Christian Jones. He was considering something. I hoped this wouldn't be the moment he said good-bye and walked out of my collective forever.

"Well," he said, tapping his fingers on the table. "Do I at least get a badge or something?"

I laughed, relieved, but there was still high embarrassment in the air. His embarrassment at being there, and my embarrassment at making him. I knew what might make it better.

"Another pint?"

"O . . . kay," said Chris, not quite straight away. "Um . . . do you mind if I call my flatmate and ask him to come over?"

I think it's safe to say I had terrified Joinee Jones.

• • •

We decided to meet Chris's flatmate, Dave, at a pub closer to their home, a five minute walk away. Possibly so that Chris would have a shorter distance to run, if it came to it. But he'd eased up now and was getting more into the idea of what we could achieve together.

The Hawley was dimly lit, and wonderfully warm. It reminded me of the kind of pub you'd see highwaymen wander into in films, a dark, but friendly place, with candles spilling miles of wax onto rough wooden tables.

"Miller?" said Chris, which kind of spoiled the effect. I was hoping for some mead, and maybe a bag of oats for my horse.

We took a seat and continued our chat. Looking back, I'm not surprised Chris decided to stay with Join Me, despite having no real idea what it was. He was already officially a charitable chap.

"I'm a property administrator for Help the Aged. It's mainly stapling, filing, the usual office rubbish. I'm a fiend at double-sided photocopying, mind. And I like it there. I believe in what Help the Aged stands for."

"It's always good to make an old man happy," I said, thinking of Gallus.

"I might have indirectly made a few of the lovable lads crack a smile in my time," said Chris. I liked his turns-of-phrase. I knew we were going to get on. Once he'd stopped being afraid of me.

"Can I ask," I said, "exactly why you . . . you know . . . joined me?"

Chris looked a little embarrassed. "I dunno. I was bored. And I wanted to see what would happen."

"Me too!" I said, delighted. Maybe I'd found a kindred spirit here.

"Hello lads," said a tall, bearded man, suddenly by our table. It was Chris's flatmate, Dave. Chris looked relieved to see him.

"Sit down," he said eagerly.

And he did.

Chris and Dave had met at university, and bonded through the constant use of a Sega Genesis. I'd worked for a Sega magazine in my teenage years, having been just as addicted as them, and so we got on brilliantly, the three of us, as we compared favorite video games and swapped stories of broken joypads and exchanges that went horribly wrong. I once swapped a *Mega Bomberman* for a *Tank Command*. I think you can see what I'm saying.

The three of us took it in turns to look at each other.

"So . . . how far's the Madras Valley from here?" I asked.

• • •

We found the Madras Valley very easily. But not because Joinee Jonesy knew the way. Oh, no. Because *I* knew the way.

It turned out that Joinee Jonesy had never even *been* there before. He'd managed to send me the wrong leaflet that day, creating yet another example of an argument with Hanne that could have been avoided by a stranger sorting their junk mail with more care.

Nevertheless, I'd decided to buy Chris and Dave a Chicken Dansak from what I'd now decided was the official Join Me Curryhouse. Dave had become far more interested in joining me than he'd been when Chris first mentioned it to him—and whether that was through meeting me, or through three pints of Stella, I felt that a spot of bribery might tip him over the edge and earn me another joinee.

Back at their flat, I was shown immense hospitality. A wonderful cup of tea. A proper plate for my curry. A side dish for my nan bread. And I was given the best chair in the living room—the electric recliner.

I decided that this was what Join Me should be all about. Friendship. Niceness. And electric reclining chairs. But this was because I was a bit drunk.

"I'll be back in a minute, I'm just going to get something," said Chris, polishing his glasses as he left the room. I spotted something that caught my eye . . . some kind of letter Sellotaped to the living room mirror. I pressed the button on the electric chair that tilted the whole thing forward until your feet touched the floor and you were more or less forced into a standing position. I started to wonder whether perhaps Chris was pilfering chairs from Help the Aged.

I read the neatly typed letter.

I, Chris Jones, bet my flatmate Dave Cobbett, that he can't have one pint of any alcoholic beverage of his choice at each tube station within zones 1 and 2 of the London Underground tube system, as shown on the map stuck on the living room mirror (above).

I looked up. There it was. Each tube station in zones one and two had been circled in red pen. I figured that was probably Dave's work. It had the look of a teacher's hand about it. I read on.

Each pint must be quaffed in the nearest boozer to its respective tube station. Mr. Jones must be present at all times to record the event for posterity. Using a camera.

I loved the fact that "Using a camera" had been added almost as an afterthought. It was as if they'd had to decide between using a camera and bringing a courtroom artist along to do sketches.

The challenge must be completed by 11:59 pm on the 24th December 2002. All other rules to be agreed as the challenge progresses between Mr. Cobbett and Mr. Jones.

Signed, Mr. Jones and Mr. Cobbett, 2002.

This was brilliant. It appealed to me immediately. It reminded me of that bet I'd had with *my* flatmate, *also* called Dave. But I was disturbed from all thoughts of that particular challenge by Chris and *his* Dave, now standing behind me.

"This is great!" I said. "Have you started?"

"Yep," said Dave.

"How many stations are there left to do?"

"Eighty-nine," said Chris. "It's a bit of a long-term project."

I knew then, beyond a shadow of a doubt, that these two men in front of me formed part of my destiny. They were dedicated and hard-working. They were up for a challenge. They would help me in my quest. They would take me closer to my goal. They enjoyed pointlessness. They were absolutely *perfect* for Join Me.

• • •

I returned to my flat that evening in high spirits. Thanks to beer and curry, I'd not only made two fine friends, but I also had another joinee. Dave had given me a passport photo as I left their flat, effectively doubling the number of joinees I had in just one short evening. I Sellotaped his photo to the fridge, and put Jonesy's there, too, while I waited for the kettle to boil.

And I smiled.

The next morning I was woken by Hanne standing over me. She'd let herself into my flat because, being deeply asleep and a boy, I hadn't heard her knocking on the door.

"Hey," she said.

"Hey," I said.

"How are you?"

"Good," I said, rubbing my eyes. "How was work?"

Hanne gets up at 4:30 every morning for work. She produces a phone-in show on LBC, a London radio station, and often pops in afterward, when I'm just about conscious and able to deal with the world.

"What did you get up to last night?"

"I was out with a couple of mates," I said. "Jonesy and Cobbett."

"Detectives?"

"Eh?"

"They sound like detectives."

"No. Jonesy works with the elderly and Cobbett works with the young. You'll have to meet them. Jonesy's got an electric chair and Cobbett has a beard."

"They sound brilliant," said Hanne, sitting down on the bed and kissing me on the cheek. "Don't forget we're going out tonight. Cecilie and Espen are going to come as well. We're meeting on Brick Lane at seven. Hey . . ."

She leaned down to pick something up. A green leaflet sticking out of my discarded jeans, with a receipt stapled to it.

"The Madras Valley?"

"Oh. Yeah. We went to the Madras Valley again."

"Again? You're obsessed with that place! Why would you go there again?"

"I . . . like . . . Chicken Dansak," I said. "And Jonesy does too. And the chef has twenty years experience of being a chef. It's good there."

Hanne just looked at me.

"I also noticed," she said, "that there are two photographs on the fridge. I recognize the first one, with glasses . . ."

"Jonesy," I said.

"Yes. Jonesy. You showed me him. But now there is another . . ."

"That's Cobbett," I said. "He's got a beard."

I wasn't making much sense yet. I hadn't had any tea.

"So why are they there? On the fridge?"

"Well . . . where else would I put them?"

"But why do you even *have* them? Who collects passport photos of their friends? And why have I never met these people?"

"They're *new* friends. What if I forget what they look like? That fridge is like a reference point for me."

"Is that why you have pictures of me in your flat? In case you forget what I look like?"

"You're not a joinee, though."

"A what?"

I rubbed my eyes and feigned waking up again.

"Oh, hello Hanne," I said. "Will you make me a cup of tea?"

• • •

I set about thinking how to get more joinees. No one else had responded to the ad as yet, but it had still worked, so I decided to put another one in *Loot*. This one would be far more specific. I drafted it up.

WANTED: 100 PEOPLE TO LIVE IN MY NEW WORLD ORDER.

Send one passport photo to: Join Me . . . xxxxx xxxxxx xxxxxxx

This is not a cult.

It was simple, it was effective, it was being phoned in to *Loot* five minutes later. I would get those hundred people for my great-uncle Gallus. Jonesy and Cobbett were just the beginning.

I thought back to what advice I'd been given by Dr. Dennis M. Hope. After all, he was a forward thinker. A guru of sorts. He'd built up a following in the US. Oh, and he owned the moon. I'd seen the proof. I'd seen his website. Ah, the Internet. A gateway to many millions of people. Real people. Real people who might join me.

I decided to start a small Internet campaign. I began by e-mailing a few of my friends. And then I e-mailed them again, and asked them to e-mail *their* friends. And then I put a small link on my own rather paltry website, encouraging anyone who happened to drop by to join me. And then I decided to go one step further, and infiltrate other people's websites, and spent a couple of hours online, copying and pasting the ad onto websites across the globe. I found discussion groups, forums, chat rooms, guestbooks. I wrote Join Me on each of them, and asked people to send me passport photos, and left my e-mail address for any questions.

I received some degree of interest and endless, tireless abuse.

E-mails came back asking me to "please not visit our website again and keep your cryptic bullshit messages to yourself." But I didn't want to be cryptic, or sell bullshit. I just wanted people to join me.

Strangers were being hostile, and I was becoming rather demoralized. And then I had an idea. I went through my e-mail inbox, which I very rarely tidy up. I found e-mails which had been sent not only to me, but to entire groups of other people at the same time. Mass e-mails from friends inviting me to birthday parties, or Christmas parties, or telling me how their trek across the Andes was going, or offering me "100 Tedious and Unfunny Things You Won't Understand About Star Wars." I collected hundreds of e-mail addresses together . . . friends of friends, people I should or could know but hadn't been introduced to yet . . . surely they'd be open to my offer of joining me? They were so *nearly* my friends already. We'd probably meet each other sooner or later, so why prolong the wait? Why not come together now?

I sent out a huge e-mail to around five hundred friends-of-friends. It was very friendly, and very open indeed. Imagine my shock, then, when I received not one friendly reply from even a single friend-of-a-friend. Oh, I received plenty of "fuck offs" and "get losts," and even one rather memorable "piss off you bosom," but not one person sent me anything I could conceivably claim was encouragement. Most people dealt me an even greater insult; they just ignored me. Why? Just who were my friends hanging out with? Several people even threatened me with physical violence. One, from a man named James, whose e-mail address I had taken from a missive my friend Steve had sent inviting us to his housewarming, went so far as to say: "Not one of my friends would hang out with someone like you so tell me how you got my e-mail address or I will find you and kick the living shit out of you."

Well, really. I hope that if I'd met him at that housewarming I'd at least spat when I talked. I vowed to start spitting on more people at housewarmings, just on the off chance our paths would cross again.

Further abuse followed. I was accused of being a cult leader, of trying to get people's credit card details, of being an American. Each of these slanderous claims hit me hard, and I realized for the first time that getting people to join me when they didn't really know who or what they were joining was going to be an uphill struggle. I had been encouraged by the ease with which I'd acquired Joinee Jones . . . and demoralized by the messages of anger I'd received from people who would ordinarily, I'm sure, have bought me a pint if they'd met me in a pub.

I felt incredibly downhearted. In a moment of sorrow, I e-mailed the man who was fast becoming my mentor, Dennis M. Hope.

Dennis,

It's not working.

After an encouraging start, I'm afraid I have been beset by misfortune. People are accusing me of being some kind of scam artist. They think I'm after their money, or I'm a lunatic, or both. I just don't know what to do.

Danny

P.S. I only have two joinees. Even Gallus managed three.

Within half an hour, Dennis had responded.

Danny,

You should only be dissuaded because of your own inner voice—not because anyone else has the opinion that you should change.

Dennis M. Hope
President—Galactic Government

P.S. If you really want people to join you, I would probably start with a website.

Of course! A website! A website was the only way I'd truly conquer the Internet. I thought about what I'd done so far and realized I'd been wrong. Maybe those people I'd e-mailed out of the blue had felt invaded. They'd felt defensive. They'd felt I'd come into their world uninvited, shouting "Join Me" and demanding their fancy Yankee dollars. They couldn't see the truth in my eyes, the hope. There was no trust there. With a website, all that could change overnight. I would be able to allow people to visit *me*. They would feel like *they* were the guests. That way, *I'd* have the authority. *I'd* be in charge. *I'd* be the one allowed to call people bosoms and tell them to piss off. *That* was the way to get them to join. Not the bosom bit, the other stuff.

So I phoned my friend Jon, a lighting engineer who's also started to dabble in web design. He met me for a coffee at Cafe Kick in Shoreditch (I had tea) and agreed to help me set up a website.

"What do you want on it?" he said.

"Well, I'm not sure. Pictures of all my joinees, I suppose. We could scan them in and stick them on, for a start. And it should tell people how to join."

"And how do you do that?"

"Well . . . I just need a passport photo."

"Sounds easy enough."

"You'd be surprised . . ."

Jon came round and started the website that afternoon. I bought the domain names *www.join-me.co.uk* and *www.joinme.info* and Jon gave the site a lovely spacelike background. We put the words "It's not a cult—it's a collective" under the title, but that was really all I'd managed to come up with, words-wise.

But Jon had cleverer ideas. He added a forum to the site, on which visitors could exchange messages and write things down for others to see. In effect, it's like having a very slow conversation. You leave a message, you come back later to see who's replied. I loved it. I was sure that this was the way that joinees could progress. They could swap notes, develop strategies and share plans.

Granted, they wouldn't actually be able to do much note-swapping or strategy-developing or plan-sharing yet—considering none of them would actually know what they had joined. But it was a gesture. A promise to them that things would become more clear. And besides, they could always use it to swap "100 Tedious and Unfunny Things You Won't Understand About Star Wars" while they waited.

I began to advertise the fact that the website existed. I left a few more messages on a few more guestbooks, and e-mailed a few friends to tell them I'd stumbled across this new website and wow—they should really check it out. Within hours of it going online, two people had used the forum. One, who simply wrote, "So what's all this about then?" (and understandably hadn't been replied to), and another, who'd found the site by accident while looking for cheaper car insurance.

In the meantime, though, I was starting to receive little trickles of interest from elsewhere on the Internet. A girl called Saskia e-mailed to ask exactly what it was I was asking her to join. A man in Cardiff had seen something I'd posted on the NME's website and wanted to know more. Someone called Jennifer asked me if I was starting a cult. And I had to start to think about how I was going to respond.

I didn't want to tell people about Gallus. That would make it too personal. I didn't want to tell them I had no idea what I was doing. That would make it too pointless. So I decided that the best course of action was to remain as mysterious as possible. I would keep my full name to myself. And I would try and give the impression that while I knew exactly what the purpose of Join Me was, I was withholding that information for the time being for reasons best known to myself. It seemed to work. I was actually convincing people . . . I could answer their questions effortlessly . . .

Q: What is Join Me?
A: Join Me is something wonderful. But something I cannot reveal much more about yet. The time will come, my people. Have faith.

Q: Is it a cult?
A: No. It is a collective. A collective of people, joined together to be as one. We will unite the world through our actions.

Q: What actions?
A: Those that we choose to take.

Q: How many others have joined you?
A: Exact figures are not helpful. We are each of us individuals; none of us numbers.

Well. It sounded better than "two." To be honest, though, I was starting to scare myself. I had started to speak out loud as I typed, in a big, booming, Brian Blessed–style voice. But people were reacting well to my replies. The more confident I appeared to be, the more open they seemed to be to my rather vague and rubbish answers.

And then it happened.

Saskia agreed to join me.

"I will trust you," she wrote. "I will send you my passport photo tomorrow."

My head nearly fell off with delight.

"You will not regret this," I replied, hiding my happiness behind mock-mysterious overtones. "Now Spread the Word. Tell your friends to join me. Together we will make a difference."

"I will," she replied, minutes later. "I will do that now."

I continued to tell the Internet about www.joinme.info late into the night, every so often receiving an e-mail about one of the posts I'd made earlier in the day, and replying to it instantly. Someone posted on the message forum, saying "How strange to have a forum populated by people whose only known commonality is their total lack of ideas about what is going on . . ."

I smiled, then laughed, then switched my computer off and stumbled into bed. It was 4 A.M., and my eyes were burning, but I was finally certain of one thing.

It was beginning. It was really beginning.

Joinee Gaz

CHAPTER · 5

5. *And it came to pass in an eveningtide that Daniel walked upon the great path of wisdom and understanding.*
6. *And beside the path he laid a stone tablet whereupon he wrote his covenant.*
7. *And a great multitude saw his words and were delivered unto him.*

It was 8 A.M. My phone was ringing. What kind of society do we live in, where someone can make your phone ring at 8 A.M.? There should be rules.

"Hello?" I croaked.

"Well, thanks a lot for last night," said Hanne.

"Eh? But I didn't see you last night."

"No, I know you didn't. We waited forty minutes for you on Brick Lane."

Argh. Shit. Brick Lane. It had completely slipped my mind.

"You should have called me!" I said.

"We did. Again and again. Your mobile was off and your home phone was constantly engaged. All evening you were on the phone. Who the hell were you talking to all night?"

"I was online," I said. "For hours and hours. I'm so sorry. Jon came round and we made a website and then I stayed online all evening and I forgot about going out."

"You made a website?" Hanne said. "What kind of website?"

"Just . . . y'know. A website. I'm so sorry. How were the others?"

"It was embarrassing, Danny. Knowing that you were just sitting there on the phone while we waited. Well, we had a very good night in the end, just so you know. We went to the Vibe bar and it was packed and it was great."

"Oh, I'm so sorry. Thank God you had a good night."

"Well, it *wasn't* a good night, actually, I was just saying that. It was a *shit* night. The place was empty. I was angry at you, and Espen and Cecilie were angry, too."

"Were they?"

"Well, no, they didn't mind. But I was *so* embarrassed. I felt like a raspberry."

"A gooseberry?"

"Don't correct my English."

"Sorry," I said. "So you felt like a raspberry . . ."

"Yes. And you did that to me. I reminded you yesterday morning, you know."

"I know. I'm sorry. It won't happen again. I'll buy you dinner. We'll go out. When are you free?"

"I'll let you know," she said. "I have to go back to work now. We're going back on air."

And she hung up.

I lay, shamefaced and embarrassed, in my bed. Which is a deeply unusual place for me to feel shamefaced and embarrassed, and anyone who says otherwise is a bloody liar.

I felt terrible for having forgotten I'd agreed to meet with Hanne and the others. It's not something I'd normally do, and it would've been nice to have been out and about last night. All I can say in my defense is I got carried away. I was enjoying myself. I had been fascinated by the responses I was getting. In fact, I'd been asleep for four hours. Surely there'd be more?

I stumbled to my computer in my boxers and switched it on. Minutes later, I was overwhelmed by the incredibly positive responses my efforts had garnered. I'd received over forty e-mails from inquisitive people around the country . . . much of my activity the night before had been on UK websites and forums, and I was now reaping the rewards. If even ten of these people joined me, not only would I have beaten Gallus's record, but I would be taking my collective up to a whopping twelve . . . equal to the number of disciples Jesus had. Not that this was about making me seem important, or setting me up as some kind of rival to the big man. No. Not at all. This was in honor of Gallus, remember. But I was energized by the interest, and my guilt for accidentally standing Hanne up all but disappeared.

I checked the forum next. There were various messages from various confused people.

I think it is so dumb to have a website about joining where all you do is talk about joining but you don't know what you are joining. I would still like to join though. Please e-mail me.

I want to join but there are no details of how to do so. Also, what am I joining?

I was hoping there'd be answers here too. Guess not. Who's running this thing anyway?

Who are you guys and what did you join? Can I join?

This was great. Complete and utter strangers were willing to Join Me for no other reason than other complete and utter strangers were doing it. I set up a proper P.O. Box address for Join Me in order to make myself seem a bit more professional, and then set about adding a little more information to the website, all of it vague and noncommital—in fact "information" doesn't seem the right word—but all of it designed to urge and excite people into joining.

As people started to mention it on other websites, or forward my Web address to their friends, more e-mails arrived throughout the day. And the day after that. And the day after that. People all over the country—teachers, students, lawyers, estate agents, even a vet—were all suddenly promising that they'd join me, and only later bringing up the rather serious question of what it was I was asking them to join.

I saved up all the offers, and at the end of the week sent one mass e-mail to those kind-hearted people who had agreed.

Dear Joinee,

Thank you. And very well done.

You are a very special person, as proved by agreeing to Join Me.

You are ace. I want you to know that.

And do not worry. You have joined nothing bad, or even slightly dodgy. This is not a cult, and will involve no space travel of any kind. Mass suicides are also positively frowned upon.

*But this *is* a collective.*

You, and many dozens of others like you, should be proud. Proud to have helped me start doing something that will ultimately make my gran smile for many months to come. Proud to be part of this wonderful brother-and-sisterhood.

And below that, I asked them to send me their passport photos, stressing that only then would they truly be my joinees.

I sat back and waited. But even I wasn't expecting, two days later, to receive, in the post, fourteen separate envelopes, all addressed to JOIN ME.

Fourteen.

All. At. Once!

Fourteen!

Imagine the delight that was spread over my face that morning as I stooped to pick up my post. Imagine the delight, and excitement, and pure undiluted joy. I had overtaken Gallus's record in a little under a week! With Jonesy and Cobbett on board, I'd actually more than *quadrupled* it! Fair enough, I was asking these people to send me a passport photo, not live on a farm in Switzerland with me, but I think it's a fair comparison nevertheless, and I think Gallus would doubtless feel the same.

On the tube, now, cruising on the Central Line toward the center of town, opening the first of my envelopes. I'd had to sneak them out of the flat, because Hanne had been round, but here, on the tube, I could open them with no fear or embarrassment.

I tore the first one open. I found a photo of a lady, in her mid-thirties, by the name of Sarah Teller. Or *Joinee* Teller, as she would be known from now on. She was a dental assistant from Shepshed, and her hobbies included musicals, videos and swimming (twice a week). Why she'd taken it upon herself to lavish these extra details on me I've no idea, but I liked her for it and for some reason committed them to memory. I couldn't dwell too much on Joinee Teller, though—I had more joinees to meet. I opened the next envelope. Another woman, this one in her late teens. Joinee Webster. She enjoys pubs, clubs and the band Idlewild. Apparently, she had a pierced tongue, though you wouldn't know it from her photo. Unless that was the reason for what appeared to be a small piece of dribble on her chin. But that didn't matter to me. It was *joinee* dribble, and thus a wonderful thing indeed.

I opened the next one. It was a man. His name was Gaz. He had sent me two photos of himself, both Blu-tacked to a letter; one, passport-sized and perfectly acceptable for his Join Me application, and another, in which he appeared to be dressed from head to toe as a Care Bear.

"It was for a bet," he wrote in his letter. "Someone bet me I couldn't fit into it. And I thought that I could. I offer you this photo as proof of my victory." I laughed. And then I noticed that the person in the seat next to me was laughing too. He'd been taking a great deal of interest in what I'd been doing while I sat next to him. It seems he'd thought I was opening that morning's responses to some kind of lonely hearts column, and while he'd approved of both the dental assistant and the girl with the pierced tongue, he rather thought I was scraping the bottom of the barrel with some bloke from Oxford called Gaz who likes dressing up as a Care Bear. Still, he can't have thought I was very fussy about who

I go on dates with . . . appearing, as it did, that I go for women, men *or* fictional cartoon characters from the early '80s.

And while his interest was welcome—y'never know, he may join—I elected to take the rest of my envelopes elsewhere in order to enjoy them. I ordered a cup of tea and sat down at the Starbucks on Regent Street to study them properly.

My other eleven joinees that morning comprised seven men and four women, living right around the country and undertaking a number of jobs. Their ages, by the looks of them, ranged from teens to early forties, and each had a warmth about them that I found hard to explain. I suppose it was because I felt such warmth toward them myself. Or maybe it's because it's always quite warm in Starbucks, and I was still wearing my parka.

I wanted to get to know a little more about these people, though. I decided that later on in the day, I'd compile and send out a detailed questionnaire. That way, not only would I be able to work out terribly interesting statistics like the average height and age of my joinees, but I'd be able to find out *why* they joined, what it was about Join Me that appealed to them. Maybe I'd arrange a get-together after I'd done that. Maybe I'd actually meet some of these people, just as I'd met Joinee Jones.

As it turned out, it wouldn't be me who suggested a meeting. It would be Joinee Haman, aka Gaz, aka the Care Bear Man.

Writing on the website forum while slightly under the influence, he said:

> *OK, well nothing ventured, nothing gained . . . (and when better to take a risk than when drunk eh?) . . .*
>
> *I'll be making my way home through London next weekend with time to kill. If there are any fellow joinees or people who want to join who fancy a pint, I'll meet you in the top bar at the Chandos pub off Leicester Square at 2 pm on Sunday next.*
>
> *I'll be the bloke reading a book trying not to look like I have no friends.*
>
> *Gaz*

I put the date in my diary. Maybe I'd go along. It would be nice to meet with my people.

In the meantime, my most important task was upping the number of joinees I had. No more envelopes had arrived in the post since that first batch of fourteen joinees, which I found rather disappointing. I suppose from that moment on I'd figured every day would be like that. But Monday, and Tuesday, and Wednesday passed by without even a sniff of a new joinee. Sure, people were *saying* they'd join me, and *promising* to send their photos off, but not one of them seemed to have done so.

I was in danger of becoming demoralized again. Especially when one person, who'd seen the advert in *Loot,* sent me a one-word, handwritten note. Still, it was the first time I'd actually seen the word "Wanker" written in crayon, so that was nice.

Another day passed and still no passport photos arrived, even when there was a dramatic and unexpected rise in the number of e-mails I was getting. It all became clear when I was tipped off and told to buy that day's copy of the *Daily Mirror*. Tucked away in a small box halfway through the paper, in a column written by a lady named Amy Vickers, I was excited to find this . . .

> *Carrying the strapline "It's not a cult—it's a collective," the bizarre Join Me website is signing up members by the bucketload. But nobody knows who's behind it or what it's trying to achieve . . . except for* The Mirror *and a few choice members.*
>
> *Rest assured, it's not a scary religious cult, but don't be surprised if it ends up in lights!*

How had Amy Vickers found out about the website? And how did she know who was behind it? I'd never met her, to the best of my knowledge, and I'd certainly told no one about what I was doing. She even hinted she knew what I was trying to achieve. Well, that was more than *I* did. I only wished that she'd been correct in what she'd said. Apparently I was signing up new members by the bucketload, and in a way I suppose I was, given that you can't really fit anyone into a bucket these days.

But still no passport photos arrived. I thought it hugely strange that fourteen should arrive all at once and then nothing at all after that.

And then . . . *bang*.

You can picture my utter delight when a large bundle of letters, held together by no less than two industrial-strength elastic bands, found its way through my letterbox late one morning.

Twenty-six letters. Twenty-six passport photos. Twenty-six *new joinees*.

Oh, joy!

A joinee from Manchester. A joinee from Durham. A joinee from Huddersfield. A joinee from Bristol. Joinees from towns and villages in Hampshire, Surrey, Oxfordshire, Aberdeenshire, and Somerset. Male joinees. Female joinees. Young joinees, middle-aged joinees and at least two who I'm sure wouldn't mind me describing them as very old joinees. And each and every one of them a *brilliant* joinee.

I now had forty-two joinees in total. Forty-two! I was nearly halfway through my own quest, and I'd hardly even done anything! But rather than please me, this actually rather worried me. Halfway. Halfway with almost no effort whatsoever. Halfway, just when I was starting to enjoy myself.

I told myself not to be stupid, to cheer up. Halfway was *good*. It meant that soon I'd have my hundred, and I could stop. My collective would be complete, and I could set about dismantling it. I would've reached my target—reached Gallus's target—and could then get on with the very serious business of living my life just as I had done before. Playing video games. Watching films. In my pants.

Sigh.

• • •

Sunday was soon upon me, and with it the promise of meeting one of my joinees. I knew Joinee Gaz would be sitting in that central London pub, at 2 P.M., waiting for fellow joinees to show their joinee faces. He'd posted again on the forum, telling people how they could recognize him, and a few people had replied, saying that as they lived in London or could get to it easily, they'd pop in at two o'clock to say hello.

At five to two I was standing outside the Chandos pub, slightly nervous. Inside could be any number of joinees, each of them full of hope and ideas and plans for the future of Join Me. What if I disappointed them? What if I wasn't what they were looking for? What if they'd imagined this was all going to be a lot slicker and more professional than it was? Should I pretend to be just a normal joinee? Should I hide the fact that I was the bloke setting it all up? All these thoughts flashed through my mind as I climbed the second staircase, up to the top bar, to find whatever lay ahead.

And there, sitting at a table in the corner, reading a book, trying not to look like he had no friends, was Gaz. Joinee Haman. The Care Bear Warrior.

"Er . . . join me?" I tried.

"Hello!" said Gaz, cheerily. "I was wondering whether anyone was going to turn up! I mean, a few people have said they will, but you never know, do you? Pint?"

At which point Joinee Haman, in what was fast becoming a traditional gesture, bought me a pint.

* * *

Now I *had* secretly hoped that by revealing that I was no ordinary joinee but Danny, the founder of Join Me, I would stir up some kind of excitement in Gaz. But no. He'd simply nodded, and said "Right," and then asked me whether I'd read the book he was halfway through reading. I hadn't. He said I should, it was a really good read. I said I would, next chance I got.

But I was genuinely hoping for some questions, this time round. Actually *hoping*. I'd prepared myself mentally for some kind of inquisition, and had my answers ready. That had been one of the first things Joinee Jones had put me through, and at least he'd seemed marginally impressed that he'd met the founder of the organization. Even though the organization, at that stage, consisted of just the founder and him.

But Gaz didn't seem at all impressed or intrigued. Not once did he ask me what Join Me was all about, or where it was leading, or why I'd started it. Not once did he try and gain some snippet of information from me, or ask for clues, or pointers. He just seemed perfectly content to have joined whatever it was I'd asked him to join. Details weren't important. He was just happy to help.

"I'm sure everything will become clear," he said, without prompting.

I'll admit it. I felt slightly deflated. The air of mystery I'd been trying to cultivate had apparently worked so well that that was all Gaz now needed to see him through the afternoon.

No one else joined us, that afternoon. Those who had said they might pop in had apparently found themselves with better things to do that day, but Gaz and I were happy, chatting, sitting by the window of this bright, sunny pub.

I said good-bye to Gaz an hour or so later and wandered back to Leicester Square, to catch a tube home. I thought again about how nonplussed he'd been by the whole meeting. I stopped off at Hanne's on the way home, had a bite to eat with her, and then returned to my flat.

Later on that evening, I checked the website forum. Gaz had posted a message, seemingly the moment he'd walked through the door of his house, back in Oxford. And there was something strange about his posting. He now seemed far more excited about the whole thing.

> *Well, although I was disappointed at the number of other joinees who turned up for a drink this afternoon (i.e., zero), I am *very* pleased to say that myself and the Leader (yes—the Leader himself!) had a very nice chat and an equally very nice few pints!*

Responses from other joinees and prospective joinees had been swift.

> *If I had known the Leader would be there I would have come along!*

> *Why did the Leader not make it known he was coming?*

> *If the Leader is there I will definitely come to the next one!*

Can we arrange another one very soon please as I would like to meet the Leader?

The first thing that shocked me about all this was that I was suddenly, inexplicably being referred to as "the Leader." I was a *Leader!* And people were referring to me as such! I felt a burst of pride. I felt as I did when Mrs. Howells asked me to be a prefect in Year Eleven at school. But there were *loads* of prefects. There was only *one* Leader. Hey—I was the new Mrs. Howells!

The second thing to shock me was the immediate backlash against Joinee Haman. Poor Gaz was now being accused of lying to make himself seem more impressive and glamorous to the group.

Sure. The Leader turned up. I believe you mate.

Someone's making up porky-pies! (lies).

Hmm . . . why do I find it somewhat hard to believe that the Leader turned up to meet you? Is it because you're talking bollocks?

Now, you, the reader, should really stop comparing me to people like Mrs. Howells and Jesus. It's not on. But I agree with you—this *did* remind me of what the first bloke to have met Jesus must have gone through, and you're clever to point that out.

Gaz, though, took it all in good spirit.

Oh ye of little faith!

Well if you really don't believe me, why not just ask Him? After all, I've got no reason to fib—and even if I was bluffing, I'd be rumbled pretty quickly!

G.

Now, I honestly don't know if this was a mistake on Gaz's part or not . . . but look at the second sentence he wrote. He'd capitalized the

"H" on "him"! Now, not only was I "the Leader," but I was worthy of a capital "H"! This was all too much. What was happening here?

That evening I did indeed receive several e-mails from confused joinees wishing to know whether Gaz's claims were fact, or the ramblings of a wishful and deluded madman. It was as if, all of a sudden, everyone was actually impressed that there was evidence I even existed. Me, a bloke they'd sent a photo to . . . a bloke sitting here, at his computer, unshaven and scruffy, with a smear of toothpaste down his front.

I wrote back to them in as mysterious and intriguing a way as I could muster. I told them that Joinee Haman spake the truth, and that they should have faith in the claims of their fellow joinees. And then I decided I should stop using words like "spake," because it really wasn't helping matters any.

But the one thing I knew *was* happening was that the joinees were becoming friends. They were bantering. They were getting to know each other, albeit electronically.

Someone else decided that a meet-up would be a good thing. Other joinees agreed. This one would be larger, and involve more than one joinee, and should take place reasonably soon.

It was all working out beautifully.

Every day more and more joinees were sending their photos and signing themselves up. Soon I had seventy joinees. Then eighty. Word-of-mouth was at work, and ten days later I had ninety. It was all getting out of control, and it made me laugh every time I checked my post.

And the best thing was, we were bonding. We were becoming a community. And I think Gallus, had he been watching, would have been smiling.

E-mail

To: Dennis M. Hope, President of the Galactic Government
From: Danny Wallace

Dear Dennis,

Since I last wrote, something has been playing on my mind. I am asking people to trust me; to believe in me. To Join Me in something which they know nothing about. To Join Me in something *I* know nothing about.

People are looking up to me as their Leader.

You too have a band of happy believers. They know that they will be joining you at some stage to travel to land they have bought on the moon.

As you know, I have no land. Interest in Join Me is growing rapidly, and I'm excited. But I'm also nervous. Where am I going with this? Where are *we* going with this? I can offer my people nowhere to live, and, to be honest, I'm not sure if I want to. I lived in a shared flat in my student days, and that was a bloody nightmare some nights.

But despite not living as a community, we seem to have started to bond as one. Is a community of the mind really enough?

Please advise.

All the best,

Danny Wallace

E-mail

To: Danny Wallace
From: Dennis M. Hope, President of the Galactic Government

Dear Danny:

The world is in turmoil. Concepts are the foundation for all reality.

I think that a community of the mind is as strong as and sometimes stronger than the real thing with geographical boundaries.

With warm regards from the Galactic Government and the Lunar Embassy,

Dennis M. Hope
President—Galactic Government
AKA: "The Head Cheese"

P.S. I may join you myself!

CHAPTER · 6

97. *And even there were fourscore and seventeen.*

98. *And even there were fourscore and eighteen.*

99. *And even there were fourscore and nineteen.*

A week later and I was back in the Horse & Groom with Ian.

"Well, I did it!" I beamed broadly, sitting down. "Buy me a pint to congratulate me!"

"You did what?" he said, blankly. Evidently he needed a little more proof of my having actually done something before rewarding me with a pint for having done it. I wish life *was* that simple; I'd probably have a lot more free stuff. "Well, I did it!" I could say. "Buy me a caravan!"

"I did what I set out to do," I said. "The grand adventure is over. I have my hundred joinees."

"What are you on about?"

"My joinees. Remember I told you about my great-uncle the other week?"

"The nutjob?"

"No, the visionary. Well, he needed a hundred joinees, and I got them for him. Job done. Buy me a pint."

"Hang on, you actually went ahead and did that? How?"

"Small ads. The Internet. Word of mouth. It grew ridiculously quickly. A hundred was nothing. I don't know what Gallus's problem was."

"Maybe it's because he didn't have the Internet, and . . . you know . . . he actually wanted people to physically live on a farm with him."

"Well, that's all in the past, now, and we can finally lay it to rest. He has his joinees. I got them for him. Pint, please."

Ian stood up, begrudgingly, and wandered over to the bar, while I sat there, still beaming, still thinking of the moment I'd got my hundredth passport photo in the post.

And the thing is, I feel I owe you an apology somehow. I didn't make the most of that moment. I'm sure if I were a better writer, or this was a made-up story, I would've prolonged the agony, stretched it out a bit, made reaching that impossible target seem all the more impossible and impressive. Maybe, in the final chapter, when I received that elusive hundredth passport photo, I'd have got a party popper out and released it, there and then, in my flat, and to *hell* with the consequences.

But the truth of it is, I'd somehow stumbled across, or uncovered, or tapped into, groups of people who were actually quite into this whole Join Me concept. Groups of people so trusting and open that they were willing to join a complete stranger for no reason whatsoever . . . all I was telling them was that I needed them . . . and they were all too happy to be needed.

Now, if it'd been *me* who'd seen that small ad in *Loot,* or found an odd request for passport photos on the Internet, or been badgered into joining by one of my more strange friends, I'm not sure I would have done anything about it. I'm not sure *you* would, either. It might sound all right now . . . but if it had happened to you, and you didn't already feel like you knew me a bit . . . would you? Honestly? Me . . . I'd have turned the page, or clicked elsewhere, or told my pal to stop frightening me and delete my number from his phone.

But the people I was now in everyday contact with were more open than I was. They all had their different reasons for their involvement, I suspect, but the sad thing is, now that I had all hundred of them, there was really no more involvement to be had. Nothing for them to do. Nothing I needed them to do. They'd done their bit. They'd joined me. And I'd done what I'd set out to do. I'd proved to myself that I could find a hundred willing joinees for my great-uncle Gallus. My tribute was complete. He had his people, at long, long last.

"So who did you get to join you?" said Ian, placing my pint on the table. "I mean . . . no offence . . . but *who'd* join *you?*"

Aha. I'd prepared for this. I'd studied my questionnaires, done some math, and made some notes. I knew *exactly* who'd joined me. I pulled a tatty piece of paper out of my shirt pocket and read from it.

"Well . . . my collective is 100 percent British. It's 54 percent male, 46 percent female, 0 percent other."

"You've worked this out?" said Ian, in disbelief.

"Yes. The average age is twenty-nine, the most common name for a boy is Matt, and the most common name for a girl is Sarah."

"I don't believe you've worked this out!"

"The average joinee also lives in the Midlands and has one quarter of a child."

"They should ask for their money back," said Ian. "This is all very odd. But . . . . y'know . . . well done, I suppose. So are you happy you've finished?"

"Kind of. I'd sort of been enjoying myself as the Leader. And it's a pity, because they've all started talking to each other and making friends with each other and deciding how to take Join Me further. When in actual fact there's nothing to move further. That's all there is. A hundred people. No reason or point. I'm going to have to tell them that."

"Seems a bit of a shame," said Ian, "to break their hearts. They were probably really hoping they were part of something much bigger. What does Hanne think?"

Oh yeah. Hanne. I'd have to tell her, of course. Have to explain the reason that I hadn't been around much lately, and why I'd accidentally stood her up a couple of times, and taken her to that takeaway in Camden. Have to tell her that those two blokes on my fridge, and, in fact, the other ninety-eight people whose photos were currently in my desk drawer, were my joinees, my followers. She'd understand. She'd forgive me. She may even find it strangely funny.

"I'll tell her. I don't know how she'll react. You know what she's like about stuff like this. She'd prefer me to collect stamps rather than joinees."

"I don't blame her," said Ian. "So you're just going to give up on these people?"

I knew what Ian was getting at. These people were too good to waste, if you ask me. Imagine what we could achieve, the 101 of us, if only there were something we *wanted* to achieve.

"But Gallus was after a hundred people," I said. "And I've got them for him."

"Well, yes," said Ian. "But they're not exactly packing their bags in order to move to Switzerland with you, are they?"

"It was a tribute. A gesture. I don't exactly want to move there myself. And to be honest, I doubt there'd be room. I've seen his land, I don't know how he imagined a hundred people living there together. What if the response had been greater? What if his whole *village* had wanted to move there with him? A thousand people all having to decide whose turn it is to buy the toilet paper."

"Now *that* would have been an achievement."

"Buying toilet paper?"

"No, getting the whole town on board. Imagine if he'd done that. A thousand people all joining him."

"I think a hundred's enough."

"No, a *thousand* would be an *achievement*. Something to be *proud* of."

"What do you mean?"

"I'm just saying. A hundred seems a bit paltry. If you'd managed to get one joinee for every man, woman and child in your great-uncle's village, well . . . I'd *definitely* have bought you a pint for *that*."

"I can see where this is headed, Ian . . ."

He looked at me innocently, but I knew what he was up to.

"No," I said. "No no no. I don't do drunken bets. Not now. I'm twenty-five. I've moved on."

"Did Hanne teach you to say that?"

Curses. Caught.

"I'm just saying. This is not a bet."

"You're the one going on about bets."

"No I'm not. And neither are you. And anyway, if that's what you think should happen, why don't you help me? Why don't you be my hundred-and-first joinee?"

"I'm not joining you! You must be mental! I may as well give you that pint right now and give up!"

"Why are you treating this as a bet? We haven't bet anything! And there will be absolutely no betting today!"

And there wouldn't. But the damage was done. The idea was in my head. A thousand joinees. One for every man, woman and child in Gallus's village. Ian was right. *That* would be an achievement. I'd have the whole *village* on Gallus's side! *That'd* make him proud!

But this could be difficult. The bigger this thing got, the harder it would be to cover up and hide from Hanne. And the bigger it got, the harder it would be to cover up the sheer pointlessness of it all. I could certainly try and get a thousand people to join me . . . but for what? I still didn't know. I just hoped my joinees weren't inquisitive types. I'd have to instil faith in them, somehow keep them interested while I sucked another nine hundred people into my world.

So I finished the rest of my pint, said good-bye to Ian and headed home.

I'd gone to the pub thinking it was all over.

Turns out, it had only just begun.

JOIN ME

"It's not a cult - it's a collective"

Hello, stranger! Did you know that all over the world, strangers just like you are uniting to the beat of a single drum? It's true! It's a **Join Me** drum, and its beat is getting stronger all the time. This leaflet has been presented to you by someone who's **Joined Me**. A proud and noble warrior, although not one who's involved in conflict of any kind. Look at their happy, laughing face. Wouldn't you like one like that? You would? Well, of course you would! Then you should **Join Me.**

Joining Me is simple. Just send one passport-sized photo to: JOIN ME, PO Box 33561, London E3 2YW, and you'll be sent your official **Join Me** questionnaire. Or check out the **Join Me** website, at www.join-me.co.uk

Please. **Join Me**. You know you want to. And, more importantly, so do I. **Join Me.**

Joinee Jones
"I Joined, and just two weeks later won £20 on the scratchcards!"

Joinee Fletcher
"Joining is brilliant! I give it the big thumbs up! You will too if you like it and have thumbs or a thumb!"

Joinee Pyle
"Only a month after Joining, I fully survived a potentially hazardous operation!"

Joinee Davies
"Since I Joined, I've been on holiday to Tenerife! Thank you, Join Me!"

Joinee Vid
"I Joined, and my band's never had so many bookings! Coincidence? No way!"

THESE ARE TRUE STORIES

JOIN ME. DO IT. JOIN ME NOW.

Please be advised: Join Me is not a cult. Space travel will not be involved. And mass suicides are, at best, frowned upon. Thank you.

CHAPTER · 7

14. *Let him that hath understanding count the number on his shoulder: for the number is PC Six Hundred Threescore and Six.*

I didn't know it yet, but we'd been sitting, in silence, for far, far too long.

"Danny, are you all right?" asked Hanne.

"Yes! Absolutely. Of course I am."

I'd been daydreaming and forgotten where I was.

"Because you've just been sitting there, staring at me, with your mouth open, for about two minutes."

"Was I doing that? Sorry. I was just thinking about something."

"You dribbled in your soup."

"Did I? Sorry."

I'd taken Hanne out for lunch because I'd had a sudden attack of guilt in the night. I just hadn't been a particularly good boyfriend lately. I was less than Hanne deserved, more concerned with strangers than with my own girlfriend. So I'd booked a table at a semi-fancy restaurant and told her to have whatever she wanted, all on me . . . I'd even pay for the starter! Oh, yes. She was going to get the star treatment all right.

"So what's all this about?" said Hanne. "Why the lunch?"

"I just decided I needed to pay you more attention. I've been a bit distracted lately," I said.

"Like when you were dribbling in your soup?"

"For example, yes. But those days are far behind us now. There'll be no more dribbling in soup, no way."

"Good. Because you're not . . . you know . . ."

"What?"

"Well . . . *up to* anything. Are you?"

"Like what?"

"Like wanting to meet other people called Danny Wallace. Or planning to bounce around from twin town to twin town. Or seeing if you can hold your breath for a total of seven hours a day."

"I never did that. I just wondered whether it could be done."

"Well, whatever. Because you know I wouldn't stand for it if you're up to anything. So are you?"

"No," I said, slightly ashamed. I think I may even have crossed my fingers under the table when I said that. Hanne brings out the child in me sometimes. In the past I've even felt I've had to ask her permission if I wanted another can of fizzy pop.

"Good. Now, I was going to ask—there's a film premiere next week. We got tickets at work. Something starring someone called Vin Diesel. Do you want to go?"

"Yes. No. Well—if you're there."

Hanne said she would be, and the rest of the meal passed without incident.

"Okay, so if you think you can make it to the film," she said, as we walked out of the restaurant, "then I'll sort the tickets out next week. Thanks for lunch today. It's been lovely. Oh, and Danny?"

"Yes?"

"You still have a bit of dribble on your shirt."

• • •

At home I changed my shirt and thought about the challenge that lay ahead. Nine hundred people to convince. Nine hundred complete and utter strangers I'd need a passport photo from. Nine hundred people I had to get to join me. I was suddenly rather daunted by it all.

And so I did what I always do when faced with a tricky predicament. I made a cup of tea and had a bit of a sit down.

How on earth could I get my collective up to a thousand people? I only had *a hunded* or so. And then I realized what I was saying. I had a hundred people. A hundred people who seemed quite open to the idea of doing my bidding. A hundred people who, surely, could *help* when it came to getting others to join me? My joinees would surely be able to help me spread the word, to get others to join our beautiful, burgeoning collective.

But how?

I studied my questionnaires and came to some conclusions. I'd asked my joinees how they thought we could best spread the word and appeal to new people. Fifty-eight percent had agreed that either leaflets or stickers would be a good idea. The joinees had spoken; I would get some leaflets made. Hopefully they'd be so impressed by receiving leaflets in the post that they'd forget about all the other, less important stuff, like the point.

So I needed a graphic designer. I could have cobbled something together myself with a Pritt Stick and a photocopier, but hey—this was Join Me. It deserved to be done properly. And it needed to look good to convince people it was important. Besides, surely I'd have a graphic designer of some kind already in the collective, ready and keen to donate their services for free?

As it happened, I did not.

The closest I could come was a bloke who designs gnomes for students.

I phoned him up immediately and he confirmed that he'd once done a night course in graphic design, and providing I had a basic design package on my computer, he'd be pleased to come round and knock something out.

The next day, at three o'clock, Joinee Bob Glanville of Putney—a young man with baby blue eyes and curly blond hair—was sitting at my desk, talking to me about designing gnomes. It's not what he'd always done, and after the winter he'd probably never do it again, but at the moment he was on a six-month contract, designing novelty gnomes to be given away at student unions with every four pints bought. If ever students had an incentive to drink, I decided, it was the prospect of a free gnome at the end of the night.

"The thing about designing gnomes," said Bob, "is you have to know what it is about a gnome that catches the eye. A lot of people would say the hat, or the fishing rod if they have one, but actually a lot of what appeals about a gnome is in the eyes."

"Yeah, I'd go for the eyes." I said. "Friendly, gnomey eyes."

"Personality is in the face. It's important. Plus, one of the great things about designing gnomes is that the companies allow you pretty much free rein in developing their personalities. You get to write the leaflet that accompanies the gnome. So, for example, I've been working this week on a gnome called Rocky. He likes eating pork pies, traditional jazz, and taking long baths. But he dislikes pigeons and slugs. So, you see, you do get a lot of input. Now . . . let's do this leaflet."

I clapped my hands together and said "Right."

"First of all, I'm going to need to know the basic premise of this Join Me lark."

"Okay."

"So what is it?"

"It's about people joining together."

"Okay. Good. To what end?"

"Eh?"

"For what purpose are we joining together?"

"To be as one."

"Right. And then do what?"

"That's difficult."

"Why?"

I decided to come clean. He'd understand.

"You can't tell this to anyone."

"Er . . . okay?"

"Well . . . I don't know what the purpose is yet."

Joinee Glanville looked shocked.

"But everyone seems to think you do! I've seen the website!"

"I know. It's terrible."

"So why don't you stop?" he said. Confusion had taken Bob's face hostage.

"I need a thousand joinees. And I don't want to disappoint anyone. I just keep saying mysterious things in a way that implies I know what I'm doing and people believe me."

"The longer you do it, the more disappointed they'll be. And what are these leaflets in aid of, if you can't explain what Join Me is?"

Joinee Glanville had a point. How could I create leaflets explaining what Join Me is, when even I, the Leader of Join Me, didn't know what Join Me was?

"Let's just see what happens when I sit down at the keyboard," I said.

And I sat down, and began to write. I didn't know where it was leading, but ten minutes later I had something.

Hello, stranger!
Did you know that all over the world, strangers just like you are uniting to the beat of a single drum? It's true! It's a Join Me drum, and its beat is getting stronger all the time. This leaflet has been presented to you by someone who's Joined Me. A proud and noble warrior, although not one who's involved in conflict of any kind.

Look at their happy, laughing face. Wouldn't you like one like that? You would? Well, of course you would!

Then you should Join Me.

I showed it to Bob.

"But that says absolutely nothing about what Join Me is," he said.

"I know. I'm going to start thinking about what Join Me is soon, I promise. But this at least sounds fun, doesn't it?"

"Well, yes. It's not enough to get people joining you, though. Why don't you reveal who you are?"

"I don't think it's important who I am. It's all about the joinees. It's about the group."

"Then I think you need testimonials. I think you need to show why people have joined you."

Then he paused.

"Actually, why the hell *have* people joined you?"

I didn't know. I looked at Bob.

"Well, why did *you* join me?"

"I . . . have absolutely no idea," he said. "A whim, I suppose. And you asked. I suppose that was enough."

I turned back to look at the screen and read what I'd written. Bob was right. We needed testimonials from happy, carefree joinees. And I knew where to look. The questionnaires.

One of the things I'd asked people was "What is the best thing to have happened to you since you Joined Me?" People had replied with varying degrees of seriousness, but what if I could somehow claim credit for all those good things? What if those people could appear to be blaming Join Me for all the wonderful things to have happened to them in life? Surely that'd get more strangers believing in what we were doing? And if it was worded correctly, it wouldn't even be lying. Not strictly speaking, anyway.

"I've got a plan," I said to Bob, before rifling through my drawer for printed-out questionnaires. "And here it is . . ."

Bob and I read through the small stack of paper before finding some suitable quotes. I gave him the passport photos and he started to scan the relevant ones in.

Soon, the leaflet had taken shape. My blurb at the top, with a row of passport photos and slightly rejigged quotes underneath them. I think you'll agree, they make quite a convincing case for why you should join me.

Joinee Jones: *"I joined, and just two weeks later I won £20 on the scratchcards!"*

Joinee Pyle: *"Only a month after Joining, I fully survived a potentially hazardous operation!"*

Joinee Davies: *"Since I Joined, I've been on holiday to Tenerife! Thank you, Join Me!"*

Joinee Vid: *"I Joined, and my band's never had so many bookings! Coincidence? No way!"*

Joinee Fletcher: *"Joining is brilliant! I give it the big thumbs up! You will too if you like it and have thumbs or a thumb!"*

Underneath, I wrote: THESE ARE TRUE STORIES.

I called each joinee and asked them for permission to use their photo on the leaflet.

It would be fair to say that I confused a few people that day. Each of them said yes, mind you. But each then also asked me who I was, and what the hell Join Me was, and what it was we were up to, and I told them they'd understand when I sent them a leaflet. Joinee Glanville looked at me disapprovingly. He'd *designed* the leaflet and didn't know what it was all about. How did he think I felt? I'd *written* the thing and still had no idea.

Bob saved the work to disk and then took it away with him.

"I'll drop this at the printers tonight," he said. "You do realize it won't be cheap. Printing thousands of leaflets which don't actually say anything about the thing they're advertising doesn't seem all that wise to me."

"Trust me," I said. "It'll work out."

Bob looked at me. "You're doing it again, aren't you?"

"Doing what?"

"You're acting all wise and mysterious when really you've no idea what you're doing. Just saying it'll all work out and looking at me in a mysterious way and hoping I believe you."

I tried to make a mysterious face but failed, and sighed.

"Yes."

"I like that about you," he said, before turning on his heel and walking off.

• • •

Leaflets and stickers designed, I returned to the everyday chores of a Leader. I checked my e-mails, and this one popped up first:

> *Dear Leader*
>
> *I have been a joinee now for a number of weeks. You have always said in your e-mails to have faith and that all would become clear. But I am facing a problem.*
>
> *I have told others about what I have joined and they say it sounds stupid and pointless. I am sure there must be a point*

otherwise why would you be doing it? However I am finding this hard because every time someone asks me what this is leading to I have to say I don't know.

I know I should have faith but it is difficult. Can you let me know some more information. What is the point of this? Please tell me.

Thanks.

Joinee Jade
Durham

I honestly didn't know what to tell Joinee Jade. I couldn't come clean to her; couldn't tell her that . . . well . . . there *was* no point. Telling her about Gallus wouldn't help, either. If I did, I'd have to admit that all I was doing was trying to collect 999 other people like her, and no one wants to be thought of as a mere number, do they?

So I told her I would be sending her some leaflets and stickers which would help explain more about the scheme. She seemed satisfied and e-mailed me back to say *"Great! I knew it'd all work out! Thanks!"*

I'd managed to put her off. But for how long could I keep these people interested? Asking them to recruit friends, neighbors and complete strangers to the cause may keep them happy for a little while . . . but then what? What exactly was I going to do with all these people I was collecting? Surely there was *something* I could do with them while I upped the numbers? Maybe we could merge with the Hare Krishnas, or do some kind of deal with the Church of Scientology? Something that'd mean we wouldn't have to believe any of their nonsense, but we could still wear the T-shirts and meet John Travolta.

Still, you'll be happy to hear that while I was worrying my pretty little face off, more joinees were embracing the spirit of Join Me and signing up on a daily basis.

And it became clear that people were joining me for a variety of reasons. Some were doing so in the spirit of adventure and fun. Others because they were just desperate to find out what "joining" meant. And others . . . well . . . others were joining for reasons all their own.

One joinee in particular was beginning to worry me. Don't get me wrong; he seemed like a terribly nice man, and terribly terribly friendly with it. He'd often send me cheerful e-mails throughout the day, and always seemed to have another little something up his sleeve in the name of Join Me.

I encouraged him and nodded him on, like a proud and doting father, until I began to realize that Join Me was beginning to take over his life. I would go out for an evening and return to find four or five e-mails from him, asking me questions, or sharing ideas, or telling me stories, or hinting that he had yet another grand scheme on the go. And it started to make me feel guilty. While I'd be out for a pint with a friend, or holding Hanne's handbag while she tried on another new skirt she wouldn't buy, it really did seem as if Whitby was devoting every hour of his day to coming up with new and imaginative ways of raising awareness. And each e-mail or letter I received from him was extremely cheerful—even when I'd refused to tell him for the fourth time what the purpose of Join Me was. He just got on with things. I liked him for that. But the sheer level of dedication he was willing to commit was—in all honesty—slightly worrying.

Again, don't get me wrong—I needed people like Joinee Whitby. People who would take me to a thousand in fine style. But still . . . listen to this . . .

Within one typical week of tireless devotion to the cause, Joinee Whitby had made his own Join Me T-shirt. He'd had Join Me business cards printed. He'd sent e-mails left, right, and center. He'd turned up at the offices of his local newspapers and e-mailed his local radio station in order to get the word out to the Hampshire masses.

And it soon became clear that his family and friends weren't too happy about it. Writing on his very own website, which he'd set up specially so he could record his thoughts and progress for all to see ("www.joinee.co.uk—where people come together . . . but aren't sure why"), he said:

I have come to discover through the wonderful world of "Join Me" that all my friends, family and work colleagues have come to the conclusion that all of this malarky has caused me to

> *finally lose the plot completely. There were pretty much two options open to me. Renounce the whole Join Me thing once and for all and return to a dull level of sanity. Or choose to fully embrace my madness. Guess which path I took.*

Did his family really think he was mad? Or—worse—that he was being *wacky?* If there's one thing that would cause me to lose sleep at night it would be people thinking I was making them be wacky. Wacky is not something I would ever willingly be involved with. Wacky people are bad. I frown upon their wackiness. I read on through Whitby's website, hoping to find evidence that would prove it would never happen. I clicked on a link which took me to a gallery of photographs he'd taken, each of them incorporating the words Join Me in some way. He'd written something at the bottom of the page. I read it and shuddered. "If you could do a Join Me picture as well, then . . . well . . . it wouldn't make *me* any less mad, but at least I'd have some company!"

No! Whitby had written the Join Me equivalent of "You don't have to be mad to work here, but it helps!"

I had to stop him. I had to stop him from doing too much in the name of Join Me. But how? For several days I ignored his e-mails. I tried to show less interest. Surely if I did that it wouldn't be long before he at least toned it down a bit?

But Whitby showed no sign of losing interest. He badgered his friends to join me. He made long-distance calls to the States to beg long-lost friends to sign up. He got up ridiculously early one morning to climb the tallest hill in Hampshire in order to put a self-made Join Me sticker at the highest altitude he could. He tried to paint the words "Join Me" on a small child's face at a school fete his son was attending. He continued to hassle his local newspaper on a weekly basis. He hired a badge-making machine for a weekend and made badges. The man was obsessed.

And he was growing impatient with me. Politely, but increasingly, frustrated. I didn't blame him. Here I was, the so-called Leader, and I was doing less than him to spread the word of my own organization.

He began to post messages on the website forum. "I am being

driven insane by a lack of information," said one. In another, he wrote "Big Brother has been silent for eleven days. Joinee Whitby worries that the world outside has lost interest and wonders whether he is alone and forgotten in the house. There is no reply from the diary room, no tasks have been set and the food is running low. Joinee Whitby paces up and down and looks sombre."

I felt incredibly sorry for Joinee Whitby. He reminded me of a puppy no one was playing with any more. It broke my heart to do it, but I still didn't reply. I had to be strong. I had to be cruel to be kind. At least this way his family might get him back for a bit.

Either way, it was for the best.

• • •

"He might start stalking you," said Ian, over a quick drink at the Horse & Groom. "Maybe he'll kill you."

"That's a cheery thought," I said. "Thank you very much. And he's not going to start stalking me. Or killing me. He's not the type. He's a good-hearted man who likes a challenge, that's all. Something about Join Me must really appeal to him. And why would he kill a stranger, anyway? Particularly one he calls 'the Leader'?"

"It's worrying, Dan. He's the most obsessed joinee you have, and you're taking his favorite toy away from him. If you keep ignoring him, who knows what he'll do?"

"He won't do anything. He'll just calm it down a bit. I don't want to be responsible for this man's breakdown. I don't want him to be hiring badge-making machines and trying to paint small children's faces when he should really be doing the washing up or pressing some buttons on his computer."

"I'm warning you, Dan. He won't let it lie. I've seen things like this before. You're not moving fast enough for him, are you? Have you told him you're after a thousand so you can get that pint?"

"I'm not doing it for the pint. Stop going on about the pint. This has nothing to do with pints. And anyway, if I tell him that he'll go mental. He'll be unstoppable. Think of the man's family!"

"But you're not letting him in on the secrets, Dan. He used to feel intrigued. Now he feels lost. And I know what his next move will be."

"What are you on about? What do you mean, 'his next move'?"

"He's going to steal Join Me away from you."

I put my tea down.

"Bollocks. He couldn't. And he wouldn't."

"You just wait, my friend," said Ian. "You just wait."

• • •

I left Ian—whose childish insistence not to join me and refer to me as his Leader still grated on me somewhat—and returned home to be surprised by a delivery driver sitting outside my flat. My leaflets and stickers had arrived from the printers. Marvelous.

I ripped open the packaging and took some delight in what I found. My leaflets were the business. My stickers beautiful. And this was just the type of thing I needed to get Whitby and his cohorts off my back. He'd said he was being driven mad by a lack of information. Well, these Join Me leaflets would surely keep him sane . . . even though there was barely any information on them whatsoever, and what little there was was hardly relevant to Join Me. But, by sending out these leaflets and stickers to my loyal joinees, I'd be sending out a message of confidence. I'd be sending out a message which said "Trust me! Things are happening! Look—have some stickers! Don't go off with Whitby, please! Does he have stickers? No! He doesn't have any stickers at all! Just some poorly made badges! Therefore I am best!" Or words to that effect.

I jogged down to the corner shop and bought myself some suitable envelopes and as many first-class stamps as I could afford with the change I had on me. Back upstairs, I hurriedly scribbled out various joinee addresses onto the envelopes, shoved some leaflets and stickers into them and left them by the door to be posted. I wanted to start the official awareness campaign in the big cities, before moving on to the towns and villages, so I chose to send the first batch of paraphernalia to joinees in Edinburgh, Glasgow, Cardiff, Manchester, Liverpool, Birmingham, Nottingham and Bristol. I figured that it would be only fitting for me to get the ball rolling in London myself. Starting with my flat.

It didn't take long. I put a sticker on my bedroom door and one on the vacuum cleaner. In no time, the word was spread right the way around my flat. But that wouldn't get me another nine hundred joinees, so I decided to move the operation to the wider world. This would take a little longer.

I took some leaflets and a few hundred stickers and wandered around the East End. I stickered lampposts, phone boxes, bollards, and a group of small children. I stuck stickers on the pavement, in case any elderly people, who often have a penchant for a stoop, decided to waddle on by. I stuck stickers on road signs, on a burnt-out Fiesta on the edge of the estate near Victoria Park, and on railings, roadworks and gutters.

I felt naughty. But I felt justified in my naughtiness. I was spreading the word, after all, and what a lovely day for it: sunny, warm, breezy and calm. I bought myself an ice cream as reward for my efforts.

I knew that what I was doing was naughty. I didn't know what I was doing was illegal.

"What's that?" said a voice, immediately behind me. On reflection, I should have skipped stickering the bulletin board outside the police station, because my doing so attracted the attention of a man in a policeman's uniform, who I think may have been a policeman, and whom I certainly took as such.

"It's . . . a sticker," I said, suddenly and overwhelmingly feeling more guilty than I'd ever felt before. Authority figures do that to me. I could have stamped on a badger and not felt more guilty than I felt right now. Put someone slightly taller than me in a hat and I'll do whatever they ask.

"And what does it say?"

I read it, just in case I'd accidentally had one printed that said "Coppers are Tosspots." I was relieved to find that I hadn't.

"It says: Join Me."

"What's that? A club?"

"Kind of."

"Where?"

"Well . . . it's . . . nowhere, really. And yet everywhere, I suppose."

"Where is it specifically?"

"Um, well . . . at the moment, it's a kind of club of the mind . . ."

I wiped what must have been quite a wistful look off my face. The policeman looked at me very, very seriously.

"A club of the mind?"

"Yes."

"What kind of music?"

"Eh?"

"What kind of music is it?"

"There's no music involved," I said. "But that's not a bad idea. Might get a few more people joining me. I need a thousand, and—"

"A club without music? Sounds very new wave. You from Shoreditch?"

"No, no, not a nightclub. Or a club night. A . . . you know . . . a club. Like the Tufty Club. Or Griffin Savers. Or—"

"Like a rambling club?"

"Well, more like a rambling club than a hardcore drum 'n' bass club."

"So it's a rambling club?"

"No, it's a . . . well . . . it's hard to explain. I just want people to join me."

"For what? A ramble?"

"It's not a rambling club. Look, officer, have I actually done anything wrong?"

"How many of these stickers have you put up?"

"It's hard to say. I've had quite a lot done, so—"

"Because you're aware that guerrilla marketing campaigns are illegal, aren't you? London's clamping down, my friend. You can be fined for each and every one of these."

"Oh." I didn't like the sound of this. "How much?"

"Potentially . . ." he paused, making sure I was looking in his eyes, ". . . £1,000 per sticker."

I physically felt my hairline recede a quarter of an inch.

"£1,000! Per sticker?"

I looked at the sticker I'd just stuck on the bulletin board. Was that worth £1,000? Would it really encourage dozens of policemen to Join

Me as they left work that evening, or arrived the next morning? I suddenly wasn't sure it would.

"How many stickers have you stuck up?"

"Er . . . well . . . I'm not sure. I've sent some to friends around the country. I've had three thousand printed."

"Three thousand? For a rambling club?"

"It's not a rambling club. And yes, three thousand."

"Three thousand . . . right. Multiplied by a thousand. So that's . . ."

He raised his eyes to the skies and did the math.

". . . that's a fine of £3 million you're looking at."

My eyes were as big as a giant squid's.

"£3 million! For these? That's more than I earn in an entire year! I can't pay £3 million!"

"Better take them down, then . . ." said the policeman, starting to walk away. "And I'm glad you've got a Web address on there, just so we know how to contact you if we see any more of them."

Curses. I felt like a schoolboy, caught apple scrumping in the vicar's garden. The policeman may as well have clipped me round the ear and taken me home to be spanked with a slipper by my mum.

Thankfully, my joinees were doing rather better. A couple of days later e-mails started to arrive telling me of the efforts and lengths to which joinees were going in order to spread the word. They'd taken on board just how vitally important it was to raise awareness of Join Me, and had been flyering hard and stickering away since their packages had arrived.

I sent more leaflets and stickers out to any joinee who requested them, and many who did not. Joinees in every major UK city were doing their bit, as well as those in many dozens of towns and villages up and down the country. New joinees were starting to send their passport photos in as a result. The leaflets—handed out in the streets, left in libraries, stuck up on walls—seemed to be working. Several people e-mailed me after being handed them, reading leaflets over people's shoulders, or even overhearing people read them to their friends. "I overheard two gay guys chatting about Join Me on a flight to Cyprus," wrote someone called Sarah. "Is it about uniting the world? Count me in!"

And I did.

A lady called Jane wrote, "So after overhearing a conversation between two people reading a flyer on the Victoria Line (they got off at Seven Sisters), I was intrigued enough to check out the website where apparently I could find out how to join up. I have done, and will be joining in the next day or so!"

And she did.

Dozens more people were reacting positively to this national campaign and signing up. My trip to the letterbox became the highlight of each morning, as I slowly and steadily racked up passport photo after passport photo from kind-hearted joinees all over the UK.

I hoped that Joinee Jade of Durham would be finding the leaflet and stickers of use.

Nope.

Dear Leader

Thanks for all the leaflets and stickers you sent me in the post the other day. I have been trying to use them and people seem a little more interested but to be honest it's not really what I'm after. I have read and re-read the leaflet and I still do not know what the point of Join Me is. I don't really know if I want to be involved in this any more so I will be leaving Join Me. Sorry.

Thanks for everything

Joinee Jade (ex)
Durham

No!

I had lost a joinee! Disaster! Having thousands of leaflets and stickers printed just hadn't been enough for Joinee Jade. She actually wanted to know what the point of what she was doing was.

I shuddered. More leavers would surely follow. I headed for the website to see if news of Joinee Jade's departure from Join Me had made it to the other joinees.

My blood ran cold when I reached the forum. There was a message from Joinee Whitby. The same Joinee Whitby that Ian had warned me would try and steal Join Me away from me . . .

> *Joinees! We can play this one of two ways. We can passively sit back and wait for answers from the "person in charge," or we can actively try and figure out what this is all about. What kind of "collective" are we? Fellow joinees . . . we need not just wait. What do we want to do as a group? Can we make decisions about our future without anyone taking overall control? Maybe! Come, fellow joinees . . . will you all decide to act?*

Oh my God. Mutiny! This was precisely what Ian had been talking about—this was the desperate call to arms of a dissatisfied joinee. It was a passionate speech. A speech designed to inspire, and unite. How could I compete with that? How could I compete with those well-chosen words of revolution?

Well, I couldn't. So to buy myself some time I deleted it from the forum and made a cup of tea while I thought about what to do.

My phone rang. It was Ian.

"Dan, I've been looking at this bloke Whitby's website," he said.

"Yes?"

"Well, that's the first thing. Why does it exist? Why does your official site need a rival? Isn't this whole scheme about joining *you?* Not setting up on your own?"

"I suppose so . . . but I've been busy, and I haven't had time to update my site much, so it stands to reason that . . ."

"And then there's Whitby's invitation to other people to join. He says if they want to join, they should click on a certain button. But when they do, it sends an e-mail to *him,* not you. And I can't find any links to *your* website, or even any mention that there's a Leader involved . . ."

Ian's voice sounded grave now.

"Danny . . . I think Whitby's out to get you."

"Not only that, Ian . . . one of my joinees has left. It's all going wrong."

"Whitby. He must have had a hand in that. Watch your back, Dan. Watch your back."

I bowed my head, said good-bye, and solemnly put the phone down. It seems that for the first time in my short life, I had found myself a nemesis. Or, more accurately, my nemesis had found me. How many more joinee minds would he poison? How many more would leave my collective and join forces with the dark side? I imagined Whitby and Jade laughing together, as they made their own leaflets and stickers, and poked fun at me for being a rubbish Leader with stupid glasses and bad shoes.

The leaflets clearly hadn't been enough. I'd been a fool to think that they'd buy me time while I decided what to do. More joinees would surely become disillusioned or bored, and I'd never reach my desired target, never complete my quest, never get Gallus his people. I knew I had to stop them from leaving. Stop them, before they ditched me, and Whitby snapped them up for whatever devious plans he was currently concocting.

I knew what I had to do. There was only one solution.

It was time to find a point to the pointlessness.

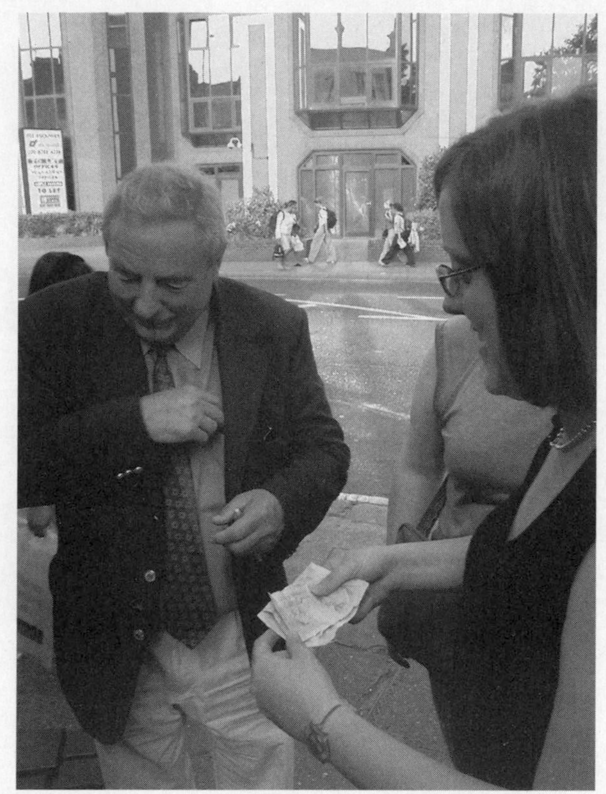

Happy Old Man Raymond Price accepts his train fare home.

CHAPTER · 8

POEM FOR THE JOINEE

Oh how we blindly join
This strange but fun collective
We're ready and we're eager
To follow each directive

In our strong and silent leader
We firmly place our trust
But as for his identity
Anonymity seems a must

And so for our tasks
We all must calmly wait
Until the man in charge
Decides our final fate

by Joinee Whitby (age 30)

Pressure on me to reveal the purpose behind Join Me was growing. Rapidly. And not only through the hard-hitting medium of poetry.

I had already lost one joinee, and I was worried that, with the likes of my newfound nemesis Joinee Whitby on my back, I'd soon be facing a bigger mutiny of sorts. It surely wouldn't be long before news of Joinee Jade's departure did the rounds, and more joinees jumped ship or legged it. Depending on whether you think of Join Me as a ship, or a more land-based collective. It'd be no good legging it from a ship. Not unless it was a ship that had run aground, anyway, and that's a metaphor I'm none too happy with, thank you very much.

I didn't know what to do. It was all my fault, this growing dissatisfaction. I began to feel like maybe I'd done all this backwards. It seems that if you're going to start some kind of collective like mine, you should really have a clear purpose before recruiting like-minded members. Otherwise you won't even know if they're like-minded or not. They'll just be members. And there's a joke there that I'm not going to do.

But that would certainly be my tip for you, if, as I suspect is the case, you've bought this book as some kind of academic research manual. On balance, I would now always suggest:

1. *Find your purpose*
2. *Spread the word*
3. *Recruit your members*

Rather than:

1. *Recruit your members*
2. *Spread the word*
3. *Find your purpose*

And it wasn't just Joinee Whitby who had been demanding more information. Dozens of joinees were constantly e-mailing me—always jokily at first, and slightly aggressively later on—to demand to know what it was they had joined. Frustration was growing; it seemed like people assumed there would be some kind of purpose to their involvement in Join Me. That had never really occurred to me at the start. But I had begun to see their point.

The fact was, I only had myself to blame. I'd thought I could probably just drop my joinees when I'd eventually had enough. But these were real people, with real feelings. I suppose I was responding to their questions in a very irresponsible way, now that I think about it. I was still acting all mysterious, trying to give the impression that everything was in hand. I sent out leaflets and stickers which gave the impression Join Me was something far bigger than it was. And all it did was build up the anticipation. My joinees had obviously taken my responses to mean that some grand plan for their involvement was in place, and now I had to think of one.

With power comes responsibility, tedious men in pubs will tell you. It always seemed slightly unfair to me, that. I think the whole point of having power is so you can delegate responsibility. I'd like to be the world's most powerful man, living in a house so big it has its own Marks & Spencer, and never have to make another decision again. That's why you never see the world's most powerful men when you're out and about—they're all at home playing on their PlayStations and eating cheese on toast. Which someone *else* has decided is what they should have for their lunch.

I sat at my keyboard with my head in my hands and thought carefully about what to do or say next. Should I come clean? I'd still achieved my original goal of a hundred joinees, after all. I could stop right now. Or I could take it to a new level. Maybe the answer lay within the joinees themselves. What did they want Join Me to be?

I went through my e-mails and letters. Some of the joinees had taken guesses at what Join Me really was.

> *I would ask whether this is some kind of statistical survey. For example, are you trying to find people who differ in looks and heights?*

> *This is something mysterious for the bored, depressed, isolated and outcast generation.*

> *I believe Join Me is a spiritual gathering of minds coming together for the greater good.*

> *This is a massive ego trip for one demented megalomaniac.*

I made a mental note that if I were ever going to start chucking people out of Join Me, I'd start with the bloke who called me a demented megalomaniac. But maybe he was right. I *was* enjoying the power. Not many people have a huge group of followers who voluntarily refer to them as the Leader. It's basically just me and Gary Glitter.

I made a cup of tea and sat down in front of my computer. I checked my e-mail, answered a few potential joinees' questions in as vague and yet convincing manner as I could (still feeling guilty about it), and then had a quick look at the website. Joinee Whitby was still on my mind. The paranoia that he might be up to something continued to bother me.

On the forum, one joinee had suggested meeting outside Harrods, and then going on to have a picnic in Hyde Park, and the idea had been approved by a few others. They'd decided that 2 P.M. on Saturday would be as good a time as any. Each was looking forward to it, and would be traveling specially from Hampshire, or Oxford, or Surrey, or various parts of London.

Part of me really wanted to go along, to say thank you for joining, and buy them a sandwich or freshly squeezed orange juice. But I knew that it wasn't time to reveal myself properly. It might have a detrimental effect. Far better to keep an air of mystery going. Far better to let people still imagine there might be some kind of robed and spiritual Dalai Lama-style figure behind Join Me, rather than some bloke with messy hair who's forgotten to shave again. Oh, and who still hasn't wiped that toothpaste off his top. And so I decided to leave my joinees be, for now.

But the one thing that rankled, the one thing I found disconcerting about the proposed meet-up was that Joinee Whitby was going to attend. I became slightly concerned that his dissatisfaction with the way things had been going would rub off on some of the others, and I would soon face my predicted mutiny. The pressure was on. I needed a point. A cause. A mission. If only to stop Whitby nicking my joinees off me. But *what* cause?

• • •

"Hello?"

"Mum, it's Dan."

"Who?"

"Dan."

"Who?"

"Dan. Mum, it's Daniel."

"Is that Daniel?"

"Yes, Mum, it's your only son, Daniel."

"Daniel?"

"Mum, put the phone to your good ear."

"Is that Daniel?"

"Mum, this is your son, put the phone to your good ear."

The phone is handed over.

"Hello?"

"Dad, it's Dan."

"Hello, Dan!"

"Hi Dad. Can you put Mum on?"

"Sure."

The phone is handed back over.

"Hello?"

"Mum, it's Dan."

"Who?"

• • •

Once my mum had put the phone to her good ear and worked out it was me, she agreed to my request straight away. Of course she did; she's my mum. I'd remembered something. I still had the letters I'd inherited from great-uncle Gallus. Letters I'd not been able to read because they were written in Swiss German, and—well—because I'd been a bit busy lately. But mum, being a fine and wise Swiss woman, told me she'd have those letters translated in a jiffy.

I typed out as many of them as I could, probably making dozens of errors along the way, and e-mailed them over. The next morning my translations arrived.

They made fascinating reading. I vowed to read them more carefully in the coming days, but now, today, all I needed was a pointer. Some clue as to what kind of society Gallus would have started, had his plans worked out and he'd had his own joinees. I hoped that within one of these letters, I'd find the guidance I needed. But, on first glance, there was nothing. Just something about never letting a cow out of a field after midnight (which, to be honest, I couldn't really imagine any of my joinees were doing on a regular basis anyway), and something about it being better to get your eggs from some woman in Frauenfeld rather than Kradolf because the woman in Kradolf doesn't wash her hands as often as she should. But then . . . in a throwaway sentence, in brackets, in the middle of a jokey anecdote about his friend Paul . . . the words: *"It is better, think I, always to make happy, those gentlemen who are in advance of you in years!"*

The words were instantly burnt into my mind. Well, polished up a bit, grammatically, and *then* burnt into it.

But Gallus had spoken. Spoken from beyond the grave.

He, in many ways the spiritual Leader of Join Me, had given me, his envoy on Earth, a . . . well . . . a Commandment.

It's important . . . to *Make an Old Man Very Happy.*

I hatched a plan.

• • •

That afternoon, I bought the things I needed. A padded envelope, a cheap dictaphone, and a disposable camera.

Back in the flat, I recorded a message onto the dictaphone. Involuntarily, and slightly bizarrely, my voice deepened and suddenly had more resonance. Somehow, I'd developed a kind of "Leader" mode, and even pointed as I sternly improvised a message.

"Hello, Joinees. Well done on opening this package correctly. And well done on finding each other today. Perhaps you will make new friends. Perhaps, by the end of the afternoon, two or three of you may even be married."

I thought about it.

"More likely to be two of you than three, but . . . er . . ."

I snapped back into Leader mode.

"I have a task for you," I boomed. "I want you to undertake one of the very first Join Me Commandments. I want you . . . to Make an Old Man Very Happy."

It sounded good. It sounded right. I continued.

"You can choose any pensioner you like. One in a park, maybe, or that one smoking a fag on a bench. It doesn't matter—so long as they're happier after having met you than they were before, that's fine. Take pictures with the enclosed camera as proof of your endeavors, and return it forthwith to Join Me HQ."

That's how much I sounded like a Leader—I was using words like "forthwith."

"Go to it, joinees. I . . . am *proud* of you."

I finished with a final "Good luck!," then tucked the recorder and camera into the padded envelope. I sent it special delivery to one of the joinees I knew was going to be there, figuring it would get there before he left for London, and there were strict instructions not to open it unless in the presence of all those joinees who had agreed to attend.

I was excited.

I sat back and I waited.

• • •

Saturday. 7 P.M. I received the following e-mail.

Dear Leader,

Joinee Davies here. We have had the most exciting day in the name of Join Me. Thank you for assigning us a task. I hope we have not let you down.

Myself, plus Joinee Whitby, Joinee Vallance, Joinee Jess and Joinee Nedelec met as agreed outside Harrods at 2 pm. From there we moved to Hyde Park where your package was opened. We were deeply excited when we heard your voice—the voice of the Leader!

Anyway, things were progressing nicely and we found a great deal of old men to make happy. In Hyde Park itself we found several old men on deck chairs and bought them cups of tea. We took pictures and will send them soon.

Once we had run out of old men there we got on a train to Hammersmith, and tried to find hospitals, rest homes and shelters, or anywhere we thought old men might hang out. As we passed a McDonald's, we spotted an old American man buying a cheeseburger, so we ran up and paid for his meal for him. He was very surprised but rather delighted.

But then we were walking past a pub in Hammersmith, and . . .

. . . and this is where I started to smile a very big smile indeed. Looking back on it, this was quite a turning point. Something which would help shape the future of Join Me forever.

The joinees were getting toward the end of their day together. They were satisfied. They'd done as I'd asked, they'd made some old men very happy and they'd been enjoying themselves.

Just as they were about to stop for the day, though, they spotted an old man, in a blue blazer and with white hair, trudging into a pub in Hammersmith. They followed him in, and observed him for a little while, from a table on the other side of the room.

He looked sad. He'd bought himself half a lager—never a good sign—and was now sitting in a corner, lost in thought, a look of concern all over his old man's face.

The joinees considered him for a while, then discussed what actions, if any, they should take. They chose to approach him.

"Excuse me," said Joinee Whitby. "I'm from something called Join Me. I was wondering if there was anything we could do to make you happy?"

The old man looked up at my joinee, and tried a smile.

"I don't think so," he said. "I don't think there's anything you can do to make me happy."

"Why not?"

And the old man—an old man named Raymond Price—told him.

"My car's broken down. I live in Teignmouth in Devon. I've had to spend all my cash to get the car towed away. I've got no way of getting home. I've just spent my last pound on this half of lager. I was just sitting here wondering what on earth I'm going to do. I can't get home."

Whitby looked over to the table of joinees and then back at Raymond Price.

"I think we can help," he said.

• • •

Joinee Whitby e-mailed me to tell me he'd be sending the dictaphone back to me straight away, and that Raymond Price had recorded a special message on it for me. I told Whitby that I was keen that the dictaphone arrived safely, so I would trust him and tell him my home address, rather than have him use the P.O. Box number. He told me he'd already found all my personal details some time ago on the Internet, through some kind of domain name search. This worried me. For a start, he'd already lost me with the phrase "domain name search." But was this the beginning of the stalking Ian had talked about? What was he doing, tracking down the home address of his usually anonymous Leader? What were his plans? And why had he told me that rather scary fact? I tried not to think about it for long, and the package arrived safe and sound the next morning.

I took the dictaphone out and pressed play. There was a muffled, pub atmosphere . . . faint music . . . someone's mobile phone playing the *Murder She Wrote* theme tune in the background . . . a fruit machine . . . and then the soft, Devonshire accent of Mr. Raymond Price.

"I'm in the doldrums," it started, which made me laugh, because the only other time I've heard anyone use that expression was on an episode of *Take the High Road*. "My car's broken down. They've taken it to New Morden. I live in Teignmouth in Devon. I was sitting in this pub, having a half a lager, thinking how on earth am I going to get the cash together to get back to Teignmouth in Devon. Within seconds of that thought a gentlemen came up to me and asked 'Can I make you happy?' And I said to him, 'No. I've got a real problem here.' And then I explained to him, and he said that he and his friends thought they would be able to help me. From whence they all clubbed together to get me my train fare back to Teignmouth in Devon . . ."

How great was this? There are three things I'd like you to take away from Mr. Price's statement. One: on a whim, and for no personal gain whatsoever, my joinees had got their wallets and purses out and pooled their resources in order to give a random old man £38—enough to cover his train fare, and buy him some dinner for the journey home. Two: Raymond Price can't say "Teignmouth" without saying "in Devon" afterwards, which I love. And three: he used the word "whence," proving beyond all doubt that he is, indeed, a very old man. I loved Raymond Price. And I loved my joinees for helping him out.

The recorded message continued:

"It is an unbelievable story. It is as if somebody has sent these people into my life at this time, just when I needed help. It is as if someone from above has sent them to give me aid. And I have never been so happy as I am now. And I'm an artist and already have everything I need. But they have helped me. I am so happy."

Well, there you have it. I was now, officially, a Higher Power. *I* was that someone from above, sending my angels into places of despair. I was the Orson to my joinees' Mork.

The joinees took Mr. Price's home address, and told him that I would almost certainly write him a letter. He thanked them again and again, and promised to pay them back, and thanked them again, and shook their hands, and said he'd be getting in touch with the *Teignmouth News* to tell them of his experience in the usually cold, usually unfriendly London.

The joinees returned to their homes around the country having made new friends and done something truly worthwhile with their day. This had been an important event. For one thing, I knew now beyond a shadow of a doubt that Whitby was back on board. There'd be no more mutiny now. But more importantly, we had made an old man very happy. We had done a good deed, for a random pensioner, and brought an unexpected ray of sunshine into his life. We had made a difference.

I knew then that we had found our purpose. We had found our cause. We would make old men very happy.

And then we would start on the rest of you.

HOW TO SUCCEED WITH GIRLS
JOIN ME
Join Me HQ
London
JOIN ME

CHAPTER · 9

11. *Daniel did bring forth bread, and cheese of kine.*
12. *And Daniel laid the cheese upon the bread, and placed them in the oven.*
13. *And presently out of the oven issued fire and brimstone, and the smoke thereof ascended as the smoke of a furnace, and verily, the kitchen did quake mightily.*

Now, my American friend, I don't know if *you've* ever started a cult, but there are certain things you have to take into consideration when doing so.

The first is whether or not you refer to it as such. Others may have continually referred to Join Me in this way, but I was sticking with "collective." Partly because I prefer it, and partly because that's the kind of thing a cult leader does.

Secondly, you have to decide whether to use your powers for Good, or for Evil. I suppose in some ways this was the dilemma I had been facing, but now Raymond Price had made the decision for me.

I would be lying if I told you there wasn't a part of me that wanted to use my joinees to spread mischief across the land. I would love to be able to tell you, for example, that I and two hundred followers had arranged the largest-ever post office robbery, with 201 masked raiders invading some sub-branch in Tooting and making off with roughly a tenner each. I was also starting to daydream about booking every single ticket for the opening night of the next Ben Elton musical and then getting everyone to stand up and leave just as the curtain was going up for the first song. But alas, it wasn't to be. Because I, Danny Wallace, was to be at the service of All Things Good.

Old men the length and breadth of this country wouldn't know what had hit them. I was absolutely determined that overnight, their lives would improve. And why? Because the sheer excitement of the Raymond Price initiative was yet to die down. Maybe it was because I couldn't really tell anyone, or share my excitement. I was hoarding it and, consequently, it was lasting bloody ages. I was as close to being giddy as it's possible to be while still maintaining a fairly masculine air. A plan had formed in my mind. I'd already written a lengthy letter to Mr. Price, explaining who those five joinees were and why they had done what they'd done, and even invited him to join me. I posted it off with a spring in my step and a whistle on my lips. As it turned out, the whole thing had been a handy trial scheme. A useful experiment. And all the signs were pointing to the fact that I could now do it on a much larger scale.

I really could improve the lives of hundreds—if not thousands—of old men.

But it would cost money. I'd already shelled out for all those leaflets and stickers. Surely it was someone else's turn to pay? All this was kind of in honor of Gallus, though, I kept telling myself. And let's not forget—he was an old man himself. This is something he would love. It wasn't about me. Not really. Just because I was enjoying it . . . well . . . that shouldn't even come into it. It was just a by-product of the real quest, a bonus. If I was serious, I would have to be prepared to sacrifice a little something. In this case, some money. But, as I think you are beginning to understand, I *was* serious. In fact, I was becoming very serious indeed.

So I found a company, phoned them up and ordered a hundred brand new disposable cameras.

"A hundred?" said the man.

"A hundred," I said.

"Big wedding, or something, is it?"

"Nope. I'm going to send them all to strangers and make them take pictures of old men."

"Cool," said the man.

• • •

Two days later the cameras arrived in a big brown box, by special delivery. I lugged them upstairs and unpacked them carefully. I now had a hundred Pro-Image Flash cameras. Oh yes. *Pro*-Image. I'd even gone the extra mile and paid for ones with flashes. Now it wouldn't just be the daywalking pensioners we'd be making happy—we'd be able to make the hardcore, nocturnal ones happy, too.

It was all very exciting. The only thing that put a downer on it was a discovery I made a little later that morning. The only other mail to arrive that day, you see, was one that on first glance seemed very familiar to me. There was something about it I recognized. It had my handwriting on the front, for a start. And an official Join Me rubber stamp mark on the back. I realized with a growing sense of unease that it was the letter I'd sent to Raymond Price. This was odd. I studied it.

Someone had scribbled out his address and written "PTO" on the front. I did as it said. I turned over and read. I was shocked and disappointed.

No one by the name of Raymond Price is known at this address.

I'd got the address wrong. Bugger. I went back to the original e-mail sent to me by the joinees who'd met him and checked where I'd gone wrong. But I hadn't. I'd written it out exactly as they'd sent it to me. Which was strange. Because they'd copied it straight off Raymond's driving licence.

My joinees were intelligent people. They knew how to copy stuff down. Surely they couldn't have got it wrong? Hang on . . . what if Raymond Price had . . .

No. It didn't bear thinking about. Surely not.

But what if?

What if Raymond Price, our happy old man, had given us a false address? What if the cheeky old devil had nicked our money and legged it back to Teignmouth in Devon? If, indeed, that was where he was from in the first place . . . he could well be, right now, sitting in the finest restaurant in all of Hammersmith, smoking cigars and wearing a new silk top hat, lavishly tipping people left, right and center—and all with *our* £38!

That surely couldn't have happened, could it? If it had, then my faith in humanity, in the future of Join Me . . . it'd all be shattered in just one awful moment. It didn't make sense to me. Who would *do* something like that?

Anyway . . . think about it from *his* point of view. What if Joinee Whitby and pals hadn't come across as simple, trusting folk, Good Samaritans, bringing hope into this bleak and ever darker world? What if Raymond Price had thought they were some kind of happy-clappy extremist Christian group? What if he thought they were nutters? They'd certainly been *very* keen to help him—maybe *overly* keen. What if he'd felt bullied into accepting money from these "Joinees" acting under a "Commandment" from an unseen "Leader"? That poor bloke! He must have been cacking himself. His voice had certainly wobbled slightly on that recording, but I'd put that down to emotion; I hadn't even considered it might have been sheer bloody terror.

Or . . . more likely . . . what if it had all been just a silly mistake? What if Raymond had shown them the wrong piece of ID? One with an old address on? We've all got them.

I decided that was the most likely occurrence of all, and that nothing would deter me from my mission. More old men *would* be made happy—whether they liked it or not.

And so I bought a hundred jiffy bags and printed out a hundred letters, then wrote a hundred addresses of a hundred random joinees onto each, and put a hundred cameras in them, along with their mission statement. Find an old man. Make him very happy. Take a picture as proof. Job done.

I took six plastic Tesco bags, each full of jiffy bags, to the post office down the road and bought seventy-eight pence worth of stamps for each. My arms were already tired from all the packing, but this was nothing compared with how tired my tongue became after licking three stamps per envelope for a hundred envelopes in a forty-minute period. I had so much glue in my mouth after that you'll be glad to hear it put me right off the whole gluesniffing scene for good. I started to walk home and felt my mobile going off in my pocket but ignored it. You try licking three hundred stamps of a morning and see how bloody chatty you are.

On reflection, I should have answered it. It was Hanne. She'd left a message, saying, "Hi, look, I thought you were going to give me a ring about the film premiere. Do you want to go or not? Let me know or I'll give your ticket to someone else. I know that Steve from work would love to go. He likes Vin Diesel."

Who was Steve? She'd never mentioned a Steve before. Surely I'd have remembered she worked with someone with a name as distinctive as that. And who the hell's Vin Diesel? I called her straight back, but her mobile was off. She was probably on air. I should have left a message saying yes, of course I'll be there, and I love Vin Diesel too, but I decided I should probably find out who Vin Diesel was first, just in case he wasn't a film star but a mate of Steve's and I'd just declared undying love for him.

I got home, stuck some cheese on toast in the oven and thought about Raymond Price some more. Paranoia set in again. Could he *really* have given us a false address? It seemed unlikely. In the pictures he looked very jolly about everything. There was even one in which my joinees gather behind him, and he crouches in the middle, with two thumbs up.

As I ate my lunch and contemplated my life, I reflected that this wasn't so bad. Being your own boss. Sitting at home. Watching telly when you wanted. Going to bed when you wanted. Eating what you liked. Having to wade through passport photos to get to the fridge. Buying disposable cameras and posting them to strangers. Making random old men very happy. Oh, I can see why so many people work from home, I really can. You get a lot done.

I decided to leave a message with Hanne, asking her when exactly the premiere was, and telling her to give me a bell that night.

Boyfriend duty done, I jogged downstairs to check the second post and was delighted to see that the P.O. box delivery, which always arrives slightly later than my normal mail, had made it through. And with it, a letter from a new joinee. My 201st.

The photograph enclosed was of a smiling man, with soft blonde hair and glasses, wearing a black T-shirt with a white collar. It made him look a little like a vicar until closer inspection . . . but in this case that was probably the point. What he was wearing could really be described as "vicar casual." Because this man, my latest joinee, went by the name of the Reverend Gareth Saunders. I read the letter excitedly. Could it really be from a proper, bona fide vicar? There was a website address for his own homepage, and I checked it . . . and yes. He *was* a vicar. A *practicing* vicar. An assistant curate, no less, at Inverness Cathedral!

Now, the one thing I hadn't been expecting was for a vicar to join me. They're already part of quite a big club, so to speak, and it's a club that's famed for its strict belief system. Surely it wasn't normal for the Church to let vicars go about joining things like this? Unless the Church was worried about Join Me, and Gareth was a vicar spy, but being a vicar he wasn't allowed to lie about it. That would really get on people's tits, being a vicar as well as a spy.

I was fascinated. Joinee Saunders's letter was polite, and funny, and engaging. He'd simply found Join Me on the Web and thought it sounded fun.

I e-mailed him immediately, just to touch base, and was surprised when, minutes later, he replied. We hit it off electronically, straight away. And he was full of good advice.

"Regarding Join Me, the one thing I can tell you I've learned from the Church," he wrote, "is that it spreads best through personal contact. That's the one thing you really need."

Personal contact. He was right. I'd been worried about revealing myself to my joinees *en masse,* but if they could look into my eyes, if they could feel the passion face-to-face, then surely that would be the way to enthuse them? To get them to spread the word even further? To let them know just how important it was to make old men happy? To really *believe* in Join Me—and make others believe? Wasn't that what Jesus had done with his disciples? And there were only a few of those—I've got *loads* more than he managed.

And before any Christian readers get all offended—relax. I'm not saying that I'm the new Jesus. I'm just saying that there's a very good chance that I *might* be.

I wrote back to Gareth to say that I agreed, personal contact was definitely the way ahead. And to prove it, with his permission, I would visit him. He said of course, and when was I thinking of? I told him I was thinking of that weekend. He appeared unfazed, and said “Okay.”

So I booked my ticket to Scotland and packed my bag.

The Reverend Gareth J.M. Saunders

CHAPTER · 10

1. *In the fiftieth year of the reign of Elizabeth queen of Britons, Daniel went forth to the land of Scotia.*

2. *And there he beheld a great temple, and before it a priest.*

3. *And the priest spake unto Daniel, saying, Hear ye the Leper Messiah, and hearken to the Phantom Lord.*

4. *And Daniel was astonished, and said, How canst thou preach such iniquity?*

5. *And the priest answered, saying, Och, well, perhaps you should start with some of their earlier stuff. Like, "Ride the Lightning." Now that's* vintage *Metallica, that is.*

6. *When he had spoken these things the priest wrought lewdness; and Daniel was filled with fear.*

7. *But the priest gave Daniel provision, and shelter, and it was good.*

8. *And at the cockcrowing Daniel went on his way.*

The plane touched down at Inverness International Airport.

I say "touched down." That really doesn't do justice to the extreme violence that the captain managed to invest in his touchdown. It's like saying you stroked a cat, only you did it with a hammer.

Oh, and I say "International Airport." It's more of a cowshed got lucky. Apparently, as well as flying to and from sunny Luton, happy Inverness residents can also fly to Malta, although if you miss your flight you have to wait a full six months for the next one. It would literally be quicker to walk.

It was stormy in Inverness and the short amble from the plane to the cowshed saw me soaked through with icy, furious water. But there was a fantastic sight to behold as I made it to the arrivals lounge: a tall man with a goatee beard, dressed in full vicar's gear, holding a small sign saying "Join Me."

"Gareth?" I said, although if it wasn't Gareth I would have been very seriously worried for the Christian faith, having to resort to my very basic tactics to get people to sign up.

"Hello!" he said, cheerily. "I thought I'd make this sign so you'd know it was me. I was worried the dog collar wouldn't be enough."

Gareth and I walked out of the airport to find his car. It was still raining very, very hard. His mobile went off.

"Yes . . . I've just picked Danny up . . . the bloke I joined . . . yes . . . well . . . we'll see . . ."

He looked over at me and smiled. Clearly there were people less at ease with Gareth meeting me than he was.

"Okay . . . yes . . . well, it's pissing down here . . . yes . . ."

Pissing down? Was this the way a vicar talked?

It was his wife, Jane, on the phone, and he continued to chat as we clambered into his sleek red Rover. The road out of the airport gives you two options . . . one sign points to Aberdeen. The other points to Inverness. Gareth slowed the car to a stop and pondered for a moment.

"Do we want fun, or do we want . . . ," he sighed, ". . . Inverness?"

"I suppose we want Inverness, really," I said. "What with that being where you live, and all."

Gareth exhaled heavily. "Okay," he said. And we drove toward Inverness.

The Rover's heating kicked in, and I started to take my sweater off, before realizing with horror that that morning I'd pulled on the first T-shirt to hand. It was a retro '70s T-shirt, with a big pointing hand, and the words "I'm With Stupid" written on it. I decided I couldn't reveal it. For one thing, it was pointing toward where Gareth was sitting, and it really wouldn't have proved a great way of endearing myself to him.

Anyone standing in front of the car would have seen one man dressed as a vicar, and another quite clearly mocking the Christian faith. I kept my sweater on.

"So, um . . . Danny," said Gareth. "Who else has joined you? I mean, what kind of people, generally?"

I took a tatty piece of paper out of my pocket and read it.

"The average joinee is thirty-three years old," I said, "and living in the Midlands with one-fifth of a child."

Gareth nodded.

"He is approximately fifty-eight percent male."

"Right," he said, as we somehow negotiated our way through the storm. "That's kind of what Jane says about me."

"How did you meet Jane?" I asked.

"I met her at my dad's funeral. She was after my brother. But I got her."

"Nice one," I said.

"Thanks," he said.

I had warmed to Gareth within seconds of meeting him. Thirty years old and with the build of a rugby player, he neither looked nor sounded like a conventional priest. He'd lived all over the country, and toured the world with the National Youth Choir of Great Britain, and, perhaps best of all, he was a laugher. He'd tell jokes, and react well to jokes, and had a quick and inclusive wit.

He drove me past Loch Ness, which was all but hidden by huge grey smudges of mist, and the relentless torrents of rain which crashed down onto the windows of the car.

"Hey," said Gareth. "One of the houses round here has a load of gnomes in its front garden, and they're all playing cricket, you'll like that . . ."

We slowed the car down as we passed the house Gareth thought it was, but couldn't spot even one gnome. Play must have been called off due to rain. But if it's garden ornaments you want, you could do worse than a trip to Loch Ness. Nearly every hotel and bed and breakfast we passed had some form of huge and inconvenient Loch Ness Monster in its garden or forecourt.

There were also half a dozen signs up and down the road, proclaiming "Loch Ness 2000! Exhibition! This way!" I love it when people still use the number 2000 in titles, as if it continues to make things sound futuristic.

We drove on, and chatted about Join Me, until we arrived and disembarked at Urquhart Castle, one of the local and hugely impressive landmarks. It's a ruin now, but still boasts a fully working trebuchet. To be honest, I think they were asking for trouble building a castle near a fully working trebuchet. No wonder it was a bloody ruin.

My phone rang. It was Hanne and I was quick to answer it.

"Hello?"

"Yeah, are you coming tonight, or what?"

"Sorry?"

"To the Vin Diesel film. Are you coming tonight or what? Because I'm getting sick of you avoiding the question. If you don't want to come to the premiere, fine, but at least let me know so I can tell Steve whether he's coming or not."

"Oh yeah, who's Steve?" I asked, then mouthed to Gareth: "Girlfriend."

"Doesn't matter who Steve is, are you coming or not?"

"I thought you were going to call me last night," I said, trying to deflect some of the obvious anger.

"I wanted *you* to call *me*. You know. Like you used to? So are you coming?"

"Er . . . no."

"*Jesus,* Danny . . ." Gah! Hanne had just taken the Lord's name in vain! In front of a vicar! There was no way he'd have heard it, but still, it's just not done, is it?

"Hanne," I said, blushing.

"Where are you? Tell me where you are and why you can't come. Make it good."

"Where am I?"

Well, this was tricky. I wanted to make something up. Some valid-sounding excuse that would have placated Hanne and saved me some strife. But I was standing right next to a vicar. A vicar who would have known I was lying about where I was for precisely the fact that he was there too. You can't lie in front of a vicar. Not without offending Baby Jesus, and we all know where that leads.

"I am . . . in Inverness."

"Where?"

"Inverness. At a castle. Just near Loch Ness."

"Loch Ness! Why? Who with?"

I chose to answer the who with, rather than the why.

"A friend of mine." I winked at Gareth, letting him know everything was a-okay.

"Which friend?"

"Gareth," I said. Gareth smiled at me. I smiled back.

"How long have you known this one?"

"Oh . . . just . . . recently."

"Another new friend? And what does this one do?"

"He's . . . a vicar," I said. I was trying to say all this as if it was the most normal thing in the world for me to be at a castle in Loch Ness with a vicar I hardly know.

"Danny . . . this is not normal. This is not normal, to be in castles in Loch Ness with vicars you hardly know."

I should have tried harder.

"Are you telling me the truth? Where are you really?"

"That's really where I am. Look, Hanne, take this Steve bloke to the film. If he likes Vin Diesel, so be it. I don't even know what one is. I'm back tomorrow morning, I'll come round, we can . . ."

"Tomorrow morning? You're staying with this vicar in Loch Ness? Jesus, Danny—"

"Hanne, please, try and tone the blasphemy down," I said, hanging up and turning my phone off, but not before catching an astounded *"Wha . . . ?"* coming out the other end.

I could now give my full attention to this most intriguing of joinees. We carried on walking around the castle.

"I've not been here since I was a kid," said Gareth excitedly. "I always used to get taken to castles when I was a kid. Jane's family had a kind of National Trust membership, so I think she's visited every bloomin' castle in Britain . . ."

We wandered around in some of the heaviest rain known to man, but our spirits weren't dampened. We explored like kids, marveling at the dungeons, climbing high up the towers, studying the signs. Each sign told you which room you were standing in, and had a braille translation written underneath, despite the fact that as we were in a ruin and therefore outdoors, these were pretty useless. "Oh," the blind people would probably say, "this room appears to sound exactly the same as all the others."

"Hello, sirs," said a man, all of a sudden immediately behind us. He appeared to be some kind of tour guide. Unless he just really, really liked neon jackets.

"Hello," said Gareth and me, in perfect unison.

"We'll be closing up in ten minutes," said the man.

"Okay," we said.

"Where are you two from?" he asked.

"I'm a priest over there at Inverness Cathedral," said Gareth.

"Ah-huh," said the man.

"And I'm a Satanist," I said. "And we're just having a discussion, just thrashing a few things out."

"Ah-huh," said the man. "And how long are you in Inverness for?"

Gareth and I looked at each other. It seems that priests and Satanists are quite the common thing at Urquhart Castle.

"Well . . . I *live* here," said Gareth. "What with me being a priest at the Cathedral and all."

"And I'm from Hades," I tried. "It's near Swindon?"

"Ah-huh," said the man, now looking at his watch. "Well, we'll be closing up in ten minutes, gentlemen, have a good day, now . . ."

• • •

The Reverend Gareth J. M. Saunders, as I have already told you, is thirty years old. He's been married for three of them to Jane, a "drunken alcohol counselor."

"A what?"

"A drug and alcohol counselor."

"Oh. I thought you said 'a drunken alcohol counselor.'"

It was lucky he hadn't, and luckier still that she wasn't. I imagine if she was, most of her advice would have been "Oh, sod it, just have another drink . . ."

"It's very nice of you to let me stay the night," I said. And it was. Gareth and I were virtual strangers, but he'd more or less insisted I make use of his spare room and the futon therein.

"Both Jane and I come from homes where our parents always had folks to stay," he said. "Or for tea, or coffee, or whatever. My mum never used to lock the front door, so we'd often come home to find that friends had invited themselves in, and were making tea and toast in the kitchen, or were watching TV while they waited for a bus. So it's no bother . . ."

Gareth made some tomato soup and we sat in his living room listening to sheets of rain batter the windows. It was cold and dark outside, but we had soup, and bread, so all was well with the world. Gareth took his dog collar off, and it prompted the inevitable.

"So . . . when did you decide to become a vicar?" I asked.

Gareth thought about it.

"I suppose it was when I was nine. I didn't know any better. I'd always wanted to be a doctor, but then one day I decided I wanted to be a minister. My mum was a nurse who worked with old people and a lot of them died. Not because of my mum, I'd like to point out. But that possibly gave me a sense of what it was to comfort people, and certainly since my dad died, there was a recognition that even when he was at his most ill, he was still a whole human being. It was just a different aspect of being a person. And I remember coming home, and telling my mum over lunch that I didn't want to be a doctor any more. I wanted to be a minister. Because I wanted to heal the *whole* person."

"You were a very wise nine-year-old," I said.

"I haven't said anything wise since," said Gareth, and I laughed.

Gareth's dad died in 1998, from kidney failure. "But he had Alzheimer's Disease, too. He often used to queue at the fridge, waiting for the next train."

Gareth smiled.

"But watching my dad as he was ill had a lot to do with what I am today, I suppose."

As did Gareth's choice in music. Because Gareth—probably like *your* local vicar—is a massive heavy metal fan.

"It was a way of dealing with things," he said. He picked up his guitar from the corner of the room and began to play. "Now, this is Metallica's 'Welcome Home (Sanitarium).' " I didn't recognize the tune, but then that's because I like normal music. But Gareth played confidently, and well, and in his hands it sounded good.

"I'll introduce you to a few things," he said, putting his guitar back down and sliding a CD into his stereo. "This is Voivod. They're French-speaking Canadians. They're very . . . passionate."

Gareth pressed play. If this was his idea of passion then I'm very surprised he's still married. It was loud, it was confusing, it was all guitar screams and near-hysterical shouting.

"What's the name of this track?" I yelled.

" 'Cockroaches.' In a minute I'll play you 'Too Scared to Scream.' "

I had a feeling I would be.

Gareth was head-banging now. He picked up his guitar again and I noticed there were two more behind him.

"How many guitars have you got?"

"Eight," he said, still head-banging to the terrifying sound of Voivod. "This acoustic was my first, then I got that one secondhand, then I moved to London and bought the Strat. Then I was working in a textile mill in Selkirk and bought myself the CC157, with ballback. It's electro-acoustic, steel strings."

I nodded approvingly.

"Then I needed some extra stuff so when I was working in Bermondsey I bought this, the GC80; haggled that down from £540 to £380 . . ."

"Nice one," I said, not really knowing what I was on about.

Gareth had noticed the time. We'd been so busy messing about that we'd lost track of it. In twenty minutes Gareth was due to take the evening Eucharist Service at the cathedral. He switched the stereo off and sprang into action.

"We'd better go," he said, finding his shoes and trying to find the keys to the cathedral. Inevitably, they were attached to a scratched plastic Metallica keyring.

It was still raining heavily as we jumped into the car. And I mean heavily. We turned on the radio to hear the rain described as "torrential" and the winds described as "storm force." Rivers had reached bursting point, and severe flood warnings had been issued. Had I traveled by train, I wouldn't have even made it into Scotland, let alone the far *north* of Scotland.

And then Gareth uttered a sentence I had never heard before, and dare say I will probably never hear again.

"Shit! I forgot my dog collar!"

Truly, he is the face of the modern clergy.

"Shall we go back and get it?" I asked.

"Too late now. I'll have to try and find one in the cathedral . . ."

We arrived, and ran from the car into the cathedral doorway to negotiate the locks in the downpour. Once in, Gareth opened the main door for the only person who'd turned up for the Eucharist, a friendly, elderly lady by the name of Cynthia.

Cynthia busied herself at her pew, and Gareth pointed out a statue of the cathedral's founder, Robert Eden, before sneakily attaching a Join Me sticker to its lapel. Moments later a man in a hat, who'd just popped in, noticed it and said, "Now, who's done that? Why would people do such things?" Gareth put on a concerned, vicar's face, and said, "I don't know, it's terrible, isn't it?" and reached up as if to take it down. The man turned away, satisfied, and Gareth simply smoothed the edges of the sticker down.

"There," he said. "Now . . . I'd better get ready . . ."

I'd never been to a church service like this before, never broken the bread and drunk the wine, and certainly never read out loud from the Bible in front of others. But it would have been rude not to have joined in, and Joinee Saunders was someone I was fast becoming firm friends with. I took my place on the other side of Cynthia, and the three of us began the service.

Gareth's voice immediately softened as he began to read. I wasn't sure what part of the Bible he was reading from, but it was about friendship, and it struck a chord. One passage in particular . . .

Pleasant speech multiplies friends
And a gracious tongue multiplies courtesy
Let those who are friendly with you be many
But let your advisers be one in a thousand

Gareth was right. Not that he'd made it up himself, but I figured if anyone in the room believed it, it was probably him.

Gareth left to get changed into his fancy cassock, and in the meantime we were joined by another lady, late and damp thanks to the fierce rain, and she sat at the pew in front of me, her head bowed. Gareth returned and continued the service.

But then the woman in front of me stood up, very quickly. I looked at her as she turned toward me, and fixed me with an icy stare. It was like she thought I'd touched her arse, or something. I was very uncomfortable, and just stared back at her, with wide eyes. She held her hand out to me.

"Peace be with you," she said.

I shook her hand, but I'd misheard her.

"Pleased to meet you," I said. The woman wrinkled her nose at me.

"No . . . *peace be with you,*" she said again.

"Peace be with you," said Gareth, suddenly there, taking her hand, rescuing me. "It's something we say," he whispered. "Only say it if you want to."

Two visiting American men arrived—Will and Scott—and took a pew. Gareth welcomed them and I shook their hands, saying "peace be with you" like I'd been saying it all my life.

"Peace be with you," they both said back. To be honest, if it was peace we wanted, we wouldn't get it by going on about it all the time, but it was quite pleasant nevertheless.

Gareth continued the service, and before too long we were all kneeling, eating our bread and sipping our wine. And then it was over.

• • •

"What did you think?" asked Gareth.

"Good gig," I said. "I liked the wine. Didn't think much of the sandwiches."

"We need a new caterer," he said. "Hey, Cynthia. Come and meet Danny. He's the guy that founded Join Me."

"Oh," said Cynthia, "yes, I did wonder whether that was you. Gareth has talked about you. About halfway through the service I did wonder whether that was you."

"When you should have been focusing on Jesus?" said Gareth, mock-sternly.

Cynthia looked ashamed but then laughed.

"How many people have joined you?" she asked.

"It's just me and Gareth," I joked. She didn't seem to think it was a joke.

"Well, the best of luck with it, both of you."

Cynthia wandered off and Gareth started to get changed. We were alone in the cathedral and suddenly it seemed okay to talk at a normal volume. I'd only just noticed it, but apart from during the service, people didn't feel comfortable if they weren't whispering in this place.

"It's ridiculous, that," said Gareth. "People get annoyed with me for just chatting in here. But it's just a building. We should be able to use it as one."

"You know what you were saying, in the service, about letting your advisers be one in a thousand?" I said.

"Yes?"

"Well, I'd like *you* to be one of my advisers."

"How many do you have?"

"Well, there's this one bloke called Dennis. He owns the moon. But I'd like to know how *you* think Join Me should progress. In a kind of non-religious way, I mean. We're making old men happy, but . . . you know . . . what's the future of Join Me?"

Gareth scratched his head.

"This is something I've thought about. Y'see, the whole thing about the Church is that it spreads best through personal contact. You're far more likely to respond to a person than you are a theory. So you should up the personal contact to get people to join you."

"Right," I said. "I will, then."

"And that's what intrigues me about this whole Join Me thing, and kind of why I joined. I did a term at theological college on 'Sociology and Religion,' and our lecturer kept banging on about how no one is joining anything any more. That explains why church membership is declining, and why membership of political parties is going down, and so on. So I was interested in what you're doing, because the sociological theory says that people just will *not* join you."

"Well, I fly in the face of that theory," I said. "But as a vicar, how have people reacted to you joining? I mean, what do they think of a vicar joining something like this? You're already part of something, after all . . ."

"Essentially, there's something about Join Me that appeals to my faith as a Christian priest. You know? The Church is not a cult; it's a collective of Christians who are joining together to spread the word about Jesus Christ and improving people's lives a little. Maybe Join Me will get there first. But Join Me is also about faith. Faith in one another. Faith and trust in following something you don't really know completely."

I considered Gareth's words carefully.

"I suppose that makes me some kind of Jesus figure," I said.

Gareth didn't look too sure about that. I continued anyway.

"But . . . y'know. He's had a bit of a headstart on me. Two thousand years or so. No wonder he's so far ahead. You shouldn't compare us, really."

"I didn't."

"I'm just saying, you shouldn't."

"I didn't."

"Well, good. Because you shouldn't."

"Mmm."

Despite his somewhat churlish reluctance to herald me as the new Jesus, Gareth was my kind of vicar. Cool, down-to-earth and utterly inspiring in that, at the end of the day, he's just a normal bloke, with no airs, graces or pretentions. The most ordinary people can easily be the most inspiring, and while you couldn't call Gareth one of the most ordinary, there was certainly something inspiring about him.

On the way out of the cathedral, though, I spotted a sign that didn't seem to sit well with Gareth's more relaxed way of life.

ATTENTION
DO **NOT** PARK ON THE GRASS.
DO **NOT** PARK YOUR CAR IN FRONT OF THE CATHEDRAL.

All very unfriendly. All very old-fashioned. All very stern. I'm not a churchgoer, as you may have guessed, and I suppose it's partly to do with the attitude I've found that the people who run it usually have. I pointed it out to Gareth.

"Yes, I'm replacing that, with something far nicer. I did do a draft the other day actually, in the style of the original. It said:

ATTENTION
DO **NOT** PARK ON THE GRASS.
DO **NOT** THROW THE HYMN BOOKS.
DO **NOT** PASS WIND.
DO **NOT** SHIT ON YOUR PEWS.

"I showed it to the Bishop, but he didn't seem keen."

I really, really liked the Reverend Gareth Saunders.

• • •

That night we ate dinner with Jane, and then they taught me how to play Mah Jong. We drank red wine, and ate cheesecake and laughed. Gareth played me home videos from years back, and I sat on their sofa and stroked their three cats.

I slept well that night. I'd made a good friend. And I'd had lots of wine too.

In the morning, Gareth dropped me off at the airport, and we began to say our good-byes.

"You taught me something vital," I said, in a moment that wouldn't have seemed out of place on *Highway to Heaven*. "About personal contact. I'm going to try and keep that up."

"Do that," said Gareth. "I think it's important. Promise me you'll meet the next person who says they'll join you."

"Sure," I said.

"No, actually promise me. There's a lot of good can come from Join Me. Not just the old man thing, but if you extend it."

He was looking at me, deadly serious.

"If you're honestly going to continue with this, I think it's important that you visit people. So promise me you will."

"Okay. I promise."

And with that, I climbed out of the car, waved him good-bye, and flew back to London.

I knew that that had been an important moment for Gareth, and I knew I would carry out his wishes. I would visit the next person who said they'd join me. It would become part of my brief. I'd go anywhere, meet anyone. It was for the good of Join Me.

I got home to my flat that night and checked my e-mails.

I clicked the first one open. It was from someone offering to join me. A girl. A girl with an exotic name.

I remembered my promise to Gareth.

But you'll never guess where she lived . . .

JOIN MOI
THE FRENCH

CHAPTER · 11

16. *And Estelle the Parisian was very wroth, and her countenance fell.*

17. *And Daniel said unto Estelle, Why art thou wroth? and why is thy countenance fallen?*

18. *And Estelle said, Intendest thou not to bless the female stricken in age as thou blesseth the male stricken in age?*

19. *And Daniel lowered his eyes and was speechless without all hope of life.*

The fact that word had spread across the English Channel to France thrilled me beyond belief. And the fact that a chic Parisian girl by the name of Estelle was offering to join me thrilled me even more. And not for the normal reasons being joined by a chic Parisian girl would thrill a boy for.

I was thrilled because she was my first international joinee. No longer was the collective a hundred percent British. We were breaking down the boundaries. Reaching into Europe. Becoming a global entity.

Granted—she'd only *offered* to join me so far. But that was reason enough to meet her—particularly after my promise to Joinee Saunders—and I was certain that once I'd explained a little more about the scheme, she'd willingly hop on board. So we'd arranged to meet, and two nights later I was clambering off the Eurostar and making my way into the heart of Paris.

I'd told Hanne with a certain amount of guilt that I had loads of work on, and would have to spend the evening on it, and she'd said that was fine. I hadn't, strictly speaking, lied. Meeting Estelle would, in some odd, roundabout way, be work, even though it was actually happening in Paris, over a coffee. It's just that, if there was ever a time to tell Hanne about Join Me, it wasn't just before meeting a strange French girl in the city of love.

Now that I had arrived in the French capital, my plan was to entertain myself tonight, then meet Estelle the following day and charge her with the enviable duty of spreading the word of Join Me throughout France. I was sure she'd be only too happy to oblige. In fact, I was sure she'd buy into the whole Join Me concept wholesale. From our brief correspondence, I'd learnt that she was an artist and amateur poet. She'd been told about Join Me by a friend of hers in England (who, incidentally, hadn't joined), and liked the idea of strangers coming together for a single purpose. Whatever that purpose was. And now that we *had* a definite purpose, I was keen to tell her more about it, face-to-face. But that was tomorrow.

I dumped my rucksack at my inordinately grubby hotel, and went out in search of food. This I found at a little restaurant tucked around a corner in the Latin quarter of town and, sated, I wandered around, every so often pausing to look into the window of a bar or restaurant to see happy faces laughing and talking and laughing some more.

Oddly, all these faces were middle-aged. Where were all the young, hip Parisians? Was this one of those cities where no one bothers to go out before two or three in the morning? I walked down a few more streets, away from the more touristy-looking spots, to see if I could find them, but to no avail.

Then, down a sidestreet, I passed a tiny, thriving bar. I peered through the window. It was packed with young, cool Parisians—almost intimidatingly young and cool, in fact. But it still appealed more than the cold night air, and so in I went. I attracted a few looks as I walked in, being alone as I was, but I strode confidently up to the bar, not making eye contact with any of the people I sensed were studying me.

I stood at the bar and immediately saw that there were no beer pumps. No problem. I'd go for wine.

"Vin blanc, s'il vous plaît," I tried.

The barman, who appeared no older than eighteen, looked at me with confusion in his eyes. Maybe it was my accent.

"A glass of white wine, please."

"Er . . . *je* . . ." He trailed off and shrugged.

"Vin?" I tried. Come on, this was France. They've definitely got wine here. I've seen it on programs. I persisted.

"*Vin?* Wine?"

The barman picked up a laminated menu and showed it to me.

"Only this," he said. "Only this."

It was a cocktail menu. Well, that was fine. I studied the list, but didn't recognize even one of the cocktails. They were all named after things that were familiar, though, like Asterix, and Pocahontas, and Goofy, but I'd never had them, and I couldn't read what was in them because it was all in French. So I decided to just order anything and try my luck.

"Snoopy," I said.

"Okay," said the barman. "Snoopy."

And he began to make me a Snoopy. And while he did, I looked at the decor behind him. It was all a bit odd. There were lots of small toys and models decorating the shelves. A large plasma screen in the corner showed strange Japanese cartoons. There was a coat rack with people's names written above the coats in childish scrawl. On the bar was a bucket of lollipops. It all reminded me of being at primary school.

I turned around and looked at my fellow drinkers, and was horrified to see that they all looked like children. Not little children, but not proper grown-ups, either. What kind of bar was this? Everyone appeared to be about sixteen. I was undoubtedly the oldest person in the entire bar, by some margin.

I turned back to the bar to see that the barman had finished mixing my Snoopy. But rather than putting it in a glass . . . he'd . . . my God. What had he done?

This man had poured my drink into a baby bottle. A baby bottle complete with sterilized teat. And was now looking at me expectantly. He was expecting me to start sucking down my cocktail like a baby.

"What the hell is that?" I demanded. Was he taking the piss? Was the Snoopy regarded as the most childish of drinks? Was he saying I was a baby for ordering it?

"Snoopy," he said, pointing at the strange blue drink in its strange transparent bottle.

"Yes, it may well be a Snoopy," I said, outraged. "But what the hell have you put it in? Why have you put it in a bloody baby bottle?"

He looked frightened now, like I was about to strike out at him. It was probably the first time in ages he'd been scolded by an adult. It was probably the first time in ages he'd even *seen* an adult. He pointed at the toys around the bar, then at my fellow drinkers.

I turned round and noticed what I had failed to notice the first time. Everyone in the *entire bar* was drinking their cocktails out of baby bottles. I was shocked. What kind of place was this? It must have been some kind of fad bar, but if it was, it was a fad that's yet to hit London.

Embarrassed at my outburst, and even more so by my cocktail, I sat, cheeks burning, at a table. The youths at the table next to mine started to sing "Happy Birthday," and it became shamefully clear that I'd gatecrashed someone's seventeenth birthday party. It was horrible.

I tried to suck away discreetly at my drink—which turned out to be disappointingly non-alcoholic—but, being someone who has in the past struggled and failed to even give a hickey, I am sorry to report that drinking that Snoopy out of a rubber teat was extremely slow going. Mind you, it wasn't a bad cocktail. I dare say that if my mother's milk had tasted like a Snoopy, I might still be breastfeeding to this day.

Needless to say, I wasn't going to stay for more than one, and stood up and paid as soon as I'd made decent headway into my drink. I needed the toilet before I went, but decided against it, given that what with their chosen theme and decor, they would probably have replaced the toilets with potties, and upon trying to leave I would doubtless be stopped by a stern-looking woman who'd demand to inspect me to make sure I hadn't got any down my trousers.

I went home, went to the toilet, and went to bed.

• • •

Now, if I were a proper travel writer, I would tell you that that I spent my time before meeting Estelle discovering unseen parts of Paris, and strayed from the tourist trail, and discovered unique and original and delightful things. But I'm not a proper travel writer. I'm a bloke. So I went to the Eiffel Tower and had a scout about.

I'd be meeting prospective Joinee Estelle in a couple of hours, so to kill time I just stood, staring, at the giant steel tower. It was once, at three hundred meters high, the tallest building in the world. Nowadays, some hats are bigger and more impressive. But it's the feeling of being near the Eiffel Tower that marks it out as special. I love the fact that places like this bring together tourists from every part of the world. So special and iconic is it that on any given day there will be people from every corner of the earth drawn to it. People stand in queues next to other people who logistically and by rights they should never even have *seen,* let alone stood next to. It's only at times like this that a family from a village in Italy can meet a family from some town outside Yokohama without it seeming even slightly extraordinary to anyone that they should have crossed paths. No one treats it as special, or in fact with any degree of interest at all, but I love it. Landmarks bring the world together.

And that's when it hit me—a place like this is *precisely* where I should be spreading the word of Join Me. Landmarks!

This was brilliant. I'd been excited enough to get a French person interested in Join Me. But this place attracted people from all over the world. Germans, Italians, Dutch, Finns, Danes, Swedes, Japanese, Chinese, Americans, the lot! I'd get my thousand joinees in no time here!

I knew what I had to do. I had to send them a message. Get them intrigued. I needed some paper and a pen.

I dashed to the gift shop under the tower. They had no paper, nor any suitable pens, but I bought a large print of the Eiffel Tower for three euros simply because its reverse side was white and blank. Now all I needed was a pen. Souvenir Eiffel Tower Biros were too thin, and there were no stationery shops for miles, so I asked the lady behind the counter whether I could buy some lipstick off her. She must have thought it was a rather strange request, like I was late for a transvestite's ball or something, and she smiled politely and said she didn't have any. But sensing my disappointment, she pulled out an eyeliner from her handbag.

"Would you like this?"

It was perfect. I thanked her, and handed her a couple of euros, then found myself a bench. I sat down and thought about what to write. JOIN ME. There. That would do.

And so I sat, on the bench, holding my sign, waiting for people to approach me. No one did. In fact, all of a sudden, no one wanted to come anywhere near me. My sign seemed to be having the reverse effect from the one it was designed for. People were sitting on *other* benches, mind you—it was just that for some reason my bench didn't seem quite so appealing any more. So I moved. I didn't want to be sitting on an unappealing bench, after all. But still no one came up to have a chat.

No one, that is, until a lone Chinese girl with a huge pink rucksack approached me with great caution.

"What does this mean, please?" she said.

"I'm trying to get people together," I said. "Trying to create a kind of club."

"What kind of club?" she said.

"One based on good deeds, I think," I said.

"No," she said, and walked off.

Well, at least I'd talked to someone. That was progress of sorts.

I decided, however, that maybe I just wasn't being specific enough. Maybe that was why people weren't coming up to me. I had to appeal to certain *groups,* rather than just to a vague mass of people.

So I bought another picture of the Eiffel Tower, and wrote on it:

JOIN MOI
The French

I thought they'd appreciate the effort I'd gone to, to speak their language. I stood, holding my sign, in the square directly beneath the Eiffel Tower. And then the heavens opened, the rain lashed down, and everyone ran for cover. I gave it a minute, ditched my sign, and then ran for cover with them.

Bugger.

• • •

Prospective Joinee Estelle and I were to meet near the Pantheon, on Rue Soufflot, in a small café she couldn't remember the name of but which I'd apparently recognize by its orange and brown facade. At quarter to two I was sitting, ready, by the window of the café, watching people running by outside, umbrellas obscuring their faces, free hands tucked up in waterproof pockets. Estelle was late, but it didn't matter. The rain was doubtless to blame, and I was happy enough, with a hot chocolate in front of me and the warm light of the café.

A group of Americans sat down at a table behind me and began to talk about their day, loudly and with the confidence of people who think no one else in the country can possibly understand them. They weren't particularly impressed with Paris. Or the food. Or the French. The croissants weren't as good as the ones you get in America, it seems. Nor the wine. I imagine you probably also got better French people over there. You certainly get better Americans.

I swirled the last of my hot chocolate around the bottom of the cup and looked up to see a girl walk into the café. She had a fake-fur-rimmed parka much like mine, and long, wet brown hair. Her face had the unmistakable pout of the Gallic. I raised my eyebrows at her and she said "Ah!" and walked toward me.

"I am late," she said, shaking my hand and taking a seat.

"Doesn't matter," I said. "Thanks for coming!"

"Yes," she said, looking around the café distractedly, as if she was still looking for the person she was supposed to be meeting.

"I'm Danny," I said.

"Yes," she said. "Estelle."

She wiped some rain from her face with a tissue from the table, and said, "So . . ."

"Would you like a coffee?" I asked. "Or a tea? I just had a hot chocolate, but I think I'll have a tea next."

"No, thank you," she said, screwing up the tissue and popping it in the ashtray. "I can only stay a few minutes."

Eh? A few minutes? Was she serious? She certainly didn't seem to be making any effort to take her jacket off. She was dripping wet, and slightly sniffly—I'd have thought this was the ideal place for her to be.

"Oh," I said. "I see. That's a pity."

"Mmm," she said. "I have to go to meet a friend in a little while. But it was nice to meet you."

What? She already seemed to be wrapping this up! She'd only just sat down!

"Er . . . are you sure you don't want a coffee? I could tell you more about Join Me," I tried. She looked impatient and a little testy.

"Maybe I will have a glass of water," she said, flatly, before turning to one of the waiters and beckoning him over. She spoke in French, presumably ordering her water, and turned back to me.

"Okay," she said. "So tell me a little about this Join Me."

"Well, I'm asking people to join me," I said. "To work for good. At the moment we're making old men very happy, and—"

"Why not old woman?"

"Er . . . well, there was this bloke called Raymond Price, and—"

"Why not old woman?" she interrupted, again.

"I'll tell you . . . there was this bloke called—"

"So you make old man happy, but why not old woman too?"

There was no stopping her. She was feisty and abrupt. She seemed angry with me, and I'd barely said a word.

"We're going to get to that," I said. To be honest, I hadn't planned anything along those lines yet, but fair enough. If old women had to be made happy just to keep Estelle from beating me up, we'd do that as well.

"Why do you do these things for old man but not for old woman?" she persisted. "Are they not people too?"

I had to think quick.

"Well, statistically, old men don't live as long as old women," I tried. "We have less time with them. We have to act now, to make these old men happy while we still have them. Only then can we move on to the old women. We've got more time with them. The pressure's off."

It seemed to make some kind of sense to her and she stuck her bottom lip out and nodded.

"So you want me to help you to do this? Okay, I will help you."

"There's one thing," I said. "I need a passport photo from you."

"No."

"Sorry?"

"No. I will not give you my passport photo. Why should I give you my image? Why should I not give you just my word? Is it not enough?"

"It's just tradition."

"No. You will have to take my word."

She shook her head and picked up another tissue. She dabbed it on her forehead.

"Erm . . . I really do need a passport photo. It shows me you are serious. And all the other joinees have done it."

"No. I will give you *a* passport photo. A blank one. I will not give you *my* passport photo. I will send it to you, okay?"

The waiter arrived with her glass of water and she took one small sip, and glanced up at the clock above the door.

"I have to go now. I am sorry, Donny."

Yes. She called me Donny.

"But you've only been here a minute!" I said. "I came all the way from London to meet you!"

"I will send you the photo, okay? Good-bye."

"Hang on—have you even got the address?"

She sighed. She was clearly in a hurry but grumpily got a piece of paper out of her bag and took down the P.O. Box address.

"It's on the website, in case you lose it, and—"

"Yes, okay, thank you," she said. "Have a nice stay in Paris, okay?"

And she was out the door. I watched as she jogged through the rain, holding her hood to her head, and disappeared around the corner. I was deflated. I had come all the way to Paris. Paris! And all for a two-minute meeting with a woman who wouldn't even join me properly. Sure, she'd said she'd help make old men happy, but *would* she? I just didn't know. And now, here I was, sitting in a café in Paris with nothing to do and no one to meet and nowhere to go until that evening when I'd hop back on the Eurostar and travel back to London, empty-handed. I felt stupid, now that I thought about what I'd done. Estelle had sent me an e-mail on a whim. She hadn't expected for me—a complete stranger—to drop everything and tell her I was going to dash off to a foreign country to visit her. Gareth had been sincere in his advice, but the truth of it was, unless I did a better job of selling Join Me, this meeting-people lark just wasn't going to work. Estelle and probably hundreds of other potential joinees just didn't share my enthusiasm for the project. Not yet. No one did. Not really.

The waiter asked me if I wanted anything else, and I suddenly didn't want to be there any more. The Americans had become louder and I didn't like this café now.

Across the street was another café, this one called Café Guize, and I decided that maybe all I needed to cheer me up was a cup of tea in a place without the negative memories the previous one had suddenly developed. You'd be surprised at the miracles that tea can pull off.

So I ran through the rain and into the café. I sat at a table in the middle of the room, ordered my tea, and simply watched the wet world go by. There was hardly anyone else in there. Just a French lady smoking and reading her paper in one corner, and a man on the table next to mine who, in the following minutes, would come to fascinate me.

He looked every inch the struggling French artist. He was wearing a smart, black beret for one thing, and around his neck was a long, flowing scarf, tied in a loop at the neck to make it look like a tie. His face had the pained expression of a man trying to remember a word forever just on the tip of his tongue, and he scribbled feverishly with a Biro into a battered blue notepad. Words filled each page at pace, and his was a hurried handwriting, as if he just couldn't get all his thoughts out fast enough. Then every so often he would stop, gaze into space, consider something, and carry on. His hair was long and unruly, and the plastic casing on his Bic Biro had split from the top down, with shards of clear plastic jutting out to make it look like an ancient quill. He looked like he was writing a novel, or film, or a passionate, poetic play about love and the injustice of the world. And I just watched him. This was undoubtedly the most French man I had ever seen in my life. And yet it was almost like he didn't belong here. He belonged to a different France, a black-and-white France. He belonged to a scene from a '40s French arthouse film, filled with cigarette smoke and light jazz, and moody French glances. This was a Frenchman born out of his time.

I had to speak to him. I had to see if he was real.

"Excusez-moi . . . parlez-vous anglais?"

He looked up.

"Oui?" he said.

Good start. Except I didn't know what else to say. I'd established he was real. If it had turned out that he wasn't, I would've probably ended the conversation there and then.

"Oh," I said. "Great. I was just watching you, and was wondering what kind of thing you're writing."

"It's a novel," he said. "I am going to write a series of novels."

His voice was deep and thoughtful. And—to my complete and utter surprise—English. This was a Frenchman born not only out of his time, but out of his country.

"You're English?" I asked.

"I'm from Norfolk," he said.

This wasn't right. He had a beret on. What was he playing at?

"What are you doing in Paris?" I said, almost offended that he wasn't being more French for me.

"I'm an artist. I write, and paint, and I sing. I play the guitar too, but I hurt my arm recently, so I can't busk any more. I *really* hurt it, actually."

He certainly had. His name, it turned out, was Paul Francis, and the sorry reason his arm hurt so much was that two days previously he'd wanted to check whether his mobile phone was working. So he went to a phone box to give himself a ring. However, when he dialed his own number and his mobile had gone off in his pocket it gave him such a fright that his arm involuntarily flew up and he smashed his elbow against the phone box window. He hadn't been expecting any calls, you see. Not even from himself.

I immediately liked Paul. There was a kindness in his eyes and he spoke slowly and with great care and grace. I moved to his table and we talked about his past. I was amazed at what I learned.

He'd begun a long musical career in 1976, in Norwich, by forming a punk band called the Toads, but had eventually been thrown out of his own band, because "the others didn't understand me. They said 'You're too strange and we don't understand your lyrics, get out.' They wanted to go commercial. I wanted to remain an artist."

"But I've gone back to my troubadour roots now," he said. "And I feel that France is the one place in the world that really appreciates my artistry, so that's why I now live in Paris. And as soon as my arm is better I'll be back out there, on the streets. But for the moment I'm consigned to cafés, and writing. Anyway. Enough about me. What are you doing here? Holiday?"

"Not really," I said, taking a hit of my tea. "I was here to meet someone but she could only see me for two minutes."

"Oh," he said. "A friend?"

"No. Not really. I'd hoped we'd become friends, but there wasn't really time."

"Who was she?"

Ordinarily, I would have been a bit cagey about explaining this. But I felt that I could trust Paul not to find it too odd. Particularly as his other name was Doctor Spacetoad.

"I'm asking people to join me," I said. "I'm forming a collective of a thousand good-hearted people. We do good deeds toward old men, but I'm going to extend that. Estelle was my first foreign joinee, and I was hoping that she'd help me spread the word internationally. But I'm not even sure if she'll join me, now."

"Hmm. What does joining involve?"

"I just ask people to give me a passport photo. Then they're in. That's their initiation."

Paul nodded.

"Like a cult," he said.

"No, no," I said. "Like a collective."

"This reminds me of something I got into once," said Paul. "Years and years ago, I was really very depressed. It was just after the Toads split up, and a friend of mine wanted to cheer me up. He believed in—and still believes in—this Indian guru who's come to the West and made a lot of money and gained lots of followers by giving them a few meditation techniques. He conveys this sense to them, that he knows something that they don't, but he never says what it is."

"That's like what I do!" I said brightly. Maybe I'd been unwittingly doing things right all along. "I've kind of been acting all mysterious, and people have started to really believe in me. They call me the Leader!"

"Well, exactly. I went along to this meeting, and there were all these people getting up and telling each other how fantastic this thing was, but that you had to join before you could find out what it is."

"That's what I do too! Did you join?"

"Oh yes."

I started to sense that all wasn't lost; maybe I could learn a lot from him. Far more than he could learn from me. I was a mere amateur at this. He had years of experience. It is amazing, I thought, who you can meet in a Parisian café on a rainy day. It was as if fate had brought us together. And before he continued with his story, I had to tell him that.

"Well," he said, wisely. "Today was a good day for us to meet."

"How do you mean?"

"Yesterday I checked the stars. Today is a fortunate day for meetings."

"You're an astrologer, as well as all that other stuff?"

"Yes. And a tarot card reader."

It just got better and better.

"Anyway," he said. "I went to this meeting, and I said I would join. They sent someone round to where I was living and he initiated me. As I say, I was depressed at the time and in need of something, and I'm naturally very curious as a person. They taught me the meditation they said I needed, and they said that once I'd done it I would be given 'The Wisdom.' They told me I had it, but to be honest, I didn't really feel any different."

I considered this. What wisdom could I bestow upon my joinees? Virtually none. Not unless it was facts about helicopters and lions they were after, and very few people are, these days. A waiter appeared and we ordered more tea. I continued to listen, intrigued.

"I kept up with the meditations, but they started to make me crazy. I had some quite bizarre out-of-body experiences. At one point, I saw myself from above. My soul had left my body, and it was just hanging there, about three feet above me. I panicked, and eventually I got it back in, but I never felt quite right after that."

"Blimey," I said. If ever there was a time for a "blimey," it was now.

"I'd joined this other sect as well, and it made me realize in the end that the vast majority of people are sheep. It's depressing."

Paul took a sip of his tea.

"So when I was out of it all I decided to start my own religion."

My eyes widened. "How do you mean?" I said. "How do you mean, you started your own religion?"

"It started out jokily, but it soon got out of hand. Have you ever heard of coypu?"

"No," I said, figuring it was probably some kind of term for a higher consciousness, or philosophy on life.

"It's a small hairy rat-like thing that lives in the Norfolk Broads."

"That could be anyone," I said.

"But this was something that was brought over from South America, and then ran riot in the Norfolk area. The council tried to kill them all, and I felt sorry for them, so I started Coypu Consciousness."

"What . . . like an animal welfare thing?"

"No. I started telling people I'd met a coypu called Guru Ma Coypu, who was still living there and had been sent to save the human race. But he couldn't speak the human language and he was communicating telepathically with me. I told them I'd written this book of his wisdom and it was up to me to spread the word. His philosophies were simple—like 'Love Everybody Except Those You Do Not Like'—and it seemed to strike a chord with people. Coypu Consciousness spread like wildfire, right across the Norfolk area. And then it started to get out of hand because people started to really believe in it, and were asking to meet Guru Ma Coypu, and so I had to stop it."

Paul looked at me, deadly serious.

"I actually wrote a song about him. It went like this . . ."

He put one finger in his ear, and closed his eyes, looking every inch the seasoned folk singer.

He wears a paisley waistcoat
And psychedelic beads
He built himself a guitar
Out of bullrushes and reeds

The French lady in the corner had put down her newspaper and was staring at us, with deep concern in her eyes.

"I didn't mention the fact that he was a guru, this coypu, because I didn't want to bring the song down and make it too heavy. Better to get people interested in the coypu and *then* hit them with the philosophies. But the coypu is just a tool to get people involved. He doesn't really exist. I made him up."

I nodded to show I understood, and that I didn't really think he'd met a coypu in a paisley waistcoat.

"And it caught on?" I said.

"Oh yes. I could have cashed in. I could have made a lot of money from Coypu Consciousness. Especially if I'd taken it to America. I would say I would have been a millionaire within the year. But I didn't want to take on the karmic consequences."

"Quite," I said, and looked over at the French woman. She was still staring at us. "Do you want to get out of here?" I said.

• • •

I wanted to pick Paul's brains some more, and, to be honest, I was grateful for the company, so I offered to buy him dinner.

Times were hard at the moment, he told me. Because he wouldn't be able to busk for a while, he was going to have to rely on his other skills, including the aforementioned tarot card reading. I felt bad, so I asked him to do a reading for me. He agreed, enthusiastically, and we walked from the café, up Rue Soufflot and on to Rue Saint Jacques. He's lived, for the past couple of years, in a hotel just down the road from here, and we chatted amiably as we walked toward it, him in his jaunty beret.

We arrived at Paul's hotel and I agreed to meet him in the Indian restaurant opposite—Restaurant Sabraj—while he went upstairs to get his tarot cards.

Ten minutes later he walked in and sat down. I'd already chosen what I was going to eat—the Chicken Dansak—and I explained its significance to Paul. He decided that in that case he would order the same. Chicken Dansak was fast becoming the official Join Me meal. I envisaged a grand Join Me meet-up in some posh London curryhouse of the future, each of my thousand joinees digging into a special edition Chicken Dansak, with Joinee Jones perhaps delivering a short speech or presentation on the history of the dish.

"Now," said Paul. "Have you thought much about music? Because music would be a great way to get people to join you. You should have a song. Something catchy, so that when people whistle it as they walk down the street it catches other people's attention. We could write it together. And when my arm is better we could play it in Paris. What do you think?"

"That's a great idea. A Join Me song. That'd get 'em joining! We could get Raymond Price involved."

"Who?"

"He's an old man some of my joinees made happy recently. He was stranded in London with no money to get home, and my joinees bought him a ticket home. They found him completely by accident, looking sad in a pub."

"He must have been very grateful," said Paul, having a sip of wine.

"Well, yes, but when I tried to write to him the letter was returned. I'd like to thank him for inspiring me to get more joinees to help old men."

"I have a feeling he'll turn up. And yes, maybe he can sing in the song too. When you come back to Paris one day, we'll work on it," said Paul.

"Okay, now let's do your tarot reading," he said, getting his cards out. "These will tell you how your future is going to turn out. If you've any questions, mentally ask the cards as you shuffle them. But really concentrate. Put as much energy into it as you can."

I started to shuffle the cards, and Paul closed his eyes and clasped his hands together, as if summoning up something from deep within. I handed them back to him a few seconds later, and he slowly, calmly dealt the top few out onto the table. The restaurant manager walked by our table and stopped to see what was going on.

"What are you doing?" he said.

"I'm having a tarot reading," I said happily.

"I am not . . . you mustn't," he said, concerned. "Is this an occult? You cannot do this here."

"It's fine," said Paul, and there was a creepy moment when their eyes met and nothing was said. A second later the manager simply walked off. It was like Jedi mind control, only more curry-based.

"Your first card," said Paul, "is the card of Fate and Change. It says you are at an important point in your life. You're searching for your direction, but there are certain forces at play that are beyond your control. Things can really happen now."

He pointed to the next card.

"This is the direction you are going in. There is a period of solitude coming up. Do you have a girlfriend?"

"Yes," I said. "Hanne."

"Oh," said Paul, looking uncomfortable.

I didn't like the sound of this. I rushed him on.

"What about the next one?" I said.

"Yes . . . this one . . . 'Harvest' . . . this means you can reap the rewards of certain seeds you've sown in the past. Certain ideas begin to come to fruition and develop."

Next card.

"This one is your desires, hopes and fears for the future . . . This speaks of grandiose ideas that you may well realize. Especially given the next card, which is the Sun. Now, the Sun is the card of awareness, optimism and joy . . . it's the card of good luck. So things are looking good, for Join Me . . ."

Maybe a part of Paul was reading the cards in a way that told me what I *wanted* to hear. Maybe, in reality, the Fool meant just that—that I was a fool. And maybe the Sun meant I should get out more. But I was grateful for what he'd told me. If nothing else, it had cheered me up and given me renewed energy for what I was doing.

As I finished my meal, there was just one thing left to ask.

"So . . . would you consider joining me?"

Paul put his fork down.

"I would," he said. "I think what you're doing is important. My advice, as someone who's been there, would be this. Keep Join Me as a force for good in the world. If you want to expand this good deeds thing, now is the time to do it. The cards told me that much. And whether people believe in what you're doing or not doesn't matter. So long as it's having a positive effect on the world."

I shook Paul's hand outside the restaurant and we exchanged numbers and e-mail addresses. He had inspired me. I watched as he strolled, carefree, down the street, beret balanced precariously on his head.

I had met the last of the great French thinkers. It was just a pity he wasn't French.

I boarded my train and rode home to London, happy.

original
salted peanuts
KP

CHAPTER · 12

2. *And Haley Joel Osment spake unto them, saying, This is me, and this is three other people, and I'm going to help them.*
3. *And the multitude were aggrieved, and put their fingers in their throats.*

I returned from Paris refreshed and inspired. Joinee Estelle's photo arrived a day or two later, as promised, and—as promised—she wasn't in it. But her hand was, so I let it go, partly because I was in such a good mood; meeting Joinee Spacetoad had given me renewed energy and hope. And it had thrown up a very interesting idea. Music.

A Join Me anthem was something I was sure could help get people interested in what me and my joinees were doing. I could send it to radio stations worldwide. The impact on the peoples of this earth would be massive. It was just a pity that Paul had hurt his arm and couldn't play the guitar any more. I mean, I knew that one day I'd go back to Paris and we'd write a song together, but things move fast in the world of kindness-based collectives, and I decided I needed a song right now.

But who could help? A friend of mine, Tony, had a smash hit in the '80s with a song called "Stutter Rap." Maybe I could ask his advice? Or did I have any joinees who'd admitted in their questionnaires to being in a band?

I went through them carefully, before being distracted by my e-mails. News had started to come back to me of old men suddenly being made happy in the Wandsworth area of London. A joinee by the name of Baxter was doing his very best to improve the lives of the pensioners down his street. And as I read of his exploits—cooking meals, buying biscuits—all thoughts of music left my mind. Instead, thoughts of dozens of happy old men crept in, as they were doing all too often these days.

It was when I could no longer look at a passing pensioner without wondering whether there was anything I could do to make him happy that I realized the kind of effect that the Making Old Men Happy scheme must be having on my joinees.

The old man I'd passed had been standing outside Woolworth's on the Roman Road, minding his own business with a dog leash in his hands, but in the ten seconds since noticing him I'd come up with dozens of potential ways of making him happy.

Could I carry his shopping home? Should I buy him some Pick 'n' Mix? Old men enjoy Werthers Originals—should I see if Woolworth's sold them? And where was his dog? Had he lost it? Should I mount a campaign to find it? Or should I just stop staring at him quite so intensely and walk away before he thinks I'm about to mug him? I went for the final option, and he certainly seemed relieved, if not happy.

And it wasn't just me. I was receiving e-mails on a daily basis from joinees just like Joinee Baxter, each of them eager to tell me of their good deeds toward this country's aging blokes.

A joinee in Coventry had befriended his elderly neighbor and mowed his lawn for him. A joinee in Leicester had cooked a big bowl of soup and left it outside an old man's bungalow for his tea. A joinee in London had helped remove a bulky yucca plant from an old man's landing. A joinee in Colerne had noticed an old man in a sandwich shop and put a fiver behind the counter to take care of whatever pastries, teas and sandwiches took the old chap's fancy. Elsewhere in the country, old men were being made happy at an almost alarming rate, with smiles being raised, friends being made, pints being proffered.

Even better, I had the proof of all these actions. Photographs of various smiling pensioners were finding their way back to my flat and every time I had another of my disposable camera films developed I knew I'd be in for quite a treat. An old-man-based treat, but a treat nevertheless. One of my joinees had even enjoyed the experience of making an old man very happy so much that he was now actively encouraging everyone he knew to do it whenever they could. "It's a brilliant feeling," he wrote, in an e-mail to his friends and me. "Just sit down on a park bench next to one of them and talk to it for a while."

I don't think he really meant to write 'it' there, but there you go. He continued: "You'll learn loads. I've started taking them to the pub by the park. It's a great way to spend a Sunday afternoon." But how sweet was this? He was nineteen, and worked in telesales, and from his picture looked as much like a beery, clubbing lad as you could wish for, and yet now he was even getting his mates to hang out with the elderly.

I thought of Raymond Price and smiled. This was all because of him, in a sense. His plight, and his willingness to be helped by strangers, was what had encouraged me to encourage others to do what they were now doing. The fact that he was open to help, and unembarrassed by unexpected acts of kindness, was what kick-started all this. If only more people could be like Raymond Price.

How frustrating it was that my letter hadn't reached him. I really wanted him to know how important he'd been to the cause. I wanted him to know that some real, undeniable good had come from his actions.

I thought I'd have another crack at tracking him down. I dialled 192 and tried to find a number for a Raymond Price in Teignmouth. He wasn't listed. I considered jumping on a train to Teignmouth—I already knew exactly how much it would cost, including sandwich—and spending a day tracking him down. But then I suddenly remembered his promise to talk to the *Teignmouth News*. I went to their website and searched for his name in their news archives, but to no avail. Still, if I was going to track him down, his local paper wouldn't be a bad place to start. After all, local journalists have local knowledge. Surely someone at the *Teignmouth News* would have an idea of how to get in touch with Mr. Price in order to thank him?

I found the number and dialed it. I spoke to a reporter called Adam.

"Well, that's a nice story," he said. "Pity you couldn't get in touch with Mr. Price. I think we should print something about that. You tend to hear such bad stories about London, so this makes a change. I'll call you back in a minute, I'll just have a word with my editor."

A minute later Adam called back.

"Thing is, my editor doesn't want to run the story unless we can have a chat with Mr. Price himself. Give me the address you had for him and I'll do some investigating."

An hour later Adam called back.

"Well, there *was* a Raymond Price who lived there, but that was some years back. How did you get that address?"

"I think it was on his driver's license. He'd shown it as proof to the joinees that he was who he said he was."

"Probably an honest mistake. We've all got things with old addresses on, haven't we? Listen, give me a couple more hours and I'll come back to you with whatever I find out. In the meantime, you said you had pictures of Raymond accepting the cash. Could you e-mail those to me?"

I did as Adam asked and even put a couple of them on the Join Me website, primarily to show joinees what had occurred.

Adam rang back later on to say that he was still checking a few facts, and just had one question: was it only old men that my joinees were making happy?

I'd spent the afternoon deciding how best to extend the work of my joinees, just as I'd promised both Joinees Saunders and Spacetoad I would, and chose this moment to reveal my decision.

"Adam," I said. "I want you to know . . . this is a world exclusive. Do you understand? A *world exclusive*. Not even my joinees know this yet. I have chosen to reveal it to the *Teignmouth News* first. Thing is, I want my joinees to be responsible for a wave of good karma all over the world."

"Karma?"

"Yes. We're not going to concentrate solely on old men any more. That was just the first Commandment of Join Me. I've always known we would extend our work to the public at large. It was just a question of when. I feel the time is right. I feel we can do this. Me . . . and the Karma Army."

" 'The Karma Army'? I like that!"

"Thank you. It took bloody hours to come up with."

"I suppose you could say that when your joinees helped a bloke whose car had broken down, they were a bit like karma-chanics."

"Eh?"

"Car mechanics. Karma-chanics."

To be honest, I've only just got Adam's joke this minute. At the time, I thought he just liked saying the words "car mechanics." Some people do. But it works better written down than on the phone, so maybe I'll phone him back today and laugh, so he doesn't feel stupid.

"Well, listen," he said, as I remained puzzled, "it sounds great, and I'll get on to finding Raymond Price for you . . ."

And that was that. The news was out. The Karma Army was launched, in a blaze of Teignmouth-based publicity.

Now I just had to fine tune the scheme.

• • •

It was Friday night, and Hanne and I wanted to meet up. So we found each other at seven, in a café just off Hoxton Square.

"So did you get all your work done the other night?" she asked.

"Yup," I said. "All done. Tough going, though."

"So you just sat in and worked all evening, yeah?"

"Yeah."

"Because I called you at home and you weren't there."

"Er . . . wasn't I?"

Nope. I knew full well where I was. I was in Paris drinking cocktails out of a baby bottle.

"I called twice. In case you were out getting milk or something."

"Right. Well, what happened was, I had loads of films to review, right?"

"Okay . . ."

"But I was cold, as well, and stuff. So I moved the TV and the video to the hallway and then I watched them from the bath and just sort of took notes with a pen that I had."

Hanne looked nonplussed.

"And then when the phone rang I probably didn't hear it because I actually was in the bath, you see, at the time, with my pen."

"But presumably you had the door open so that you could see the telly. And you have a phone in the hallway so you would have heard it."

"Yes. That's right. So I probably heard it ringing. Yes. But I was in the bath, and it's dangerous when there's electricity around, and—"

"I thought you were probably just so busy with work that you'd turned the ringer on your phone off."

I thought about it. Yes. That would have been a better thing to have said.

"So what films were they?"

"Oh. You know. New ones."

"Like what?"

Think quick, Dan.

"The . . . er . . . Karma . . . Army."

"Never heard of it."

"It's a film."

"I gathered that."

"It's very good. It's about a man."

"Right."

"He's very handsome. A very handsome man. Quite rugged. With glasses."

Hanne waited for me to continue, but I found having to think on my feet utterly exhausting and very nearly passed out.

"Is that it?"

"I haven't finished watching it yet."

"But what's the premise? How can you review films if you can't even describe what happens in them, other than they're about men with glasses?"

Right. She'd asked for it.

"Well, this bloke wants a thousand people to join his club. But he doesn't know what that club is, really, and nor do they. But they still join. And before he knows it he's got hundreds of people who have joined him. Two hundred forty-eight actually. And they all want to know what they've joined. So he's under all this pressure and he has to come up with a reason for their very being. So he makes them all go out and make old men very happy. And then he extends it, and all his joinees have to go out and do random acts of kindness for complete strangers, each and every . . ."

I struggled to come up with something, and settled for . . .

". . . Friday. Yes. Fridays is when they do stuff."

"Why Fridays?"

"Because that's what day it was when he decided that."

A thought struck me.

"Oh. And 'Good Fridays,' he calls them. On account of people doing good, on Fridays."

In some way, subconsciously, I suppose I was seeking Hanne's approval by telling her this. I was testing things out on her. Nudging the basic idea into her head and seeing how she'd react. I mean, I was *hoping* that she'd say it sounded *great,* and when could she watch it, and how quickly could I lend it to her? And then *I'd* say "But it's a *true* story, and *I'm* the man who's doing it, and I'm *so* glad you like it, because I've been *so* scared of telling you!" And then we'd hug and we'd kiss and she'd join me.

But she didn't say the first bit, so I couldn't say the second bit.

Instead, she shrugged her shoulders and said: "It sounds a bit derivative to me. A bit like that *Pay It Forward*."

"What? It's not derivative!"

"Well, I'm just saying—"

"How dare you say it sounds a bit derivative! And how do you mean it sounds a bit derivative?"

"Just that it sounds like that film *Pay It Forward*. This teacher asks his pupils to come up with ideas that will make the world a better place, and the kid comes up with the idea of passing good deeds on. It's that Haley Joel Osment kid. And he says that if someone does a good deed for you, then you have to do one for three other people. And when they ask you what they can do in return, you say 'pay it forward.'"

"That's a stupid idea," I said, pouting. "I prefer mine. At least with mine, people will be doing it off their own backs. They're not doing it to repay anyone, or because they feel *obliged* to because of some evil little child actor. They're doing it because they genuinely *want* to. In the . . . er . . . film, I mean."

Hanne looked intensely concerned, and I suddenly remembered who and where I was.

"I don't know why you're being so upset. It's not like you directed it, or wrote it, is it?" she said. "I think you've been working too hard, Dan. Let's go for a meal. Calm you down. I think you need to relax more. You're always working these days. We hardly see each other."

"I know. I'm sorry. We will. But I should go now. I should finish that *Karma Army* review."

I kissed her lightly on the cheek and stood up. She'd be meeting her friend Claire in a bit, so I felt it was okay for me to leave.

"Before you go," she said, "don't forget it's Jon's wedding next week."

"Of course not. How could I forget?"

I'd forgotten, of course. I didn't even know who Jon was.

"Who's Jon again?"

"From work," said Hanne, annoyed. "I really want you to be there. I don't want to go on my own. And did I tell you, Jon's going to get you and his younger brother to be the best man?"

Eh?

"Eh? How can we *both* be best man? And hang on—how am *I* meant to be best man? I don't even *know* this Jon bloke! I can't begin my best man speech by saying 'In the five minutes since I've known Jon, I've witnessed lots of embarrassing things to tell you,' can I? Why on *earth* would he want me to be his best man?"

"No, Danny. Not *you and* his younger brother," she said. "*Ewan,* his younger brother. He's coming all the way from America."

Again. That one works better written down than it does said out loud. The concern on Hanne's face still wasn't budging.

"Go home and get some rest, Danny. You're starting to behave a little oddly. And I really don't like it."

That night I rented *Pay It Forward*. It was rubbish. Relieved that I wasn't the new Haley Joel Osment, I e-mailed my joinees . . .

> ***To:*** *Joinees*
> ***From:*** *The Leader*
> ***Subject:*** *The Good Fridays Agreement!*

Joinees!

It is I! The Leader!

For a while now you have been asking me who or what you have joined! Well, it is time to reveal all . . .

You are . . . The Karma Army!

As a joinee you are now duty-bound to undertake at least one Random Act of Kindness each and every Friday and report back to me on your actions. Henceforth, these Fridays will be known as "Good Fridays," and this e-mail represents the first step of the Good Fridays Agreement!

Those of you who believe in karma should take comfort in the fact that if what goes around really does come around, you'll be assuring yourself a great weekend. Those of you who don't should take comfort in the fact that you'll be improving someone else's weekend in whatever way you choose.

Go to it, joinees! Go to it, Karma Army!

Danny
The Leader

The joinees responded in their droves. They were very, very excited about our new direction, while I was relieved that there was now actually something for them to do while we edged closer to our thousandth member.

And oddly, although I'd only mentioned the what-goes-around-comes-around aspect of things on a whim, and because the phrase "karmic consequences" was still in my mind from my meeting with Dr. Spacetoad, it actually seemed to be working . . .

"Instant karma!" wrote Joinee Gibson. "I was in the pub and bought my mate a packet of crisps as my first Random Act of Kindness, and there was one of those little blue competition packets in it. He opened it, and there was £20 in there! He gave it to me, and for my second Random Act of Kindness, I bought this old man a pint with some of the profits. He was really pleased and talked to us for ages, and it turned out he'd lived on my street a few years before and knew my mum. So now they're back in touch. I'm going to do loads more Random Acts of Kindness this week!"

Joinee Downs wrote: "Hello Boss. Yesterday I bought a colleague some sweets because she was upset. Today I found a tenner on a petrol station forecourt."

And while it was great that joinees seemed to be benefiting like this, I didn't want it to become their reason for doing the good deeds. It was about spreading good karma, but not creating good karma for selfish means. It was about sharing kindness through completely random and unexpected ways. There would be no political, religious or monetary motive for any of these deeds. All they'd gain was perhaps a warm feeling in the pit of the stomach. It would just be outrageously random, and embody the same spirit of randomness that had led those five brave joinees to Raymond Price that famous day in Hammersmith. That was pure pot luck and cherished chance, and they'd embraced what fate had presented to them. Their paths might never have crossed, and Raymond might still be stuck in London to this day.

Ah, Raymond. Where are you now? What are you doing? Are you aware of how you've helped kick-start the Karma Army? Do you know how many old men we went on to make very happy because of that one fateful meeting?

Little things were happening everywhere. Little things that, if they happened to you, you'd tell whoever you got home to that night all about. Little things that'd make you smile. Things that would have improved your day, or put you in a better mood, or maybe far more. From the person behind you in the queue offering to carry the flatpack wardrobe you'd just bought from the shop all the way to the carpark, as Joinee Flannery of Luton tired himself out doing, to someone in a busy café giving up their precious seat because you're looking for one, as happened in Worcester thanks to Joinee Berham.

And it was all happening because of Join Me. I was ecstatic.

"The thing is," Joinee Flannery put in an e-mail one night, "I often think to help people like this, but I never do because society deems it wrong or odd. Now I have an excuse to do it and that's great."

I knew what he meant. The sad thing is, I was discovering that you almost have to make a joke of being good to strangers. Up and down the country, these people doing their good deeds were doubtless being seen as slightly eccentric, when in reality and in an ideal world they should be deemed the most normal people of all.

Good deeds continued to happen on every subsequent Friday too. While some joinees waited for opportunities to present themselves, others actively sought out good deeds to do. Joinee Whitby admitted to struggling slightly for ideas, while Joinee Saunders couldn't stop thinking them up. I suppose this whole kindness business is just more suited to the work of a priest than that of a computer programmer. In fact, Gareth had even convinced a vicar friend of his—the Reverend David J. Meldrum—to join up too. Now I had two vicars! Two! I made a mental note not to allow Join Me to become a mouthpiece for the Christian faith, and to try and convince two Satanists to join up in order to balance things out. Not that they'd be doing many random acts of kindness, but you know what I mean . . .

"And it really is the randomness of all this that I'm really enjoying," said Joinee Saunders, when I phoned him up for a quick chat. "At first it was slightly awkward. I bought a box of Roses chocolates, and I was walking down the high street here in Inverness, just looking for someone to give them to. And I felt incredibly self-conscious. I almost gave them to a man in a music shop, but he looked very stern and I bottled it. I would have felt less embarrassed *robbing* the place."

I laughed.

"And I thought, 'This is stupid—this is just a random and unexpected good deed. I *have* to do it.' So I walked onto an industrial estate where I felt more at ease, and I found this security guard sitting on his own, and I strolled up to him, and gave him the chocolates. The look on his face was amazing! And then I walked away thinking, 'This is great! I could do this more often!' And he was over the moon, and said he'd share them with the other lads!"

And that wasn't all Gareth had done.

"Today I was buying someone a wedding present online. And on the John Lewis website, you can type a number in, and get people's wedding lists, with all the things they want their friends and family to get them for their wedding day. So I typed a random series of numbers in, and found the wedding list of some young couple who are getting married in the next few weeks. Sophy Moore and Mark Stephens, I think their names were. And I read their list, and bought them something that they wanted, and wrote 'Courtesy of Join Me' on the card."

"What did you get them?" I asked, impressed.

"Brass numbers, for outside their house. Number one, and number zero. I almost got them the full set, in case they ever move."

Gareth was enjoying himself, and I was pleased to hear it. Performing these random acts of kindness, in fact, had started to mean so much to him that nowadays, whenever he was asked to give a speech or take a school assembly, he talked not about the Christian faith, but about Join Me. He didn't even wear his dog collar to most of them, opting instead for a Join Me T-shirt.

And not wishing to be left out, and in order to lead by example, I myself did a random good deed, early one Friday lunchtime.

"Excuse me," said the lady who had suddenly appeared by my side, at Mile End tube station. "Is this the Central Line, or the District one?"

"It's the Central Line," I said, and we both got on and sat down next to each other.

Her name was Helen and she was a social worker. She asked me what I did. And because I'd forgotten that what I actually did was watch films and play games, I told her about Join Me.

"That sounds lovely," she said, after I'd told her about random acts of kindness, and making old men very happy. "Especially the old men bit. You should make my granddad happy, if that's what you do!"

"What would make him happy?" I asked.

Helen laughed. "Well, he quite likes peanuts!"

So I took his address from a giggling Helen—who clearly didn't understand the seriousness of all this—and set to work. I knew I had to work quickly in order to get my deed in place by the end of this Good

Friday, and once I was in town I headed for an Internet café on Bond Street and sat myself down. I had a bunch of passport photos in my bag and a bunch of letters from joinees new and old. I found whatever e-mail addresses I could from them and sent an urgent appeal out, telling them about this old man in Sheffield who needed us to make him happy.

And over the course of the next few days, that old Sheffield man received, in the post, completely anonymously, over eighty packets of peanuts from random joinees all over the country.

And was he happy? Yes, I believe he was.

So all was suddenly going incredibly well with Join Me. And, in fact, with me. I had found an odd kind of purpose in life. One that made me feel very good indeed. One that, in a roundabout way, I owed to a man named Raymond Price.

Sure, things with Hanne were a little rocky, but all that would settle down soon enough. Just a little more effort and the whole thing would start to run itself. People would be climbing over themselves to Join Me. I'd reach a thousand joinees and then I could be done with it.

In the meantime, I was satisfied.

Because I had created something wonderful.

E-mail

To: Dennis M. Hope, President, Galactic Government
From: Danny Wallace, Leader, Join Me & The Karma Army

Dear Dennis,

Hello from London again!!

I just thought I would let you know that everything is going very well with Join Me!

I now have hundreds of followers who do my bidding every Friday. I ask them to do unexpected good deeds and random acts of kindness, and then tell me about it.

The world is improving as a result!

With my best regards,

Danny Wallace

E-mail

To: Danny Wallace, Leader, Join Me & The Karma Army
From: Dennis M. Hope, President, Galactic Government

Dear Danny:

Thanks for the update on Join Me. Sounds like you are actively pursuing your dream.

You should continue this until you decide it is not producing the results you are looking for.

I have always found that when we pursue what we love doing that the challenge is easily accomplished.

Good luck!

Dennis M. Hope
President – Galactic Government

Signing up to 'kindness' collective

A CLERGYMAN serving at Inverness Cathedral has been recruited into a new flock.

Rev Gareth Saunders, a curate at the Cathedral, is now a man with a double mission, spreading the word not only about the Church, but about "Join Me" — an informal group which started almost as a joke but is now bringing people together from across the world.

Join Me was created when advertisements appeared in London newspapers asking people to "join me" by writing back with a passport-sized photograph.

The person whom respondents found they were joining is Danny, who prefers not to give his surname although he does reveal he used to work for catalogue sales firm Argos.

"The reason I did this was part boredom. I just wanted to see what would happen," he explained.

"I didn't expect anyone to write back, to be honest. Then a few days later people started writing in. It spread and now I have got hundreds of followers, as it were, throughout Europe.

Danny describes Join Me as a collective, not a cult, and told the Courier: "One of the dilemmas I had was to use my powers for good or evil and you will be glad to know I decided on good."

He is encouraging his joinees to carry out "random acts of kindness", but insists Join Me is not a religious organisation. "I'm not religious in any way, but funnily enough, I've had two vicars join me," he said.

...of Join Me's two vicar fol-

❑ Rev Gareth Saunders sports his 'Join Me' t-shirt.

join him," Gareth (30) recalled.

"It seemed like a good idea and could lead somewhere positive, so I said 'Yes', although ob-...ously I didn't know much ... then.

...wasn't too sure

Heavy-metal fan Gareth, who has been at the cathedral for three years, has been undertaking missionary work on Danny's behalf, not only wearing his Join Me t-shirt, but distributing leaflets about the group

"It seems a good idea. Something to get people together to do some good work is what the church is supposed to be about."

Although the two men have

CHAPTER · 13

1. *It came to pass that the words of Daniel were heard by a second Daniel, son of Ander.*
2. *And Daniel—nay, but the other one—was mending a chariot brought out from the land of the Ikeans.*

I awoke in the morning because my head appeared to be vibrating. My phone was under my pillow, for some reason, and a text message had arrived and wouldn't go away.

It was from Joinee Saunders, my priest up in Inverness.

LOCAL PAPER HEARD ABOUT MY GOOD DEEDS FOR JOIN ME. THEY MAY CALL YOU FOR QUOTE. IS THAT OKAY?

I texted him back to say that it was, and within an hour I was talking to a journalist from the *Inverness Courier*. I answered his questions to the best of my ability, while at the same time upholding an air of mystery.

"So what's your full name, Danny?"

"Oh, I'd rather just be known as Danny, if that's all right."

"Er, okay. And how old are you?"

"Twenty-five."

"And what do you do for a living?"

"Um . . . well . . . I don't really want to say . . . but I used to work at Argos."

It was true. I did. When I was fourteen. It was all I could think of to say. Anyway, the journalist seemed happy enough and told me he was off with a photographer to take a few pictures of Gareth now, and wished me good luck with it all.

The next day I was in the minimarket on the corner buying a few groceries when I got another text message from Gareth.

IT'S IN TODAY'S PAPER, it said.

Wow, I thought. That's good. Joinee Saunders was definitely doing his bit throughout Scotland.

I CAN'T WAIT TO SEE IT . . . , I wrote back.

Moments later, he replied.

. . . AS THE ACTRESS SAID TO THE BISHOP.

All vicars should be like this man, I thought, and plonked my groceries on the counter. I was cooking for Hanne tonight, and I was making a little extra effort because of being so preoccupied of late. And extra effort for me means actually buying some fresh vegetables and cutting them up all by myself. I did it once in the late '90s, and it worked out quite well. Tonight I would recapture that vegetable-based magic for the benefit of my girlfriend.

I looked up to see that the girl behind the counter was having a little trouble. She'd taken the rather small onion I was buying out of its bag and was comparing it to little pictures she had on her till. She didn't seem to be able to find one to match.

"S'cuse me," she said. "What's this?"

"That's an onion," I said, wondering whether this girl harbored any real ambitions for a long-term career in the minimarket business.

"Right," she said. "Only it's not on here. I don't know what price it is."

"Oh," I said, looking at the onion in her hand, like that would give any clues as to its price.

"So it's an onion?" she asked. Well, it was worth asking again, just in case I'd got it confused with a box of Coco Pops or a copy of *Front* magazine.

"Yes," I said. "It's an onion."

"But what would it be called on *here?*" she asked, indicating the price list Sellotaped to the front of her till, as if they'd have provided her with a list written in Spanish, or something.

"Well . . . probably 'onion,' " I said. I wasn't being very helpful, but to be honest I shouldn't have needed to be.

"Right. Yeah, it's definitely an onion," she said. She re-scanned the list. "Nope. I'm sorry, I don't know how much this costs, so . . ."

She shrugged her shoulders and raised her eyebrows in a what-can-ya-do? way, and put the onion to one side.

"Hang on," I said. "I need that onion. You can't not sell it to me."

"I've no way of knowing how much it is, sir."

"Well . . . take a guess, or something. I can't be the first person to buy an onion in this place. You've a whole bag of them over there."

"Tell you what," she said, glancing from side to side even though we were completely alone, "have this one on me." She chucked the onion in the bag, smiled, and continued packing my bags.

"So . . . are you cooking tonight?" she said.

Apparently the fact that she'd saved me about 12p in onions meant that we were now bosom buddies, and would presumably be going out clubbing together later.

"Yes, I am, I'm afraid."

"You're probably a much better cook than me," she said.

"At least I know what a fucking onion is," I said, and headed home.

I didn't say that really. I mumbled something about not being very good really, blushed, and *then* headed home.

Once there, I gave Joinee Saunders a call.

"Danny! Hello! I'm just scanning the front page of the *Inverness Courier* in to e-mail to you. Join Me's front page news!"

"Front page?" I said in disbelief.

"Well, like I told you, the paper heard about the good deeds I was doing in the name of Join Me, and wanted to interview me. They sent a photographer round and took a picture of me in front of the cathedral wearing my Join Me T-shirt under my dog collar! I had a bit of explaining to do today. It took me by surprise a bit, because I walked into Safeway and there I was—all over the place! I look like a fat Gary Barlow. Not that there's any other kind. Anyway, the Bishop thought it was fantastic. Ooh—hang on, I just got a text message."

The Bishop thought it was fantastic! Brilliant. I waited while Gareth fumbled with his mobile.

"It's from my mate Johnny. It says 'CLERGY BRAINWASHED IN CULT SCANDAL!' He's a joker!" And then we both laughed and said good-bye.

I virtually skipped to the kitchen, chopped my onion up and heated a pan to fry it in. But then curiosity got the better of me and I went to my computer to see if Gareth's article had arrived in the sixty seconds I'd been in the kitchen. It hadn't, so I kept pressing "Send & Receive" until it had.

There he was, proud, noble Gareth, staring into the middle distance in his Join Me T-shirt, with the magnificent cathedral towering over him.

SIGNING UP TO "KINDNESS" COLLECTIVE

A CLERGYMAN serving at Inverness Cathedral has been recruited into a new flock.

Rev Gareth Saunders, a curate at the cathedral, is now a man with a double mission, spreading the word not only about the Church, but about "Join Me"—an informal group which started almost as a joke but is now bringing people together from across the world.

Join Me was created when advertisements appeared in London newspapers asking people to "Join Me" by writing back with a passport-sized photograph.

The person whom respondents found they were joining is Danny, who prefers not to give his surname although he does reveal he used to work for catalogue sales firm Argos.

Surely it couldn't be long before the Argos people got in touch with some kind of big-money sponsorship offer? But the article continued . . .

Danny (25) is encouraging his joinees to carry out "random acts of kindness," but insists Join Me is not a religious organization. "I'm not religious in any way, but funnily enough I've had two vicars join me," he said.

One of Join Me's two vicar followers, Gareth (30), says: "It seemed like a good idea and could lead somewhere positive, so I said 'Yes,' although I didn't know much about it then."

Heavy-metal fan Gareth, who has been at the cathedral for three years, has been undertaking missionary work on Danny's behalf, not only wearing his Join Me T-shirt, but distributing leaflets about the group.

Fantastic. Join Me was indeed front-page news! Gareth revealed in the accompanying e-mail that he had further plans. In the days that followed, news of Gareth's involvement in Join Me had made it to local radio stations, church websites, cathedral newsletters and even the *Daily Express*.

I was inspired by Gareth's efforts. And I thought back to our time together. He'd been so insistent I listen to his advice, and although I'd met the fantastic Dr. Spacetoad off the back of it, I hadn't done as much meeting and greeting as I'd thought was appropriate, since I'd given my word to a man of the cloth. There just hadn't been time to do it.

I had to continue to apply that to Join Me. There was a chance that people not as dedicated as Gareth would begin to lose interest. I couldn't allow that to happen. Before, I hadn't wanted to go out and meet too many people, because it was easy to be mysterious from behind a keyboard. And I had to be mysterious, because I hadn't known what to tell them; we didn't, after all, have an aim. But now, *now* we had a purpose. We had a *mission*. I felt far more able to go out and meet people, to tell them about the way of Join Me, and urge them to do their good deeds on each and every one of our Good Fridays. I was going back to basics, taking the message of the Karma Army on the road. I worked out a route that would take me past the home towns of several joinees, and ordered my tickets.

That night over dinner (I burned the onion) I told Hanne that the following day I would be popping back to my parents' house in Bath to say hello to my mum and dad. And I would be. But I would also be going in order to meet two of the founding members of the Bath Collective: Joinees Sansom and Jones. They'd written to me requesting an audience. They wanted to collaborate to do good deeds, but they wanted my advice on how to do it. A trip to Bath was the least I could do to guarantee their loyalty and help stir up some goodness in the Southwest. But

I wouldn't just be in Bath. Oh no. I'd be working hard on the campaign trail, meeting as many joinees as I could in a day and ensuring their continued commitment to the cause.

The next morning, I jumped on an early train out of London and an hour and a half later I'd arrived at Bath Spa train station. I walked the five-minute walk to my parents' house, said hello, had a quick cup of tea, and then headed into town. I met Sansom and Jones outside Bath Abbey. We headed for the Pump Room to have a cup of tea and a sit down. I chatted to them quickly and efficiently. Sansom works in Web design. Jones works for a labor counselor. I gave them some extra leaflets and stickers to aid their word spreading, and they thanked me as if I'd just given them each a check for two hundred quid. Then it was time to be off. I had a long day ahead of me.

Joinee Jonathan and I met after a twenty-five-minute train journey out of Bath, in the small town of Chippenham. We sat in a café near the station and he revealed to me that he wanted to play a bigger part in the world of Join Me. In many ways, he wanted to be the Watson to my Holmes.

"I think it's great that you meet your joinees," he enthused. "It's inspiring. I think more people should know about it. I want to chronicle your journeys. I want to chart them. All this good that's happening—it should be told to the wider world. There could be a book in it!"

"Trust me," I said. "There's not."

"You never know! I'd like to write a kind of modern-day Bible about what you're up to. The Book of Joinees. I'm fairly sure we could get a publisher interested. If you could spare me just a few minutes every week to tell me what you've been up to I could write it up for you."

I told Joinee Jonathan I'd e-mail him when I could, and he should feel free to send me his interpretations. I had a feeling he would anyway. And then it was time to get back on the train and leave Chippenham far behind.

Well, several miles behind.

My next stop was Swindon. A joinee named Ms. Taylor had been trying to convince her friend Rachael that she should join . . . but Rachael wasn't sure. I agreed to stop off at Swindon not only to meet

Joinee Taylor—an English teacher—but to help badger her mate into signing up too.

After a chat and a photo, Joinee Taylor and new Joinee Rachael waved me off as the train moved away, and I sat down and awaited my arrival at Didcot Parkway.

There, I stood in a thin rain until I was met by an unsure looking man with a wispy moustache, who turned out to be Joinee Anderson, a part-time mechanic who'd traveled to meet me from Banbury.

We sat in his car in the car park and he offered me one of his sandwiches.

"So, I must say, Danny, I didn't really know what I was getting into with this whole Join Me business. But I've been trying to do my bit for you. Last Friday I repaired a car and didn't charge for the oil change."

"Did the car belong to quite an attractive woman?" I asked, having met mechanics before.

"Well . . . yes," said Joinee Anderson, and we laughed.

"So you started giving free oil changes to women you fancy?"

"Among other things."

I felt good. Thanks to me, fit birds in Banbury were getting free oil changes. Not many people can say that.

It was soon time for my next train, and I bid Joinee Anderson goodbye, telling him to spread the free oil changes around a bit, and not just give them to girls he fancied, and he promised he would.

At Reading Station, I'd arranged to be met by Joinee Thomas, a student at Reading University. I say "arranged." She obviously thought it was a far more casual agreement, because she didn't bother turning up. Either that, or she'd told one of her friends that she was planning to meet some bloke she'd met on the Internet.

"That's nice," her friend would have said. "And how very modern of you. I assume it was through some kind of secure, official dating service?"

"No," Joinee Thomas would have said, "he is a sort of cult leader and I have agreed to do his bidding."

Her friend would have then called the relevant university authorities and had Miss Thomas sedated.

I kicked about Reading Station for half an hour or so. I had to be on the 18:34 train in order to make it back to London in time for my final appointment of the day.

As I sat there, though, I had time to think about my next joinee visit. I was supposed to be meeting Joinee Benjamin. I had the feeling he would be rather more difficult.

His e-mails were always slightly cryptic, for a start, and his attitude sometimes rather suspicious, but I kept telling myself not to be silly. He'd joined me, after all, and if that wasn't enough to recommend a chap, what was?

I'd printed out his questionnaire in order to bone up on him before we met, and I read it on the train back into London. It was strange. While most people were inclined to give me their life stories, Joinee Benjamin had chosen to leave many questions blank and answer other questions with questions. It was all very odd, and I learned virtually nothing from it.

I dashed through the slanting rain, out of Paddington station, and across the road, where I found the tiny café we'd agreed to meet at. Five minutes passed. Then ten. I was sitting in a prime position—no one could miss me if they walked in, and I could see anyone approaching the café for quite a distance. Surely I wasn't going to get stood up again? Was someone bumping off my joinees before I got to meet them? Unless the person I was going to meet was already here. I looked around. The couple and one of the men had gone, which only left the two Italian students, and the bloke who looked like a bored commuter, eating a baked potato and reading the *Evening Standard* on the other side of the room. I thought about leaving. But moments later the man I would come to know as Benjamin walked into the café, brushed the rain off his shoulders and strode purposefully toward me.

"You're Danny?" he asked.

"Yes," I said.

"Benjamin," he said. I was slightly taken aback. He certainly looked very different from how I'd expected. He looked nothing like he did when his passport photo was taken. He had a different hairstyle, for a start, and he had an earring, and he'd even gone to the trouble of having a completely different face.

"I watched you, er, walk in," he said. "I was in the, er, café opposite."

"Oh. Am I in the wrong one?"

"No. I was sitting there, just watching, just watching."

"Oh." I said. There was an awkward silence. I didn't really want to ask him why he'd been sitting there, just watching, just watching.

"So . . . it's nice to meet you," I said.

"Mmm. I've been looking forward to meeting you too."

Another awkward silence.

"You're not quite as I imagined you," said Benjamin.

"Well . . . you're not quite the same as you look in your photo," I said.

He laughed.

"That's not a picture of *me*. I'm not a *complete* idiot!"

I imagine I looked quite confused at this stage, but Joinee Benjamin continued.

"I'll cut to the chase. I've been keeping my eye on your Join Me thing. I keep an eye on a lot of things, and Join Me is one of them. I applied to join you, I answered your questionnaire, and I'm fascinated. I thought it was important we meet face to face, so you know that someone is . . . let's say 'interested' . . . in what it is that you're doing."

I nodded, but was still confused.

"What is it that I'm doing?"

"You know exactly what you're doing."

I bloody wished I did.

"No, tell me."

"I was suspicious as soon as I heard about you."

"Well . . . how did you hear about me?"

"Your website was mentioned in the *Mirror*. *Why is he getting people to join him?* I thought. *What's in it for this guy? Politics? Religion? Money?* Then I found out some more from you and other joinees I e-mailed, and they said you used the term 'New World Order' in one of your advertisements, is that not the case?"

"Yes."

"And what does that mean to you?"

"Well . . . I just wanted to start my own thing. You know. Like a collective."

"Because to me . . ."

The waiter arrived with the coffee, and Benjamin fell silent while it was placed on the table, followed by a bowl of sugar, a spoon and a napkin. The waiter left and Benjamin felt it was safe to continue.

"Because to me, and to my friends, it means something very different. It means eugenics. The elimination of what some deem the useless."

"No," I said. "The useless are *more* than welcome. I'm useless myself."

"The New World Order is something They want to instigate with the ultimate aim of reducing those who are left on the planet to a near pre-industrial state. It's about the creation of a one-world oligarchical government."

I think my eyes were about as wide as they could get at this juncture.

"I can't even *say* 'oligarchical,'" I said, disproving my point. "That's not what I'm about at all."

Who the hell did this bloke think I was? What did he think I was up to? He was a joinee . . . and yet he didn't seem to be into the idea of Join Me at all. Why had he given me a false photo? Why couldn't he have been like all the other joinees I'd met today? Or at least had the decency not to turn up, like Joinee Thomas? I couldn't take it all in . . . and then he started to get a little odder.

"What would you say if I said the words: the Process?"

"I'd say 'What's that?'"

Benjamin was studying my eyes for any glimmer of recognition or fear.

"What about the Children?"

"I don't know."

"The Finders?"

"I've never heard of the Finders. What did they find?"

Benjamin paused. He wanted to tell me, but instead continued trying to catch me out. His eyes narrowed.

"The Sovereign Order of the Solar Temple?"

Jesus . . .

"Dunno."

"International Chivalric Organization?"

"I don't know, but I don't mind the sound of them. Chivalry is dead in this country."

Benjamin looked like he was about to agree, but remembered who he was and instead barked: "The Moon Child?"

"Never met him."

"The Golden Way Foundation?"

"No."

"The Luciferians?"

I sighed.

"No. No, I've never heard of *any* of this lot. They're nothing to do with me. I'm doing something called Join Me, and it's about good deeds. That's all. No Moon Children, Luciferians or Finders."

"You've *heard* of *the Finders?*"

Benjamin's eyes were filled with horror.

"You just mentioned them a minute ago," I said. "Look, do I look like someone who'd be in one of those things?"

"Cult leaders take all forms."

"It's not a cult. It's a collective. And cult leaders very rarely take a form similar to mine."

"Why aren't you more open about what you do, if it's all so innocent? Why the secrets, Danny? The evasive answers? Why don't you have a picture of yourself on your website?"

"Because I don't feel I look like a particularly inspiring Leader," I said. "Look at me. I'm just a scruffy bloke with specs. I don't want people going to the site and saying, 'Oh. Look. We appear to have joined one of the Proclaimers.' "

Benjamin considered this. I continued.

"And anyway, I *am* being more open. You know what Join Me's all about now. Good deeds. Nice things. And I'm meeting people face-to-face precisely *because* I've nothing to hide."

"The fact that you took out the advert worried me. The Heaven's Gate cult did something similar when recruiting for new members. They placed an ad in *USA Today* saying something along the lines of 'This is your last chance to advance beyond the human.' "

"Mine's about just *being* human," I said. "Not about advancing *beyond* it. What have I asked you to do since you joined me? Just nice things. Have I ever tried to control your mind? Have I ever once asked you to kill the president? Even the president of a small country, like Antigua? No."

"So why do you ask people so many questions? Why send out a questionnaire?"

"I want to find out a little about them. I want to know who's joined me. It's natural. And anyway, *you've* asked most of the questions today."

Benjamin looked at his fingers, drummed them on the table again, and then looked back at me.

"Are you *sure* you're nothing to do with the Finders?"

This bloke had to be winding me up.

"I promise you. I know nothing about them."

Benjamin looked around the room, decided it was safe, and whispered conspiratorially, "Since 1987, the Finders have been active, mainly in America."

The words "mainly in America" translated to me as "this is bollocks" and I sat back in my chair with a sigh.

"There are roughly forty of them, all adults. They have no visible means of support for their activity, and they appear to be worth over two million US dollars."

"What's the problem with them?"

"Well . . . their activities are worrying in the extreme."

I sighed again. "Go on . . ."

Benjamin looked around again. Apparently, "mainly in America" didn't mean that one of the forty Finders mightn't be in this tiny café near Paddington, just by chance.

"They constantly walk the streets. They follow people about all day, and they take extensive notes and pictures of everything."

"Why?"

"No one knows. But that's what they do. Always writing notes. Scribbling things down. Keeping a record. They're part of the global vision. Heralds of the coming world superstate."

I didn't really know what to say to any of this. It's not often you're sat with a complete stranger, in a café in London, discussing heralds of the coming world superstate. Not unless you're Benjamin, anyway, who I imagine spends much of his time doing just that.

"Are you sure we're not wandering into the realms of fantasy here, Benjamin?" I asked. This was all very peculiar, and I was slowly coming to the realization that this increasingly fidgety man was a complete and utter cockney nutjob. You may have realized this for yourself a page or two back, but remember: I still had my tea to finish, and I find concentrating on two things hard enough at the best of times. Nevertheless, I was fascinated by what he was saying. And I was still trying to work out how he thought Join Mc fitted into all of this.

"Let's look at how you've recruited people for your cult," said Benjamin.

"It's not a cult—it's a collective. And all I did was invite them to join."

"Yes, but let's look at what we're going to do now we've got them."

I didn't like Benjamin's use of the word "we" there.

"*We're* not going to do anything. Apart from good stuff. And what's with the 'we'?"

"I'm just saying. You obviously have plans. And it's very interesting that you chose to mention killing the president a few moments ago. Why did that pop into your head?"

"It just did."

"So the words 'kill the president' were just offered up by your subconscious? That's interesting."

This annoyed me.

"It's *not* interesting. And I'm *not* going to kill the bloody president, okay? That was just an example of one of the many things I *haven't* asked my joinees to do. Do you want more? There are *lots* more. I haven't asked them to make plans to leave planet Earth on a big bloody spaceship hidden behind a ruddy great comet. I haven't asked them to all do crazy little dances and dress up in orange and play the bloody bongo drum. Oh, and most importantly of all, I have *not* asked them all to *be in a cult*."

Benjamin looked slightly offended. There was a tense five seconds of silence, as he looked to our left and right to see who'd overheard me banging on about cults. I'd raised my voice slightly at the end of all that, without really realizing, and I calmed down, and felt slightly ashamed. It's just a bit annoying when a man you've only just met thinks you're planning to assassinate a world leader. It puts a downer on your whole day. You start wondering who *else* people think you're secretly planning to kill.

Benjamin cleared his throat and continued. "What do you do when your 'joinees' come together?"

The question was carefully put, and quietly spoken. Benjamin was now the one coming across as the sane party, and I the cult-obsessed nutter. He clearly thought he would have to treat me with kid gloves; I had just proved myself prone to unstable outbursts, after all.

"I haven't really met them as a group yet," I said. "Some of them like to make old men happy, that sort of thing."

"Chanting?"

"What?"

"Do they do any chanting?" Benjamin was stirring his coffee but looking me straight in the eye.

"Not that I know of. Maybe in their own time. But not on my watch."

"Because continual chanting is a common technique used to alter a person's state of awareness. The same is true of swaying, or clapping, or just about any repetitive movement. Some leaders make their followers hyperventilate, to reduce the level of carbon dioxide in the bloodstream, which produces lightheadedness. You then tell them they've reached an altered state or had a spiritual experience."

"But don't they just reply, 'No, I'm just a bit dizzy because you're not letting me breathe properly'?"

"I'm just giving you the facts."

"Well, I won't be telling people to hyperventilate. Because I'm not a cult leader, am I?"

"Have you ever pressed anyone's eyes in?"

I was getting annoyed again. "No I have not. Who do you think I am? I don't go about pressing people's eyes in."

"Because if you did, you'd be doing what They do," said Benjamin, flatly. "You pass along your line of followers and you press on their eyes until the optic nerve sends signals to the brain as flashes of white light. And then you tell them that you were 'bestowing Divine Light' upon them. You can also push really hard on their ears—"

"I don't *want* to push really hard on their ears!"

"I'm just saying. You can push really hard on their ears until they hear a buzzing sound and then tell them they've heard 'The Divine Harmony,' which is like Jesus humming—"

"Jesus never hummed," I said, moodily, despite the fact that He probably had, at least once or twice. I made a mental note to check with Joinee Saunders.

But Benjamin sensed my continued annoyance. He held his hands up and sat back, obviously trying to avoid confrontation.

"I'm just trying to educate you, Danny. To let you know what it's all about. I've been involved in certain things myself and I am aware of the techniques."

I think Benjamin was trying to tell me—without actually telling me—that he'd once found himself in a cult. He gave the impression of being someone who was violently against them, but he talked about them with a strange sense of glee. Like he *enjoyed* their existence. The only thing I can compare it to is when someone is telling you about a particularly grisly scene in a horror film; their eyes are a mixture of enthusiasm and disgust, and they desperately want you to share in both.

My phone rang. It was Ian, who was actually ringing to ask me if I'd tape *Die Hard 2* for him that night, but I made it sound like he was in town and demanding to meet me.

"I've got to go," I said to Benjamin. "But thanks for . . . you know . . . some interesting ideas for Join Me."

"I'll be in touch," said Benjamin, before, slightly sarcastically, "Oh, Leader!"

I nodded enthusiastically, gave him a little thumbs up (which he returned), said good-bye, and headed for the tube.

What a very odd man. And I'm sure he wouldn't mind my saying that. Because that's the kind of attitude odd people have.

I got back to the flat, head low and shoulders heavy, to find Hanne in my kitchen.

"Where have you been?"

"Bath," I said. "I told you. I went to say hello to my parents."

This was true. I had.

"Yes," said Hanne. "And I thought it would be nice to phone them while you were there, but your mum said you'd turned up for about five minutes and then gone again."

This was true. I had.

"Well, you know what my mum's like at exaggeration. I must have been there longer than five minutes."

"Five minutes, she said. From 9:30 to 9:35. She was horrified! So where did you go?"

"I went to see some friends."

"More new friends, I suppose. Where are you meeting all these people? Why have I never met any of them? It's really getting to me, Danny. We could have spent today doing something. I'm not sure how much more of this I can take. You've changed."

I said I was sorry, but I needed to see my friends, and she said she just wished I could be honest with her. I'd never been so secretive, she said, and for a moment I was utterly desperate to come clean, to just tell her what I'd been up to. Would that really be so bad? To say that I'd been spending my days not earning lots of money writing film reviews or playing videogames, but instead creating a network of joinees across the world, who do my bidding every Friday for no real purpose or profit other than to be nice? How could a girl not like a boy who did nice things? I wanted to tell her, I really did, but there was something inside me telling me I shouldn't. I knew that either I had to stop doing this completely, or carry on in secret. There was no middle ground. It was stop or be stopped, and neither option was particularly pleasant to imagine.

The truth of it was, I was enjoying myself. I had found a purpose. And, in a horrible way, I'd gained a power. A power few people have. A power I was determined not to misuse, but a power that was as addictive as it was unexpected. And so, yet again, I didn't tell Hanne.

She knew something was wrong, and I could tell that her attitude toward me was changing subtly, and it made my stomach churn every time I thought about it. I didn't want to risk my relationship, but I couldn't stop doing what I was doing. I had hundreds of people relying on me. Hundreds of good things happening as a result. If I told Hanne, I'd have to stop, and by stopping, I'd be risking preventing hundreds of good things happening in the future. Hell, hundreds of good things happening this *week. Thousands* happening in the months that followed. Maybe *millions* by the time I follow in Gallus's clogs and they pop from underneath me. Could I really risk those things not happening, just to suit my own selfish needs?

I didn't know.

Maybe?

I'd have to think about it.

Probably, yes.

No. No way.

I don't know.

Hanne didn't stay at mine that night. She said she wanted to go home and clear her head. I didn't stop her. But it made me very sad.

Later, when I was utterly physically and emotionally exhausted and getting ready for bed and had just realized I'd forgotten to tape *Die Hard 2,* I checked my e-mail. The first name up was Benjamin's . . .

Danny,

Forgot to mention earlier: everything is in place for the creation of a nega-utopian society. Worldwide slavery is not so very far off, and narcohypnotics, water fluoridization, mass observation, human robot production, microminiaturization of mind control implants (etc.) all have a little something to do with it! I'm sure you know what I'm saying . . .

More soon, *Benjamin*

P.S. We are partners now. Let's Make It Happen!!

Oh God. I'd hit a low.

What the hell was I doing with my life? My girlfriend was constantly and unfailingly angry with me, I was living the shady double life of a well-meaning cult leader, it was all costing too much money, I'd attracted the attentions of a lunatic who thought I was out to kill the president and now wanted to team up with me for God knows what dark purposes, and I was absolutely, dreadfully shattered by it all.

But not as shattered as I was about to be.

Con artist sentenced for trail of deception

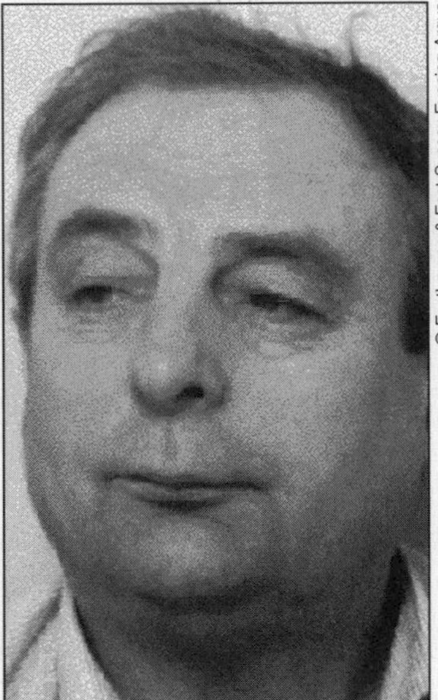

PAINTER: Price has started painting again in prison

A CON artist who accidentally became one of Britain's most wanted men has been jailed for deception.

Raymond Price, 59, specialised in cheating kind-hearted members of the public.

He toured the south claiming his car had broken down and he needed cash for his train fare home.

Price promised to send the money back to his victims, taking their names and addresses, but they never heard from him again.

But when he committed offences in Worthing he came under suspicion by murder squad detectives involved in the hunt for the killer of pensioner ████ ████.

His description was circulated nationwide and his pictured was issued to the media and was shown on Crimewatch.

Price, of no fixed address, gave himself up to police at Heathrow.

He was quickly ruled out of the murder investigation and another man has since been charged with the murder of Miss ████.

But yesterday Price was jailed for 18 months at Chichester Crown Court after admitting 13 charges of deception and asking for another 162 to be taken into consideration.

Beverley Cherrill, prosecuting, said Price gave his victims a false name and borrowed sums ranging from £7 to £20 for his bogus train fare.

Help

Mrs Cherrill said some people even went to cashpoints because they wanted to help him.

The court was told Price had previous convictions dating back to the early 1950s.

Warwick Tatford, defending, said Price had not seen his own photograph on television but went to the police when he heard rumours he was wanted.

He said that between 1973 and 1986 Price had kept out of trouble because he was a talented painter and ran an art gallery in Rye selling his own work, but the business collapsed when his marriage broke up.

Mr Tatford said Price was painting again in prison and hoped to make a living again from art.

Judge Anthony Thorpe told Price he hoped that he would use his artistic abilities to keep out of trouble in the future.

CHAPTER · 14

22. *And Daniel wept, and howled with bitterness of heart.*
23. *Then he returned unto his place.*

I read and re-read the article with wide, unblinking, disbelieving eyes. It was from *The Argus*. It was from 14 January 2000. It was real.

And it was incredible.

CON ARTIST SENTENCED FOR TRAIL OF DECEPTION

A con artist who became one of Britain's most wanted men has been jailed for deception. Raymond Price, 59, specialized in cheating kind-hearted members of the public. He toured the south claiming his car had broken down and he needed cash for his train fare home.

It was about here that I choked and coughed tea through my nose. But there was more . . .

Price promised to send the money back to his victims, taking their names and addresses, but they never heard from him again.

But when he committed offenses in Worthing he came under suspicion by murder squad detectives.

His description was circulated nationwide and his picture was issued to the media and was shown on Crimewatch.

Murder! Offences! Victims! And *Crimewatch!*

> *Price, of no fixed address, gave himself up to police at Heathrow.*
>
> *He was quickly ruled out of the murder investigation.*
>
> *But yesterday Price was jailed for 18 months at Chichester Crown Court after admitting 13 charges of deception and asking for another 162 to be taken into consideration.*

Make that 163!

> *Beverley Cherrill, prosecuting, said Price gave his victims a false name and borrowed sums ranging from £7 to £20 for his bogus train fare.*

Ranging from £7 to £20! And yet he'd tried his luck and nabbed *£38* from us! He'd seen my happy-faced joinees, taken them for simpletons, and gone for the bloody record!

> *The court was told Price had previous convictions dating back to the early 1950s.*
>
> *Warwick Tatford, defending, said that between 1973 and 1986 Price had kept out of trouble because he was a talented painter and ran an art gallery in Rye.*
>
> *Mr. Tatford said Price was painting again in prison and hoped to make a living again from art.*
>
> *Judge Anthony Thorpe said he hoped that Price would use his artistic abilities to keep out of trouble in the future.*

Well, Judge Anthony Thorpe is obviously a bloody optimist then!

Oh my God.

Raymond Price had sucked me into a world of crime. He'd served his eighteen months, walked out of jail, and almost immediately tricked my good-hearted joinees, just as he'd been tricking people since the '50s. The man had made off with our money!

This undermined *everything* my joinees and I had been working toward. How could we have taken inspiration from helping a *criminal?* How could I encourage people to go out and make random people happy, when random people would take advantage of their kindness and steal from them?

• • •

"So," said the taxi driver, as I struggled with my seat belt. "What brings you to Teignmouth?"

Well, wasn't it obvious? Couldn't he tell from the look in my eyes? From the short, sharp, angry tugs of my seat belt? I was in Teignmouth to find a man named Raymond Price and bring him to justice. I was going to track him down and demand my joinees' £38 back. And then I was going to go home and carefully rethink this whole being-nice-to-strangers thing.

"Hello?" said the taxi driver, and I realized that it's all very well having an internal monologue, but it does tend to leave the other person a bit stranded, conversationally.

"Sorry," I said. "I'm here to see an old friend."

I hoped I'd said that a bit mysteriously, in a way that I suggested I might very well be a hit man, here on a mafia contract, but I'd actually accidentally said it in a way that suggested I was probably here to see an old friend.

"And what's the address?" he said.

"Well," I sighed. "He probably won't be there, to be honest, so I don't know what the point in going there is."

I shrugged, and sat back in my seat.

"Right," said the driver. "So . . . what's the actual address?"

"Well, I can give you the address if you want. The newspapers couldn't. They thought he was of 'no fixed address.' But I've got one. Though I'm warning you, he's probably long gone, so don't get your hopes up."

"I won't," he said. "But what's the address? I need that to get there."

"Oh, mate, believe me, that's what I would have thought, too, but that's because we're too trusting."

"Well, why do you want to go there?"

"Ha! You tell *me!*" I said, with a casual shrug of the shoulders. "It's a false address. Or the address is real, but he isn't. Or he's real, but he doesn't live there."

I smiled at the driver and threw my hands up in the air, as if he knew exactly what I was on about and could relate to the situation entirely.

"Okay," said the driver, switching the ignition off, and turning to me, semi-menacingly. "Do you want to just sit here and talk about some possibly fictional man who may or may not live in a place that may or may not exist, or do you actually want to go somewhere?"

So here I was in Teignmouth, in Devon, on the trail of Raymond Price. But did he even really live in Teignmouth? The article mentioned Rye, and Worthing, but my group of joinees had met him in London . . . who knew where he was nowadays? The only thing I could do was turn up at the address I'd been given and see if I could find him.

I rang the doorbell.

No answer.

I rang it again.

Still nothing.

I rapped on the door. By which I mean I knocked on it, not that I did a little MC-ing. But if I *had've* done a little MC-ing, it would've been quite angry stuff, like NWA when they're on about the Rodney King incident. Only I'd have made it less about police brutality and more about old Devon men ripping young folk off with their made-up stories of broken down cars. And there I think you'll find the main difference between British and American crime.

There was still no answer. So I tried the neighbors.

"Nope, don't know him," said a lady in a blue dress. "There was a chap who lived there several years ago."

"When was that?"

"That would have been several years ago now."

"Right. So he doesn't live there any more?"

"Nope. He moved. Several years ago."

Leave me alone. I never claimed to be Columbo.

So I walked back into town and found a pub called the King William IV. I ordered a lager and sat by the window. So this was Teignmouth. This was where people like Raymond Price were from. I drank my pint and scowled at my fellow drinkers.

Oh, they *looked* nice enough, with their casual shirts and kind faces. But underneath it all, were they not all just the same as Raymond bloody Price? This lager cost me £2.20. How much of *that* was going in the landlord's pocket? Oh, I expect he wanted me to buy some crisps, as well. Well, no way, pal. You're not getting *my* 40p. Wait for some other London chump to walk in.

I watched as a lady with a charity collection tin wandered from table to table, asking for money. Where would this money-grabbing tyranny end? Yeah, yeah . . . she was polite to people. On the *outside*. She was probably swearing and calling them wankers on the inside.

"Collecting for disabled children," she said, when she reached me.

"A likely story," I said, eyebrows raised. "I suppose you want £38, do you?"

She looked slightly startled, and I got all embarrassed, and reached into my pocket and gave her a quid despite myself. Christ, these people were good.

So, yet another pound down, I left that pub in that town of sin. Teignmouth. Sinmouth. Put it in the binmouth. And I walked away.

I got a bus back to the station and made a decision on the way.

I was giving up on Join Me. I was giving up on the Karma Army.

It was time to stop.

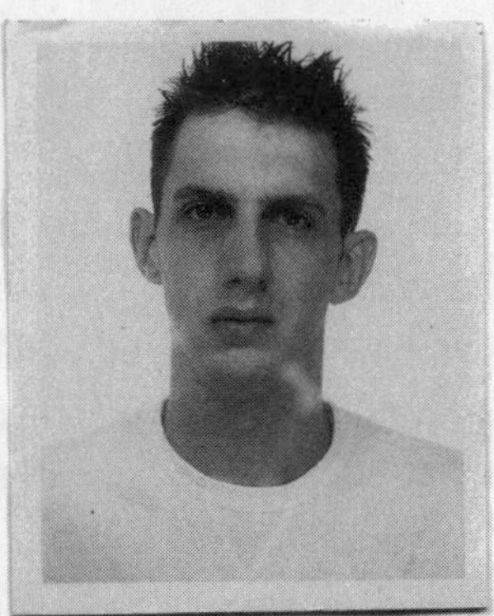

Vis à Vis

CHAPTER · 15

9. And, behold, the words of Daniel reached a damsel of fiery seasoning, not red and yet not brown.
10. And the damsel did give ear, and was beguiled.

I didn't know whether to be thankful or annoyed.

No one seemed bothered that I'd stopped having any involvement in Join Me for the last couple of weeks. I'd ignored my e-mails. I'd been absent from the website. For Gods' sake, I'd even gone on holiday to Greece. But no one seemed to have even noticed. If the Pope gave up on Catholicism for a fortnight it'd at least make the papers. If Jesus had stopped paying attention to his disciples and spent his days down the pub smoking, playing darts, and restocking the wine racks at will, I'm sure there'd have been a bloody great passage in the Bible about it.

But no. People had just got on with things. It was as if they didn't need me any more. While I'd been drowning my sorrows in Greece, drinking to forget, making friends with seven beermasters from Newcastle and waking up on muddy beachfronts with the image of a laughing Raymond Price on my mind, Join Me had, quite without me realizing, taken on a momentum all of its own. It had been good to get away, though. Make new friends. New friends who'd been quite into the idea of Join Me, and promised to spread the word around Newcastle, no matter how much I tried to look like I didn't care.

When I'd arrived home I'd checked my post and been surprised at how many people had heard about Join Me in my absence and signed up. I now had over four hundred passport photos. Four hundred! Nearly the halfway point! And not only that, but my existing joinees had been incredibly busy with their random acts of kindness while I'd been all upset and pouty on a sunlounger. E-mail upon e-mail informed me of what they'd been up to. I had hundreds of good deeds to wade through and tried my hardest to at least send a "well done" to each and every joinee who'd done something good.

And in an exciting twist, new localized collectives were forming all by themselves. Joinees in Manchester had decided to meet up and plan their movements. Joinees in Oxford had realized they'd be more effective working as a team than apart, and six of them were arranging to meet at a local pub the following Wednesday to swap notes and develop strategies. Joinees in York had met up while I'd been away and were full of ideas and game plans for new random acts of kindness. The two joinees I'd met in Bath had found a new member and were arranging to meet with her over the weekend. It was all going very well without me.

At first I didn't know how I felt about it all. My little children were fleeing the nest.

More exciting news came in the form of an e-mail from Joinee Estelle of Paris. She'd told a few friends, one of whom was from Belgium, and he'd decided to join me. So now I had a picture of Joinee Geert Stadeus, a journalist from Brussels, and he'd promised to tell his pals in the media about all this too. Brussels! The heart of Europe!

It also appeared that a dedicated joinee had called the phone-in radio station *TalkSport* and waxed lyrical about the benefits of signing up. Fourteen people did so as a result, including a curious chap called Joinee Gerstein who also sent me a rather frightening self-penned poem about a relentlessly crying baby.

Joinee Jess had sent me a photo of her at a book-signing session handing ex-Spice Girl Geri Halliwell a Join Me leaflet, along with assurance that "Geri had seemed quite interested in the whole thing and so may join you!" I am sorry to inform you that I am still waiting for her passport photo. But slowly, slowly, I could feel myself being pulled back into the world of Join Me. Surely I couldn't let Raymond Price win? By the time I finished reading my e-mails, I knew that the inevitable had happened: I was back.

Joinee Whitby had also been busy in my absence. By curious coincidence, he had recorded his very own Join Me anthem on his home computer. I popped the CD into my stereo and listened with great interest. To give you an idea of what it sounded like in the most polite way possible (because he, like you, will be reading this), I had initially thought that the CD was defective and was skipping around. In actual fact, it wasn't. In his letter, he asked me what I thought of it, and told me he would be in London very soon, and would I fancy meeting up?

I managed to avoid the first question, but not the second. And in a brave move, I agreed to meet with him. After all, he fascinated me. Ian wouldn't be happy. He still thought that Whitby harbored impure ambitions to steal Join Me away from me. But I wanted to meet him. For one thing, I'd promised myself I would meet more joinees. And for another, I wanted to set my mind at rest that he wasn't the evil-fueled joinee I'd been told he was.

So we arranged to meet the following week, when he'd be in town doing "something special" for Join Me. He wouldn't tell me what.

And then I found the business card of the Vis à Vis boys and gave them a bell.

• • •

"Come in," said Wayne. "Excuse the mess. The studio's just up there . . ."

I was in a small suburban street in Middlesex, walking up the stairs of the '60s semi that contained the Vis à Vis studio, which looked remarkably like a spare bedroom. Not many other studios, in my experience, contain a futon and an ironing board.

"Hello!" said Christopher, when I walked in. "Nice to see you again. Wayne's told me all about what you're up to. Sounds good."

"Thanks. I hope it is."

I moved some laundry and sat down.

"So what is it exactly you're after?" asked Wayne.

"Well . . . an anthem, I think. A joinee of mine called Spacetoad suggested it at first. He reckons it'll break down any cultural boundaries. And then I met you guys, and you seemed to think the same. A hum is a hum in any language, you said."

"Right. So this should be something hummable to get people joining up in their masses?" he said. "Well, I'm sure we can come up with something."

I'd brought Joinee Whitby's anthem with me to play to the boys, in case it gave them any new ideas. As it started, I saw Chris check the stereo to make sure the CD wasn't skipping. It wasn't. The boys politely tapped along in silence for the three minutes it took for the track to end. At times, I couldn't tell whether it was them out of rhythm, or Whitby's anthem.

"Would you mind if we made it a bit . . . less . . . you know . . . like that?" said Chris.

"Whatever you think."

"I have a feeling a track like that would get people thinking yours was a suicide cult."

Ideas were flung about left, right and center, and I was incredibly impressed with how quickly the boys were working with it. Wayne had his guitar out, and Christopher sat at his keyboard, and while they strummed and plink-plonked about, I tried to think of a few lyrics. I was a bit rubbish, but Chris came up with the inspired lyric *"If you're a lady, or a manny, or a granny, or a tranny, Join Danny!"* and Wayne developed a lovely hook.

To be honest, I'm very impressed with the way I got the term "hook" in there. It's one of the two musical terms I know. For a brief period, I'd worked for the music magazine *Melody Maker,* until I discovered that I found it impossible to write about music. My reviews inevitably made reference to the song's "hook," and if I could ever get the phrase "syncopated backbeat" in there, then by God I would. Even though to this day I have absolutely no idea what that means.

Wayne and Christopher, however, knew exactly what they were on about.

"Thanks for doing this," I said. "I know you must be busy."

"No problem," said Chris. "We're still having trouble with that Polish butter advert, so any distraction is welcome . . ."

Pretty soon a tune was coming together. It was jaunty, and lively, and had a lovely hook and made good use of the syncopated backbeat.

The lyrics were simple. It began with a moody, swelling intro while I talked over it . . .

The word is spreading . . . all over the earth!
Through England . . . Ireland . . . Wales . . . and the Scottish . . .
Across Europe . . . A-zee-ah . . . and the United States of Americans . . .
Everyone . . . is talking about one thing . . . !

And then the whole thing turned into a hugely upbeat, almost jazzy funfest with a great hook and a *brilliant* syncopated backbeat . . .

You gotta join . . . join Danny
You gotta join . . . join Danny
Ooh you gotta join . . . join Danny
'Cos tonight we're gonna party like it's 1983!
(Very good year for me, I was seven years old, I got a new bike!)

Join me!
You gotta join me!
You gotta . . . join me!

If you're a lady
Or a manny
Or a granny
Or a tranny
Join Danny!

It was great. I sang, then Chris and Wayne added their backing vocals, as well as pianos, a choir and drums. They phoned up a Filipino trumpeter mate of theirs who popped round and improvised around it. By the end of the day, we had something beautiful.

"That was brilliant," I said, standing up to leave. "Thank you so much."

"Before you go," said Chris, looking at Wayne, who shrugged and then nodded. "We were wondering if you could do us a favor in return?"

"Anything," I said.

"Well . . . you actually have a better voice than we thought you'd have."

This was very odd. I am famed for my bad singing voice. I am almost universally asked *not* to sing by people. And yet here were two professional musicians telling me I was all right.

"Yeah," said Wayne. "Could we borrow you for something?"

Ten minutes later I had some headphones on and was standing back in front of the microphone.

"Buh . . . buh . . . buh . . . Butter!" I sang, before, in a mock-American accent, "Yeeeow!"

"Perfect!" shouted Chris. "That's what we were after!"

"That'll make *all* the difference, mate," said Wayne. "I think we've got what we were missing."

It was amazing. I had arrived at their studio a normal man.

I left as the Voice of Polish Butter.

• • •

I was in the Horse & Groom with Ian.

"So how was your holiday?" he asked.

"Never mind that," I said. "Listen to this."

I popped some headphones on him and pressed play on the Walkman. Ian looked shocked when he heard me singing, but listened to the whole thing, tapping his finger on the table in time with the music.

"You've done a song!" he said.

"It's on the website!" I said. "I'm going to get it on the radio, too! And not just that—I'm also now the Voice of Polish Butter! That's track two!"

"So you're still doing all this? But the last time I spoke to you, you sounded like you were giving up!"

"I just needed time to get things into perspective," I said. "My holiday did that."

"So Raymond Price didn't beat you? That's good. You can still get revenge on him. Send a group of joinees after him. That'll teach him!"

"Ah, but will it? I've decided to do something else instead . . ."

And then I told Ian my plan.

When I'd been lying in the sun in Greece, I had a lot of time to think, you see. And I thought not just about Raymond Price, but about the effect he'd had on people. And not just on *my* people. But on the people of Britain.

Raymond Price had been convicted for thirteen acts of deception, and then asked for another 162 to be taken into consideration. Add to those the one he pulled on us, and a little faith in the British justice system, and that's 176 crimes.

Each crime had been worth between £7 and—thanks to my joinees—£38. That means he stole between £1,232 and £6,668 (nearly the number of the beast), which means that the good-hearted people of this country are an average of £3,950 worse off than they were fifty years ago.

Because yes—all these crimes were committed over the course of about fifty years. So that averages out at a loss to the nice people of Britain of £79 a year.

Raymond Price was making £79 a year from his crimes.

Which—as any criminal mastermind will tell you—is *rubbish*. Even if you round it up to £80. It's not exactly Nick Leeson or the Green Goblin, is it?

But through his actions, he had unwittingly spawned something beautiful. He had inspired me to ask others to do good. Surely that was worth £79 a year? Perhaps. But what was absolutely crucial was that he did no more damage.

And if we could keep Raymond Price from doing that—would that not be as good for him as for the karma of this country? If I could find a way of preventing him from committing any more crimes, we'd be keeping him out of jail! We'd be stopping an old man straying from the straight-and-narrow!

And so I started The Raymond Price Fund For Keeping Raymond Price Out Of Trouble. I suppose I could have called it Help An Aged, but, as I think you'll agree, TRPFFKRPOOT is a far superior acronym.

I opened a new bank account, and asked my joinees to set up a special direct debit. I'd only ask for around 20p per person per year. If we could raise, annually, around £79 to give to Raymond Price, then he'd no longer need to hit the streets in search of people to scam. He could stay in and watch *Countdown* instead! And the people of Britain could walk the streets knowing full well where Raymond Price was—staying indoors with a nice cup of tea and a biscuit.

Within a day, I'd raised £11, and told Ian all about it, rather excitedly.

"£11," he said. "That's very . . . impressive. But it's slightly odd . . . I mean . . . you're giving money to criminals now? It wasn't enough doing it by accident? You're now doing it *on purpose?*"

"No! Don't you see? He won't *have* to be a criminal anymore! The whole true spirit of Join Me started when I asked people to make an old man very happy. Well, we *are* doing! We're keeping him so happy he'll never have to go to jail again! And at the same time we're saving people from being ripped off! People will walk around happy without even knowing why!"

"But why will that stop him from doing more scams? It'll just be free money!"

"I'll find him one day, and I'll give him the money as long as he signs something to say he'll stop scamming people. And if I find out he's still doing it, I'll immediately stop the payments and give it all to charity. He's a clever bloke. He'll know he's on to something good. And it's so much more positive than going round there and shouting at him."

"I suppose . . ." said Ian. "But look, Dan . . . where will all this end?"

"How do you mean?"

"Well, don't get me wrong . . . but I bumped into Hanne the other day, and she seemed . . . well . . . a bit annoyed with you, generally."

"You didn't tell her about Join Me, did you?"

"No, course not. But maybe *you* should. You know? She thinks you're acting all odd for no good reason."

"I'll tell her. One day. I can't tell her now, though. I have a feeling if I did she'd make me stop, and I've only just realized how much this still means to me. And I've been *trying* to spend more time with her. You know how much I love her. I cooked her a burnt onion the other night. I saw her last night too. And I'm having dinner with her and some of her mates on Thursday."

"Which mates?"

"Just some mates of hers. New ones. Anyway, she's been on at me to meet them. So I'm doing that. And I *will* tell her. Soon. Just let me carry on for a bit longer, now that I've found my direction again."

"But how much longer? When will you stop?"

"When I've reached my target."

"What's your target?"

I didn't want to tell Ian. He didn't know for sure I'd decided to go for 1,000, and if I told him, he'd think we were having a bet. And we were *not* having a bet. I'm twenty-five. I've moved on.

"Ah!" said Ian, remembering that afternoon in the pub. "It's a thousand, isn't it? Admit it!"

Damn.

"Yes. But that doesn't mean this is a bet. Because it's not. No one's bet anyone anything."

"I said I'd get you a pint if you did it," he said. "So that counts."

"No it does not. This isn't a bet. I want a thousand because that's the maximum number of people Gallus could have got. And anyway, you're my friend—you should be helping me."

"I'm not joining you."

"Go on."

"No. I'm not helping you win that pint."

"Will you stop going on about that pint? This isn't a bet, okay? It's a tribute. A tribute to Gallus. Stop tainting it with talk of bets."

My phone rang. I was relieved. I answered it.

• • •

"What do you mean, you're planning something?" I asked.

"We just are," said Patrick. "Me and the rest of the Newcastle Collective have a little something planned for tomorrow."

Talk about Join Me gaining momentum. Now things were happening that were being kept a secret even from *me*.

The Newcastle boys had only one thing on their minds: how to carry on the good work of Join Me and the Karma Army. Even though when they'd met me in Greece I'd been more interested in beer, staring at my feet, and cursing the day we came across Raymond bloody Price.

• • •

The next morning—a Saturday—I was woken from my slumber by a reporter from the *Newcastle Evening Chronicle*. Twenty minutes after that I was phoned up by a freelancer from the *Guardian*. After her, I was called by someone from Newcastle's *Sunday Sun* newspaper. Later on I received an e-mail from a reporter from BBC Radio Newcastle. This was followed by a phone call from a researcher for a Radio 4 magazine show.

Each time I gave them the same answers. My name was Danny. I used to work at Argos. Join Me was about good deeds. And each time they told me how impressed they were by the Newcastle Collective's efforts.

As was I.

These seven lads had stayed up all Friday night—and I mean all of it—and painstakingly painted six huge, black letters on to six six-foot pieces of white cloth. Together, they spelled the words "JOIN ME."

Then, at five in the morning, they drove in two cars to the world-famous Tyne Bridge, ran under cover of darkness to its center, and hung their massive banner off the side. The words had caused fascination and confusion throughout the Northeast. Journalists accused me of being, variously, a media student, a clever marketing man about to release a new shampoo or chocolate bar called *Join Me,* and a religious nutjob. One of them made the point that if I wasn't starting a suicide cult, I really shouldn't be hanging words like "Join Me" off the side of a bridge.

But the boys had done incredibly well. They'd stayed and watched as the good people of Tyneside had stared, open-mouthed, at their achievement, right up until lunchtime when the police got involved and decided to take the thing back to the station with them.

Perhaps most remarkable was the fact that when the boys had retreated to the nearby Millennium Bridge to get a better view of their work, they spotted, glued to the side of the railings, a worn, blue, Join Me sticker. One that they'd had nothing to do with.

The word of Join Me really was spreading at an alarming rate. And the following day, articles about the Tyne Bridge event helped the word spread even further . . .

MYSTERY MESSAGE STUMPS SHOPPERS

A mysterious message hung from the Tyne Bridge over the weekend caused a great deal of head scratching.

Commuters, shoppers and the authorities were all confused after the words "Join Me" appeared hanging over the side of Newcastle's famous landmark on Saturday morning.

Police on both sides of the river appeared baffled and could offer no explanation of why the banner should be there or what its meaning was.

The mystery message, which was written on single squares of white cloth in black paint, led to speculation it could be the latest example of modern art to decorate the increasingly high-brow area of the booming Quayside.

"The latest example of modern art to decorate the increasingly high-brow area of the booming Quayside"? No! Seven idiots and me!

The *Sunday Sun* had gone one step further and asked to speak to one of the Newcastle Collective, and Patrick decided that because he was the tallest he'd do it.

"But the thing is," he said, "when he asked me my name I panicked. I don't know why I said it, but I changed my name and called myself 'Jamie.' " The intimidating power of the press, it seems, is second only to their powers of alliteration . . .

BYSTANDERS BAFFLED BY BANNER ON THE BRIDGE

A giant banner saying "Join Me" was erected on the Tyne Bridge yesterday . . . to the puzzlement of passers-by.

The banner was made by seven Newcastle members of an organization called simply Join Me.

But officers from Northumbria police will definitely not be joining up.

> *They took a dim view of the stunt . . . and quickly took the enigmatic recruiting poster down.*
>
> *One of the northern members of the group, identified only as Jamie, said "It was done for a bit of fun. It's not a religious thing but it's all about doing little acts of kindness."*
>
> *The organization was started by founder Danny, who wanted to stay anonymous.*
>
> *He said: "It's really about random acts of kindness. The Newcastle Collective is one of my most dedicated and hard-working."*
>
> *A typical example of their "work" was sending a man packets of his favorite wine gums to stop him feeling depressed.*

Wine gums? Depressed? Maybe sending an old man peanuts to make him very happy is frowned upon in Newcastle. But whatever . . . word was most definitely out in the Northeast, and within a couple of days, I received thirty joining inquiries and nineteen brand-new passport photos as a result.

It was great. And one thing was certain. I was losing control over Join Me. Things had carried on without me when I'd been gone, and bigger things were starting to happen without me even though I was back.

To be honest with you, it was all starting to get a little out of hand.

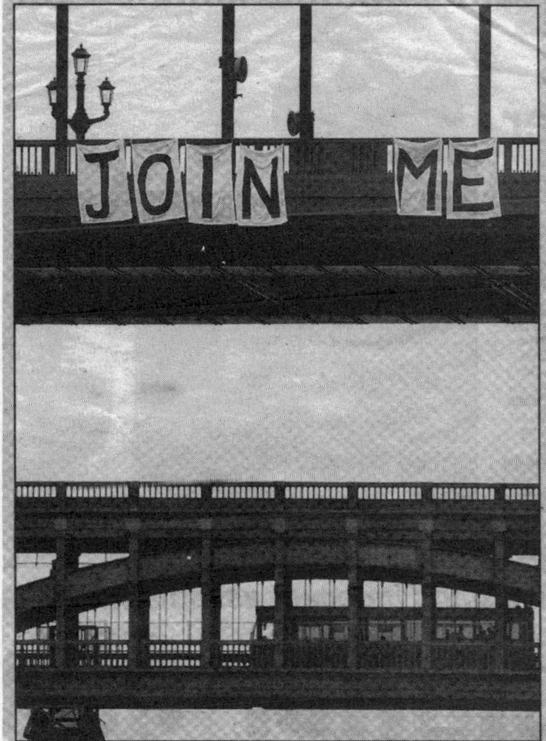

PUZZLER – the banner high over the Tyne at the weekend

Mystery message stumps shoppers

A MYSTERIOUS message hung from the Tyne Bridge caused a great deal of head scratching.

Commuters, shoppers and the authorities were all confused after the words 'Join Me' appeared hanging over the side of Newcastle's famous landmark on Saturday morning.

The mystery message, which was written on single squares of white cloth in black paint, led to speculation it could be the latest example of modern art to decorate the increasingly high-brow area of the booming Quayside.

Police on both sides of the river appeared baffled and could offer no explanation of why the banner should be there or what its meaning was.

● If you know the meaning behind the message call the Chronicle newsdesk on (0191) 201 6446.

BELGIANS
DOE MEE, BELGEN

CHAPTER · 16

15. Then Daniel met with Annalies, an exceeding beautiful maiden whose height was threescore cubits.

There were two e-mails I clicked open straight away.

Well, two e-mails I clicked open after having a sip of the first cup of tea of the day and trying to stop my boxer shorts from exploring areas of my body usually reserved for someone with a qualification.

The first was from Hanne.

"Just a little reminder," it began sweetly, "about Thursday. Dinner in Finchley with Mike and the others. Hope you're still up for it. xx."

I replied instantly.

"Yep!"

The next e-mail was from a name I didn't recognize. That was happening all the time now, though, so I thought nothing of it. But it was marked "Highest Priority," which was unusual, and had an intriguing subject line.

"Belgium."

I clicked it open . . .

Dear Danny,

It was a good friend of mine who has "joined" you, Geert Stadeus, who draw my attention to what you do. And believe it or not, but we love you.

So much that I dare ask you two questions:

—Have you ever been in Belgium?
—Would you like to come to Belgium?
There is a reason I ask.

I work in Belgian television. I would like to invite you in the most famous Flemish talkshow there is.

Can you believe this? A Belgian TV executive, inviting me onto the most famous Flemish talk show there is! Not one of the *less*-famous ones (and I think we all know which ones I'm referring to . . . !) but one that we *all* know the name of! What was going on with my life?

De Laatste Show *is a daily talkshow on the Flemish national channel TV1, hosted by Bruno Wyndaele. Every night Bruno invites three guests who were in the news that day (more or less) to have a relaxed and cheerful talk about the events of that day or that week. A show you could compare with it is* The Late Show with David Letterman.

Other past international guests in the show were Joanna Lumley, Tom Jones and Roger Moore.

And now, the logical extension—*me!*

Am I being unrealistic or do you see an opportunity to come to Belgium before May next year?

Please let me know if you'd like it.

Yours truly,

Sam De Graeve
De Laatste Show

Did I see an opportunity to come to Belgium before May next year? Too bloody right I did! I e-mailed Sam back immediately, saying that by complete and utter coincidence I would be in Belgium any time this week he fancied. Well, I didn't want to seem too keen.

But how exciting was this? My first international television appearance! And on a chat show! The David Letterman of Belgium was probably already as excited by my possible appearance as I was!

I re-read the e-mail. *"Other past international guests in the show were Joanna Lumley, Tom Jones and Roger Moore."* Well, I was in good company. Me, Jo, Tommo and Rog.

I checked and re-checked my e-mail every five or ten minutes, hoping that Sam would reply . . . but nothing. Nothing for hours. I found myself unable to leave the flat. Always connecting to the Internet. Always hitting "Send & Receive." Always hoping that the next mail would be the one confirming that his message hadn't been written in a moment of madness.

I started to worry that Sam was regretting his offer. Perhaps he'd just been carried away after listening to an enthusiastic friend. Or maybe he was an imposter. A joker. Perhaps he was a mental. Or what if he'd been drunk when he wrote it? I checked what time it had been sent. 9:17 A.M., Belgian time. The Belgians like a beer, but surely not that early in the morning? Mind you, this man worked in television. A lot of late nights. A lot of post-show drinks. I mean, maybe he really had drunk a little too much after yet another award-winning edition of *De Laatste Show*. Maybe Roger Moore had suggested going on to a nightclub, and Joanna Lumley had said, "Sod that, I've got a bottle of vodka in my room," and they'd all gone back there and polished that off, and then Tom Jones had arrived and said, "I've found some drugs from the '60s in my pocket," and Sam had just been carried away with the whole crazy vibe of the thing, and then there was a knock at the door and it was someone like Tom Selleck, who was in Belgium to promote a new kind of moustache or something and was on the next night's show, and he'd turned up late and said "Hey Jo, Tommo, I've heard about this thing called Join Me, it sounds brilliant and I might write a Hawaii-based detective series about it," and Sam had said, "Yeah, my friend Geert was on about that," and Roger said, "You should get the bloke behind it on the show," and Sam had said, "Okay Roger, I'll e-mail him in a minute," and now he was sitting at his desk in a TV studio in Belgium wondering how on Earth to tell me he'd changed his mind, and then I received his reply.

Danny,

Great! How about Thursday? We have a slot free then, but after that not for quite a while. If you are planning to come to Belgium, tell us where to pick you up from in Brussels and we come to get you at 17.00h. You are very welcome. I look forward to your visit very much. Also, I have been looking at the Join Me website and I like the song very much!

Sam

Argh. Thursday. The night I was supposed to be spending meeting Hanne's new and impressive friends. It was important to her, that much I knew. But could I really afford to turn down an opportunity like this? This would take some consideration. I did what I always do in situations like this—I tried to imagine what Roger Moore would do. But clearly, I'd already been given the answer. He'd appear on *De Laatste Show*. That was all the guidance I needed, because I realized there and then that if I analyzed it too deeply, I'd start to feel guilty. If I started to feel guilty, I wouldn't go to Belgium. And my gut was telling me that Belgium could be very, very good indeed.

I immediately jumped online and bought a very cheap ticket to Brussels, and an even cheaper hotel to stay in once there. I was going now, whatever happened. I would fly there on Thursday afternoon, do the show, and return not on Friday, but early on Saturday morning . . . because I'd had an idea. Quite a good one. Imagine what I could do with a whole day in Brussels. Especially if I'd had television exposure the night before. I hatched a plan. I would go on to the chat show, and then extend an invitation to the Belgian people to join me. I'd choose a place in the middle of town, and then tell them to meet me there the next day. For a moment, I felt quite sure that the entire population of Belgium would turn up, passport photos in hand, in order to join me—and all thanks to the all-powerful influence of television. I would conquer Brussels, the city at the heart of Europe, and then surely it wouldn't be long before the rest of the EU would crumble and follow suit.

But obviously, I had some excuses to make, Hanne-wise. It was now Wednesday. How could I get out of the dinner on Thursday? I'd left it late to cancel, but only because I really hadn't been expecting to be offered a spot on one of the most popular shows on Flemish TV. There was only one thing for it. I would have to be ill.

I phoned Hanne.

"Hanne, I'm ill."

"What?"

"I'm ill."

"You don't sound ill."

"That must be part of the symptoms or something."

"You'll be okay for Thursday, though, won't you?"

"Let's cross our fingers, but it's not looking good."

"But I've just had an e-mail from you saying you'll be there!"

"It's only come on in the last ten minutes. Listen to this . . ."

I attempted to cough a little. It sounded rubbish.

"Danny, you've *got* to come on Thursday. I can't be there with those people on my own."

"But I thought they were your friends?"

"No—I'm only going because Cecilie wants me to be there. They're *her* friends, not mine."

"Why didn't you say that before?"

"Because I thought you wouldn't come."

Treachery!

"So you'd force an ill man to go to a boring dinner with people he doesn't know just because a friend of yours wants *you* there?"

Nice reversal of guilt, I thought.

"I'm sorry, Danny. I should have been honest."

"That's what a relationship is all about, Hanne," I said, making myself cringe. "We have to learn to trust. Now, if you'll excuse me, I have to go and blow my nose and be sick or something."

Yes. I felt guilty. But needs must. At least now I could crack on with things. I knew that I had to make the most of my trip to Belgium. I couldn't claim to be ill again. Hanne would be sure to notice, and might make me go to a doctor who'd want me to take my shirt off and put cold things up me. I had to make this count. And to make it count, I'd need the help of the media. I had a plan; I just needed an outlet. I found the name of the biggest Belgian paper I could—*De Standaard*—and gave them a ring. I spoke to a reporter called Frank.

"Yes, I see, but why did these people join you?" he said. "I really don't understand . . ."

"They joined me just because they wanted to."

"I really don't understand at all. They joined you just because you asked them to join you?"

"That's right."

"But why? Why do they join?"

"Because they want to. Because they're good people."

"I don't understand. This is stupid. I don't understand."

"Will you write an article?"

"I think I had better."

I explained the work of the Karma Army to Frank, and then told him my next plan—to initiate a meet-up of potential joinees, somewhere in the heart of Brussels. Frank suggested that outside the town hall would be good, but that "I still don't understand this at all." I told him it didn't matter—and if he helped bring me Belgians I'd consider him an honorary joinee. This seemed to make him happy, although I'm sure, when he thought about it later, he wouldn't understand why.

"Listen," said Frank. "What about a photo? Could you e-mail one over? We go to press very soon and we need to get this into tomorrow's paper if the appeal is to work properly."

I am afraid that I neglected to mention that throughout this conversation I was still wearing nothing except for my boxer shorts. It's hot in my flat sometimes. Anyway, I ran to my bedroom, pulled a shirt on, set my digital camera up on a suitable shelf, and took a picture of myself, pointing at the lens, and holding up a sign saying "JOIN ME, BELGIANS." I e-mailed it straight off to Frank and then set about packing for my trip.

On the plane, I couldn't help but notice that the lady in the opposite aisle was looking at me slightly oddly. Only *slightly* oddly, mind. Every few seconds she would lean forward very gently and cast me a curious sideways glance. At first I'd thought she was trying to take a look out of my window, but no, we were definitely making eye contact.

And then I noticed what she was reading. In her hands was a copy of *De Standaard*. Of course! The Join Me story was in that! They'd have brought that morning's papers over on the first flight of the day, in order to keep returning Belgians happy. And they must have printed the picture—how else would the lady have recognized me? I stopped one of the cabin crew as they shimmied by and asked for a copy of *De Standaard*. Dutifully, they brought me one and I turned the pages until I saw myself staring back at me, under the headline:

KARMA ARMY RONSELT LEDEN OM GOED TE DOEN

No, I didn't understand, either. But embarrassingly, I was still wearing the same shirt as I had on in the picture. I'd just pulled it on again that morning, and, consequently, I must have now looked like nothing more than some kind of filthy cult leader. But it was quite a distinctive shirt, which must have been what alerted the lady opposite. I looked over at her and did the same pointing gesture as I was doing in the picture. "Join Me," I mouthed, and smiled. I'd expected her to smile back, to be honest, but she didn't. She just looked at her companion, and back at me, horrified. What had Frank written? I couldn't make head nor tail of it, but I hoped he hadn't described me as some kind of odd-shirted, pointing murderer.

"Excuse me, can I help you?"

The lady's companion, a biggish man in his early thirties, was speaking to me.

"Er, no, I was just saying 'Join Me.' "

"And you were pointing at my mother. What did you want?"

"Nothing. I was just pointing."

"And saying 'Join Me.' "

"Yes." I looked to the man's mother, hoping that she would fill in the gaps in the story. Surely she'd have to now mention the fact that she'd just read about me in her paper? She didn't.

"And why did you do those things?"

I tried to think of an excuse. My mind went blank.

"I ask you again: *why did you do these things?*"

"I'm sorry," I said, before, *absolutely inexplicably,* "My leg hurts."

I turned away, and stared at the seat in front of me. I was going bright red. What the hell had I just said? *My leg hurts?!* Why had *that* popped out? Why had I thought that there was any way in which that could come across as a valid excuse? Why couldn't I have just told him about the newspaper article? I could have come up with *any number* of believable excuses to get me out of a potentially embarrassing situation like that, and I'd chosen "My leg hurts."

The man and woman said nothing, and I continued to stare straight in front of me, my cheeks burning. I noticed the man in the seat right next to mine bristle with embarrassment as he glowered intently at his book.

"Sorry," I whispered, as much to myself as to him.

He said nothing, not wanting to be connected to me in any possible way.

I remained silent and well-behaved throughout the rest of the short flight, not looking over at that troublemaking old woman even once. I didn't know what her problem was. What had she been playing at? I waited for everyone else to get up at the end, so that I could be the last to leave, and could do so relatively unseen. Why hadn't she spoken up? Why had she denied all knowledge of me? I found out as I reached to get my rucksack out of the overhead locker. I looked down to where she'd been sitting and went bright red again.

She'd been reading the previous day's *Standaard*.

• • •

"Danny, I'm Sam, come in," Sam said to me, asking me to come in. Which I think you may have already got from what he said, but it's best to make sure you understand, what with his accent and everything.

"Everybody, this is Danny Wallace from the UK."

I had now arrived at the studios of TV1, a neat gray concrete box at the end of a clean suburban street, and had been offered beer, sandwiches, a chair and a tour in the time it took me to take my jacket off and blink a couple of times.

Sam De Graeve, a friendly faced man in a rollneck top and combat trousers, cracked open a bottle of water and sat himself down next to me.

"I'm a big fan of Britain," he said. "I've been there often. Once, I hitchhiked across the country. It was only in Milton Keynes that no one stopped to pick me up."

"Really? But you got out eventually?"

"Yes. But strange people there. We were there for a day and a half."

"Blimey. Not even the people who *live* there stay longer than that."

Sam nodded, and glanced downward. These were obviously painful memories for him.

"Now, you know who else is on the show tonight?"

"Yes. A politician, a depressed footballer, a comic and a newspaper editor."

"He only edits a newspaper, not a comic too."

"No, I mean a comic, like a comedian."

"That's right. I am joking with you! Now, you're the first guest on, because we have to have technical time to get you subtitled."

"I'm going to be subtitled?"

"Yes. The show goes out a couple of hours after we record it, and we need to make sure the Flemish people can understand you. Anyway, you are on first, and you will walk onto the stage while the house band plays some appropriate music."

I made a mental bet with myself that it would be "Danny Boy."

"And then Bruno, the host, will shake your hand, and you will both sit down and talk for maybe ten or fifteen minutes about this whole Join Me thing. Hopefully, there will be some applause at the end, and that's you finished."

"Great. Where's Bruno?"

Bruno Wyndaele had been described to me as the Belgian Terry Wogan, which is quite a terrifying thought, but one that was thankfully far less terrifying in the flesh. Inordinately tall and with the look of a consumer affairs presenter about him, he had a reassuring smile and a firm, manly handshake. And that's about all I got out of him. He was a busy bloke, and had to prepare for the show, so we talked for maybe five seconds before he was ushered out of the room by a Belgian, and into make-up. I, meanwhile, was left to talk very slowly and carefully with the Belgian Minister for Culture, who told me he'd once been a boxer and later in life hadn't been allowed to join the priesthood. I told him I used to work at Argos and was now a kind of cult leader. He didn't say much after that.

"Danny? You're on."

I was marched downstairs, through a maze of corridors, past a lady sitting in the subtitling room (whom I wished good luck) and round the back of the studio where I waited, behind a black curtain, and studied the monitor to await my introduction. Predictably, it was in Flemish, and I had to wait until I was prodded in the back by the floor manager before I walked on stage to the applause of about fifty Belgians and the sight of big old Bruno Wyndaele. All my concentration had been on connecting my hand with his and carrying out a proper handshake. It wasn't until I was sitting down that I remembered to listen out for the appropriate music the house band was playing. And I was amazed.

You gotta Join . . . Join Danny . . .
You gotta Join . . . Join Danny . . .
Smoke a joint . . . Join Danny . . .
You gotta Join . . . Join Danny . . .
'Cos tonight we're gonna party like it's 1983 . . .

The band had learned the official Join Me song!

Fair enough, they'd changed part of the lyrics to suit their rock 'n' roll image, but still . . . I was impressed. And touched. They'd downloaded it from the Join Me website and set about learning, practicing and adapting it for their own house band stylings. What would Joinees Wayne and Christopher think when I told them the work we'd completed in their Middlesex spare bedroom was now being enjoyed by millions of toe-tapping Belgians? The lead singer looked over at me proudly as the guitarist put the final improvized flourishes on the end of the song and the drummer finished with a crash-bang of the cymbals, and before I could say anything, Bruno exclaimed: "It's your Join Me song!"

He was evidently just as proud of the performance as the band.

"It certainly is," I said. "And played beautifully."

"Join Danny . . . so what does it actually mean, this Join Me?"

It was my first question. My first question on international television. I decided to play it vague.

"Just what it says. I want people to join me."

"But for what?"

Be mysterious, Danny. They love that, the chat show hosts.

"Well, we can discuss that when we've all joined together."

I saw a look of blind panic in Bruno's eyes. Was this all he was going to get out of me? Was he going to have to spend ten minutes asking the same question and receiving incredibly vague and nonspecific answers in reply? No, of course he wasn't. I'm British, and I've been brought up properly.

And so I set about telling Bruno, and the assembled crowd, and the people of Belgium, all about Join Me. Bruno seemed entertained, but that was because he spoke perfect English. I started to worry about the people at home.

"Am I speaking too quickly, by the way?" I asked. "Because I walked past the subtitling room on the way here. This will have subtitles, won't it?"

"Yes, it will."

"Because I was thinking, maybe I should just start making up words . . . so that the people next door go 'What the *hell* is he saying?' and have to get a dictionary out . . ."

Bruno laughed.

"But I won't do that."

"No," said Bruno.

"That would be lebstromonous of me."

Phew. I'd got a big laugh out of the audience. And I'd confused at least four of them, who each leaned to the person next to them in order to ask what "lebstromonous" meant. But now I'd gained their trust, so I could tell them about the small ad. About Joinee Jones. About the Karma Army. And about Good Fridays. Bruno asked about international joinees. About good deeds. About making old men happy.

"So it's like the boy scouts?" he asked.

"I s'pose so. But more grown up. More like the Man Scouts."

Bruno nodded thoughtfully. I felt sure that I was getting through to him, and getting through to the audience too. I felt sure that some of them would be joining me by the end of the interview.

"All I require for someone to join me properly is a passport photo, and tomorrow, at 6 P.M., I'll be standing outside the town hall, in the Grand Place, in Brussels, holding a small sign, saying 'Join Me Belgians.' "

"Right . . ."

"And if any Belgians *do* wish to join me, all they have to do is turn up. It'll be lovely."

"And how many do you want to turn up tomorrow?"

"I'd be happy if even one Belgian turned up to join me. Even just one. And I'll buy them a beer."

I suddenly realized what I'd said. Beer could be expensive in Brussels.

"But if a million turn up, they can buy their own."

"Well, Danny, I wish you the best of luck with your movement. And I wish you all the best for tomorrow, when you will be standing, very lonely, outside the town hall . . ."

"I'm well aware it might just be me and you, Bruno. But thanks."

"Ladies and gentlemen: Danny Wallace!"

We shook hands, I smiled at the applauding audience, the band struck up and before I knew what was happening, my spotlight had disappeared, the cameramen had run off and Bruno was sitting down on a sofa in order to counsel the suicidal footballer. The floor manager whisked me backstage where I was picked up by someone else and taken back to the green room. I felt good, though. It had been a successful appeal, and I sat down with the others and opened a can of beer. The Minister for Culture regarded me with a look of deep suspicion, and I was tapped on the shoulder by a tall man with glasses.

"Hi. I enjoyed your interview very much. I think you will get some success from that. I'm Peter from *De Standaard*. You were in my paper today. But I must apologize to you. I'm afraid we got some of the facts wrong."

"Oh," I said. "Never mind. It was in Dutch so I couldn't understand it anyway."

"I'm afraid we said you had tens of thousands of followers from all over the globe."

Tens of thousands? Well, it was an exaggeration, but that was fine by me. It could be that the Belgians might be hard to win over. Maybe thinking tens of thousands of people had already joined me would be a good thing. And if Peter thought I'd achieve some degree of success from the appeal, I was ready to believe him, because once again, he was in a position of authority and slightly taller than me. It works every time. My trust was his. It really is lucky I'm not a midget, or I'd probably be serving time by now.

I ambled around until I found a restaurant called Bonsoir Clara, on rue Antoine Dansaert—an achingly stylish place on an achingly trendy street, an experience spoiled only by the fact that I'd had to leap over a suspicious stream which started rather near the trouser leg of an unconscious drunk outside a furniture shop. But inside, it was all zinc-top tables, moody lighting and huge '70s mirrors on every wall. I decided to treat myself to an expensive meal. The finest steak and chips in all of Belgium. It arrived, and it was excellent. This was the life. Here I was, making waves in Europe, enjoying a fine meal, relaxing nicely. But I did feel a pang of guilt. Right now, in Finchley, North London, Hanne would be sitting, without her boyfriend, at a table in a restaurant with a load of people she didn't really want to be with. And where was her boyfriend? Secretly on telly in Belgium. I sighed, and knew I should just come clean with her. Ian was right. I should just tell her. She wouldn't mind. She might even think it was fun. And positive. What if she joined me? What a team we'd make. We'd be here together, enjoying Belgian *frites* and buying each other posh chocolates. But the problem was, I'd already messed up. I'd kept it a secret all this time. That alone would anger her.

Back at the hotel, I fiddled with my television until I found TV1 and waited until I was sure *De Laatste Show* was going out. To be honest, I knew it would be. It would have been a hell of an elaborate practical joke for someone to pull on me, what with the whole setting-up-an-entire-Belgian-TV-station aspect to it, but with my friends, you can never be completely sure. The show started, and there I was, subtitles and all. I started to feel sleepy. It had been a long day, with one thing and another, and the next day promised to be even longer. I watched the rest of the interview, knocked my light off and fell asleep more or less straight away.

But I was woken, two or three hours later, in the wee small hours, by what sounded like a mouse scratching at my door. I sat up, reached for my glasses, knocked a bottle of water over, and found the light switch. In slightly odd hotel practice, the people at the Ibis had decided that now was the right moment to slip the bill under my door. I waddled over to pick it up and opened the envelope.

But it wasn't the bill.

It was a passport photo.

I recognized the face. It was the receptionist who'd checked me in that afternoon. She'd obviously been watching the show downstairs and then looked up which room I was staying in. There was a short handwritten note:

Hello Danny.
I found your idee very good. I would be happy to join you!
Greetz,

Anya

I had my first Belgian joinee!

I opened the door and peered out. The corridor was empty. Anya had scarpered.

I closed the door, clambered back into bed, and went back to sleep with a huge grin on my big, stupid face. I was happy.

• • •

I awoke in the morning with a huge grin on my big, stupid face. I was happy.

I switched my phone on. There was a text message from Hanne. "HOW ARE YOU FEELING? X." I replied, "BIT GROGGY. TALK IN A BIT." I felt bad about this. But, for now, at least, this was how it had to be. Especially now I'd told her I was ill, rather than in Belgium. It's not easy to mix those two up. I couldn't exactly claim she'd misheard me. "What?

You thought I said I was ill? No, no, no . . . I said I had to go to Belgium to be on the telly!" If I came clean now, I had no doubts Hanne would consider finishing with me. I'd lied, and, perhaps worse, I'd started devoting most of my free time to complete and utter strangers.

I looked at my watch. It was 9 A.M., and I had the city to see. I already knew a little about Belgium and the Belgians. They like their chocolate. And their lace. And . . . that's about it. Whether they're happy with it or not, the Belgians do have to live with the fact that their European neighbors regard them as . . . well . . . a little on the dull side.

But what I saw of the city in just one morning was enough to convince me otherwise. Never have I seen a city bustle quite so convincingly. People everywhere. Constant chatter. And it soon became clear that the best way to get around would be to walk. The trams were tempting, but only because I'm a boy and therefore quite like the look of trams. The city is so compact, though, that it's possible to get anywhere you need to with nothing above the stress you'd associate with the words "a gentle stroll." I therefore found myself strolling gently through streets teeming with restaurants and over-eager restauranteurs, past buildings of undeniable splendor and only round the corner from streets of undeniable poverty, drinking hot chocolate at cafés on small town squares, and finding things I really didn't need at a shouty, sprawling flea market.

From there, I wandered around, trying to find the symbol of Brussels—the Manneken Pis. It wasn't tough. A large crowd had already gathered around it, somehow organizing themself into some sort of order, each person striding up to have their photo taken and, five seconds later, making way for the next stranger who wanted to be pictured in front of what's essentially a statue of a small boy having a pee. The statue, it's said, is supposed to represent the "irreverent" nature of the city of Brussels, but to be honest, if having a whizz in the great outdoors is irreverence, then closing time outside my local must be the European center of irreverence, and you can keep it.

"Excuse me? Are you Danny?" It was a man in a blue T-shirt. He had a friend with designer stubble with him.

"Yes," I said, somewhat taken aback.

"I thought it was you, Danny. I saw you on *De Laatste Show*. It sounds like fun what you are doing, and I wanted to wish you luck with it."

"Oh. Cheers. Will you be coming along at six?"

"No, we can't, we're going to a party."

"Ah. Well, do you still want to join me?"

"No. We have to go now. Bye."

His friend murmured a good-bye, too, and off they went. Two potential joinees. Gone. Of course, they'd never had any intention of joining me. They just wanted to say hello to the man they'd seen on the telly.

I bought a giant marker pen and piece of A2 paper from an art shop in order to make my sign, and at 5:45 P.M. started to walk to the Grand Place. It was, and is, an extraordinary part of Brussels. I stood right in the middle of the square and turned, slowly, full circle. Once a marshland, later a market, later still the chosen site for public executions, and now . . . well . . . now it's the most photographed set of buildings in the country. And they're glorious. I'd been told that, as night falls, a kind of Jean Michelle-Jarre light show dominates the square, with the town hall, the Hotel Du Ville, standing proud as the center of attention. But which one was it? As I started to walk toward the one I'd thought was probably it, a young, slight man with glasses and a neatly trimmed goatee beard stopped me.

"Danny?"

"Yes?"

"I have come to join you!"

His name was Waldemar and he had traveled one hundred and twenty kilometers to be here.

"My name is Waldemar and I have traveled one hundred and twenty kilometers to be here."

"Brilliant! Have you brought a passport photo?"

"In my bag!"

We strolled to what Waldemar had confirmed was the town hall.

"Although I must be honest with you, I have never been here before. This is my first time at the Grand Place. Because I live one hundred and twenty kilometers away."

I found this a very shoddy excuse. I mean, I was all the way from England, and even *I'd* been there five minutes before him.

"Thank you so much for coming, Waldemar. I really appreciate it."

"That's okay. It's not so far for me. Only one hundred and twenty kilometers."

Suddenly, someone else was present.

"Have I come to the right place?"

"Are you here to join me?"

"Of course. I'm Steven."

So now me, Waldemar and Steven were standing in front of the town hall. It was working! I found it hard to believe. A part of me had genuinely thought that I would be standing, lonely, all evening—a sad picture of a man, but a man with determination. I had found encouragement in the eyes of Waldemar and Steven. I felt sure we could get others. I knelt down and wrote JOIN ME BELGIANS on my huge piece of paper. Steven translated it, and wrote the Flemish words underneath: DOE MEE BELGEN. I held it aloft and looked out at the hundreds of people currently pottering around the square.

And then there was movement. In the corner of my eye, someone was walking toward me. The sign had acted as confirmation as to who I was and what I was doing there. On the other side of the square, someone else was moving toward me, too—slowly, casually, but definitely toward me. We made eye contact as he got closer.

"I'm Wim," he said. He was a tall man with gray hair, probably in his forties. "I'd like to join you."

"My name is Katleen," said a voice to my side. I turned round and shook her hand.

"You are very welcome," I said.

She'd been there for an hour, she said, and Waldemar confirmed he'd been there since 4:30. Their keenness made me happy—it was what Join Me needed. And now, look: in the middle of the square, two men were picking up their bags and starting to walk toward me. One had a notepad, the other a camera. The press had arrived! I waved at them, and they waved back.

Before I could say anything else, next to me, two girls, giggling and short, said: "We are here to join you!"

Another lad, in skater gear, raised his hand. "Hi Danny," he said.

I was becoming overwhelmed by Belgians.

I shook hands with the journalist and photographer, who'd traveled fifty miles to be there. "Hello Danny," said the journalist, Raymond. "Can we watch?"

I started to reply but someone was putting something in my hand. A passport photo.

Another person arrived. "I'm Joan," she said. "I saw you on TV. I would like to be part of your club."

Moments later, there were two more; a boy and a girl, both bearing passport photos.

I was heartened. But I also started to panic. What did they expect would happen when they arrived here? Was I supposed to have brought sandwiches? Or make a speech? How was this going to end?

Another photographer strutted up and started taking pictures at random. A crowd of non-joinees had begun to gather around the outside of the group. I held the sign in their direction. A few turned away, embarrassed, but one man stepped forward.

"Join you for what?" he said.

"You'll find out," I said.

He hesitated, looked to his friend, and looked back.

"Okay, sure."

His friend smiled and followed him.

Two more!

A man on a bike, whose name, I would later find out, was Baert, cycled up to me very quickly, skidded, got a passport photo out of his pocket, thrust it in my hand, and then sped off again. He was like a hit-and-run joinee.

The assembled joinees, about twelve of them at this stage, chatted and laughed together. An old man had broken away from the crowd of spectators and stood by my side.

"What is the purpose of this?"

"We're joining each other," I said.

"And why does it take a British people to do this?"

"It doesn't—these are all Belgian people."

"I am very skeptic to the British. You want isolation."

"We can't help it," I said. "We're an island."

"I don't care. Why don't you join Europe?"

"That's exactly what I'm doing," I said. "I'm uniting the people of Belgium with the people of Britain, and the wider world . . ."

"Ha!" he shouted and batted me on the arm. I say "batted." It was more of a punch, hidden behind a mock-friendly veneer, ensuring he could whack me but I couldn't slap him back. I, Danny Wallace, had just been *punched by an elderly Belgian!* Days don't get much better than this.

More people approached and joined me. Some stayed, some left. The photographers were keen to take pictures.

"Danny, can you sit on the steps there, and the joinees behind you?"

This was great. Even he was calling them "joinees." And they were *happy* to be referred to as such. I had fallen in love with this country.

We got into position for the photo.

"Wait," came a voice from the square somewhere. "Can I join you?"

A young, happy-faced girl bounded toward us. The joinees cheered as one and welcomed her into the throng. "Philip! Join us!" she shouted.

Her friend, Philip, trudged toward us, coolly, with the air of an art student about him. The photographers waited patiently for him to reach us. He stood at the side and postured moodily. He was a scowler. But he had joined me.

Katleen—now Joinee Van Veen—smiled. "The power of television, huh?"

"I never expected this," I said. And I hadn't. I was now surrounded by a group of around twenty-five Belgians. Most had a photo with them, some were promising to send one along, but each was now shaking the hand of another, each was making a new friend. One joinee, Inge, said she had to go because the bar she runs should have been open ten minutes ago but she'd got carried away. I thanked her for coming, accepted her photo and a business card, and sent her on her way. I was sure her customers would understand.

I surveyed the scene, and sensed that the time had come for me to say something. I didn't know what it would be. I cleared my throat. Not because I needed to, but, I think, because that's what I've seen people on telly do when they're about to address a crowd.

"Joinees," I said, making eye contact with as many of them as I could. "I thank you. I thank you for coming today, and I thank you for joining me. As you know, each and every Friday is a special day for those who have joined. Today is Friday, and you have done something nice already. You have made me happy. But next week, I would ask you to do something nice for someone else. Something unexpected. Something random. Something that will improve their day. You are now a very important part of the Karma Army. You are the Belgian Collective. You are at the heart of Europe, and will set an example to other joinees, throughout this fine continent."

I had started to ramble. I knew I had to stop, before I started using words like "moreover" and "hence." How could I end this? I had an idea.

"Now, all that remains is for us to complete your initiation into Join Me. Joinee Inge runs a bar called . . ."

I found her business card and read it.

". . . La Sorciére De Heks. It is now the official Join Me bar in Brussels."

The crowd made a mental note of this, I could tell.

"Last night on telly, I promised you all a beer. I am no liar. Please . . . join me for a pint . . ."

The joinees applauded and whooped and I led my army of Belgians through the streets, press still in tow, until we'd found the right bar. Apart from two young men and a bloke in a trilby, the place was empty. Joinee Inge smiled a broad smile as we walked in, and the barman looked shocked as a sudden influx of people filled the room. We put four or five tables together, and sat around, talking, drinking, laughing and having fun.

We talked about Belgium, about my other joinees, about life in general. Joinee Steven talked me through one of his favourite subjects—Belgian chocolates—and the whole group chatted and jabbered like we'd been friends all our lives.

I'd been slightly worried about Waldemar, though. He was the first person to have met me at the town hall, but he'd been quite quiet throughout the evening, bordering on the withdrawn. I sensed he wasn't the type to talk over another, to be overbearing, or to force his point across, and I liked him for that, but I was concerned about whether he was having a good time or not. I was about to lean over and make sure, when he unexpectedly called for our attention, and addressed the room.

"Excuse me everyone," he said.

The tables quieteted down, respectfully.

"Who here has had a good year?"

A few people raised their hands, a few others murmured positively. All eyes were on Waldemar.

"Because I have had a *really* good year. I didn't expect to go to Canada, but I did, and I loved it. And I didn't expect to meet my girlfriend there, but I did, and she is wonderful. And I really did not expect to be sitting here, in this place, with you people, tonight, who I think are *great*. So thank you. All of you."

There was a heart-swelling second of silence after he said this; one which I'll savor forever. He'd been so quiet, and yet, inside, this had meant so much to him.

"Kaas," I said, lifting my pint, saluting this magnificent moment.

There followed another second of pure silence, this one made rather less touching by the fact that the table then erupted with laughter. The previous day, I'd asked someone how to say "Cheers," and apparently he'd thought I wanted to know how to say "Cheese." That, or he was a wanker.

"Proost!" someone to my side tried, rescuing me, and this seemed to work far better. The table raised their glasses to Waldemar, and then to each other, and then we carried on with the very taxing business of laughing and fun.

At the end of the night, I paid the bill, which, to be honest, I think Inge may have slightly "fixed" to my benefit—another good deed on her part—and Joinee Steven walked me back to more familiar streets.

"That was a lovely thing Waldemar said, wasn't it?"

"It was," Steven agreed. "I think he will be a great joinee."

I left Steven on the corner of the Grand Place, where he was going to wait to be picked up by his mum. Still a student, he also had to be up early for his Saturday job.

"If you are around tomorrow, Danny, I will be dressed as a mobile telephone and I will be handing out leaflets nearby. You could come if you like . . ."

"It's tempting, Steven, but I'm on the first flight home."

I shook his hand and gave him a little hug. "Thanks," I said, but I was really thanking Belgium.

"It's been great."

Eerst moeten ze beslissen
om mee·te doen en dan...

CHAPTER 17

COME ON, ARLENE . . .

Dear Danny

I saw you on *De Laatste Show* last week and I am now a very big fan from you. I would ask you please to send me a signed photo from you.

Arlene Baptiste (14)
Rue M**** B*****
Antwerp
Belgium

Dear Arlene

No problem. I will find something and sign it for you—if you Join Me!

Danny

Dear Danny,

Thanks but No, I don't want to join but please send me you photo.
Thanks you

Arlene

Dear Arlene,

I really must insist you Join Me. But I will definitely send you a photo and a souvenir from London too.

Danny

Dear Danny
No, I don't want to joins you, but what souvenir?
I don't want to join

Arlene

Dear Arlene
You have to Join Me to get the souvenir. That's the deal. Please Join Me.

Danny

Dear Danny
no, i wont join but what souvenir?

Arlene

Arlene
You have to Join Me.

Danny

Dear Danny
no

Arlene

Arlene
Yes

Danny

Dear Danny
STOP. NO. I DO not want to JOIN YOU. I write NO MORE.
goodbye danny. not ask me to join you any more.

Arlene

Arlene
Join Me.

Danny

Dear Danny
I am the parent from Arlene Baptiste and I would ask you please to not pester my child any more.
Greetings

Olivier Baptiste

Olivier
How about you, then?

Danny

(No reply)

VRIJE UNIVERSITEIT BRUSSEL
FIN-code: 2454
Collegekaart 1999-2000
99643031
Rolnr 64303
Philip
Janssens
geboren op 21/05/1980 te Antwerpen
voltijds
1ste jaar Kandidaat in de Wijsbegeerte

CHAPTER · 18

6. *Now Daniel's knees smote one against the other, for his cogitations much troubled him.*
7. *But there was a letter sent unto him by Katleen of Veen.*
8. *And the letter held goodly pleasant things, and words of peace and truth.*
9. *And Daniel made a joyful noise.*

I had returned to London a proud and happy man. And a man who possessed a clutch of new, colorful passport photos. Plus, I was big in Belgium. Fair enough, most of us are. But to those of you who aren't yet . . . imagine the feeling. I was now that most coveted of dinner party guests . . . a minor Belgian celebrity!

Incredibly, no one at Heathrow had recognized me. The woman on the tills at the snack bar had treated me rudely. My bus was late. I just couldn't understand it. This would never have happened to me in Brussels, back among my own people.

Shortly after I got home the phone rang.

"Hello, it's Hanne. Listen, I'm just down the road from you, and thought I'd pop in. We need to talk. Are you still contagious?"

"Nope, I feel pretty much okay now."

"I'll come round then."

"Cool," I said, looking around me to see what evidence of my trip I'd have to shove into a cupboard.

"Stick the kettle on. I'll be there in five minutes."

I sprang into action.

Half an hour later Hanne arrived at the door.

"Sorry—took longer than I thought it would."

There's a fashionable shoe shop down the road from me. The sooner they shut it down, the sooner Hanne will start making it round to my flat on time. Still, her tardiness had allowed me time to receive many e-mails to do with my trip to Belgium. Apart from the article in *De Standaard* and the appearance on *De Laatste Show,* the Belgian media had been quite into Join Me. Reporters and photographers from *Het Belang van Limburg, Gazette van Antwerp* and *Het Laatste Nieuws* had turned up at the Grand Place, and journalist Raymond de Condé—a very nice man in a yellow jacket, with a quiet, unassuming demeanor—had come along to the official joinee bar afterward too. He'd written his article and it appeared, along with a photo of me accepting passport photos and holding my sign, in *Het Belang van Limburg*. Joinee Vanden Bossche had scanned it in and e-mailed a translation to me, to the very best of her translating abilities . . .

ALREADY BELGIANS JOINED DANNY WALLACE

BRUSSELS—"Join Me!" was the call made by the amusing Englishman Danny Wallace to the viewers of "De Laatste Show" on Thursday night.

The viewers had to come yesterday at 6 pm to the Grand Place of Brussels to join this new movement. Many people came. What they were going to join or do was still not resolved, but everyone felt the good about it and the meeting was outmost pleasant!

It all began with a few advertisements in local London newspapers, in which Danny Wallace invited people to Join him, just like that. Only thing he asks is to send him a passport photo.

To his own amazement, he got massive reactions from different countries. He calls his movement "A Collective," and has given it a name in the meanwhile: the "Karma Army." They have stickers and posters and even a kind of anthem, but the members are still looking for the sense, the target of this collective.

Luckily, Danny decided to be at the service of Good Things, and for a start on every Friday. A first task was made up: "Make an old man happy." So Danny did an appeal to send peanuts to an old man who loves this kind of food. The old man received about eighty packages of peanuts.

Danny paid all Belgian joinees a drink in a local pub. Strangely enough no one really asked for an explanation, and they didn't get much of an answer either—the meeting itself was already a very positive event on itself.

Wallace himself admitted afterwards that he would love cooking, adore sharp knives, read and internet a lot.

"Belgians are a very nice people. I already got hit in every place where I showed up, but not in this country" stated this odd man.

"'Stated this *odd man?*'" Well, I'm not surprised Raymond de Condé thought I was odd—listen to how I'm talking! *"I already got hit in every place I showed up, but not this country?"* I appear to need some serious lessons in how to speak. Plus, the *only* place I'd so far been hit in was Belgium, by that furious anti-British pensioner.

But *infinitely* more worrying: what in God's name is all this about me ADORING SHARP KNIVES? I have never in my *life* stated that I "adore sharp knives!" Where did *that* come from? How strong was that beer? What element of the language barrier had caused Raymond to think I'd said that? And was *that* why he'd left so quickly afterwards? What if *other* potential joinees thought that I adored sharp knives? Add that to the fictional beatings I've apparently been taking around the world and my apparent love of the Internet and you've got a psychopath waiting to happen! It was a reputation I could well do without.

But at least Raymond had thought the meeting was a very positive event on itself and that the evening was outmost pleasant. And he was right: everyone *had* felt "the good about it."

"So," said Hanne, sitting down on the couch. "You're feeling better?"

"Oh yes," I said. "Much better now. Outmost pleasant, in fact."

"I told my dad you were ill. He said that if you had a fever, you should cut up tomatoes and then place them on your forehead."

Hanne's dad is a PE teacher back in Norway, and has rather unconventional medical techniques. And yet they nearly always work.

"I didn't have a fever. And if I did, you know what my mum would have said."

My mum, as you know, is Swiss, and has rather unconventional techniques of her own, which very rarely work. Once I had a fever and her first reaction was to wrap my feet in cabbage leaves.

"How was Thursday night, anyway?" I asked.

"It was okay."

"I'm sorry I couldn't be there. It won't happen again. I won't be ill any more. I'm on a real health kick now."

"I know what you're like, Danny. Drinking Fanta instead of Coke because it has a vague association with fruit does not count as a health kick."

"Lilt, then. There's *all sorts* of tropical fruit in Lilt. Vitamins galore. I'll be fine from now on, I promise."

Hanne smiled and I sat next to her with the tea. I turned the TV volume up.

"Belgium?" she said.

My heart stopped. I turned the TV volume down.

"Sorry?"

"What are you interested in Belgium for?" She leaned forward and picked up a map of Belgium, which lay, creased, under my coffee table.

"Er . . . I don't know," I said, brilliantly.

"Whose is this?"

I stuck my lower lip out and shook my head.

"Dunno."

Again: brilliant.

"What do you mean, you don't know? It's in your flat!"

"Well, I mean, it's mine. I've had it ages. I've always wanted to go to Belgium, you know that."

"You never told me you wanted to go to Belgium. Why do you want to go to Belgium?"

"I like . . . lace. And y'know . . . Belgium is famous for lace."

Hanne frowned.

"You don't like lace, do you?"

I realized how ludicrous it sounded.

"No." Brilliant, once more. I was good at getting out of difficult fixes. "Anyway, drink your tea."

Hanne took a sip and placed the map on the table.

"We can go to Belgium if you like," she said. "After you've taken me to Venice, of course . . ." She snuggled into my arm and I turned the volume up again. We sat, and laughed, and drank tea, and watched *Gloria Hunniford's Open House*. It was cozy and safe and nice. The afternoon, I mean, not the show. Gloria was talking about the best place in the house to put an aspidistra, or some such nonsense, so you can imagine the controversy.

But this still annoys me to this day: part of me, sitting there, was restless. I wanted to check my e-mails, or check the post, or just see how my merry band of joinees were doing. I should have been happy—Hanne was there—but my mind was in a different place. I felt like a parent on a night out, guilty for not keeping an eye on the kids, having to force himself to relax and enjoy some time off with the person he hardly ever got to see any more.

But I couldn't.

The joinees had well and truly taken over my mind. I was always thinking about them, now, always wondering whether they were safe and happy. Their short, regular e-mails provided tantalizing glimpses into their lives. I knew Joinee Austin was going on a date on Wednesday night, with a man she'd met somewhere recently. She'd been through a lot lately, what with the break-up and all, and I hoped things would go well for her. Joinee Whitby had just found out he needed seventeen fillings—how would he pay for that on a computer programmer's wage, especially with little Max to think about? Joinee Anderson's car had broken down a week before . . . had he found a replacement? How was he getting to work? That car was his lifeline, especially now Gemma had a new job in the city.

"You look worried," said Hanne.

"Oh, it's nothing," I said. "I'm just probably still recovering a bit."

Hanne looked disgruntled. That's not to say she'd looked particularly gruntled beforehand, because, to be honest, I wouldn't go out with a girl who had a gruntled face, despite the fact that I have no idea what one would look like.

"Well, do you want some soup or something?" It was a nice offer but she said it impatiently.

"No, no, I'm fine. Let's watch Gloria."

"Danny," she said, switching the TV off. "Just tell me. Is something wrong? Something between us?"

Uh-oh . . .

"What? No! Nothing at all. I'm just a little distracted!"

"By what? Because whatever it is it's been distracting you for a while now. You're not behaving normally. You just sit there not talking to me, always thinking about something. And you don't seem all that ill for someone who couldn't get out of bed on Thursday night. Is it me?"

"No! Not at all—it's not you. It's me. I'm just sort of busy a lot."

"With what? Playing videogames? Watching films? You weren't like this when you had a proper job. I'd really thought things were back on track for us."

"They were. They are. Don't worry about me. I'm just tired or something. How about tomorrow? Give me one more day to recover and then tomorrow we'll do something nice. Dinner or something?"

"Not a curry, okay?"

"Okay. Anything you want."

Hanne smiled, almost reluctantly.

"Fine, okay. Tomorrow it is. Shall I meet you in town? I finish at five."

"Cool. I'll call you and we'll hook up."

But I felt bad for making Hanne feel bad. She didn't deserve that.

She deserved a boyfriend who would sit there, and talk to her, and make her the center of attention whenever she came round.

I walked, head heavy with guilt, to my computer, and downloaded my e-mail. There was only one. It was from Joinee Katleen Van Veen, of Belgium.

Danny,

I want to say something about Join Me. It has become a way for me to show that I care for other people. Since I have given you my picture I am being more open and I am trying to meet more people and that makes myself very happy. Thank you for this fantastic initiative that changed my life.

Katleen

PS. You can do with my photo what you want except for publishing it on a website of prostituts.

I was touched. Not by that last bit, obviously, but by the rest. This is what it was all about. I felt immediately less guilty about the Hanne situation.

It suddenly hit me that what I was doing was . . . well . . . important. At least in a small way. It genuinely was improving people's lives. Not through anything *I* was doing or saying—but through what *they* were choosing to take away from it all. Perhaps that was the key to the whole thing, even in the beginning. People were joining something they knew nothing about, and applying their own meaning to it. Joan and Katleen were both doubtless gaining different things from their involvement in Join Me . . . but so long as the end result was positive, who cares?

WANTED

Are you happy? If you think I could make you happy then please contact me at the following address.

areyouhappy@hotmail.com

CHAPTER · 19

5. *And, lo, the words of Daniel were heard in London; and in the shire of the Hamps; and in the shire of the Berks.*

I looked up and down the street. There was no sign of Joinee Whitby yet. I began to wonder whether perhaps Ian had been right about Whitby all along. Was this a cunning ruse? While I was sat here, on this picnic bench, outside this pub, was Joinee Whitby rallying the troops? Was he stealing my joinees while I was out and about? Surely someone would have phoned me by now to tell me.

My phone vibrated, giving me quite a surprise. A message had arrived. Would it be one of my joinees warning me of Whitby's actions? Or a mysterious voice, telling me my days as Leader of Join Me had come to an end, just when I'd rediscovered the pleasures of power? I found myself scouring the rooftops and windows of Langham Street, just in case Whitby had decided a simple assassination was all that would be necessary.

The message was from Ian. MEET FOR COFFEE? AM IN TOWN. I texted back. COOL. STARBUCKS CARNABY STREET. 3 P.M.?

I looked up as I pressed send, and there, about twenty feet away, was Joinee Whitby.

"Hello," I said, standing up.

"Hello," he said, shaking my hand.

So this was he. Whitby. My nemesis. At last we meet.

• • •

Matthew John Whitby prefers stout to beer, and likes composing music, as well as playing the piano. Oh, and the *jembeh,* an African drum, not entirely dissimilar to the bongo. As my friends will tell you, I think I have, in the past, made my position on matters of the bongo quite clear.

He also enjoys mugs.

"I like winning them. I'm up to six now. My local radio station gives them away. I'd prefer to have ten, because then I could build a bigger pyramid, and of course, the ultimate would be to have fourteen, because you'd have a very strong, wide base."

I made a mental note not to criticize mugs or mug-based pyramids while in his presence. I sensed it was a battle I wouldn't be able to win.

Matt's thirty years old, lives in a pretty Hampshire village with his girlfriend and young son, and works as a computer programmer. "But music is my passion. I played the piano when I was about ten. Not that I've ever been any good. I started learning again recently. I feel that there's so much good music out there, and I just want to add to it, you know? My work is so dull. Programming day in, day out. I need a creative outlet. That's why I enjoyed doing my Join Me anthem so much."

"Now, I have to say," said Matt, "I'm finding it hard to do good deeds."

"Are you?" I said. "I remember you saying that in an e-mail, but are you really?"

"Yes. People just don't seem to want me to do any for them. What are other joinees doing?"

"Well, one bloke cleaned his neighbor's car," I said.

Matt raised his eyebrows.

"Someone else sat with an old man on a bench and then took him to the pub for a pint. Someone else bought a homeless lady a sandwich. Someone else helped the cooks at his university canteen tidy up. Stuff like that."

"Right. Well, I've had to come up with a plan of my own. I've been putting up posters like this . . ." He indicated a small piece of paper, Blu-tacked to the side of the pub, ". . . all over the place."

He'd placed it there while I got the drinks in. I stood up to read it.

WANTED
CAN I HELP?
Are you happy? If you think I could make you happy then please contact me at the following address.
areyouhappy@hotmail.com

"Wow," I said. "That's nice of you."

"I'm going to spend the afternoon putting them up all over London. I've pretty much deluged Berkshire and Hampshire."

"Any responses?"

"Mainly from people being a bit critical. Just saying 'What on earth makes you think you can make me happy?' And one from someone claiming to be Robert Mugabe. But I think that one's fake. And if it isn't I'm not going to help him. Sorry, but that's just the way it is."

"How many of these have you got?"

"Hundreds." He opened his bag to reveal a thick wad of photocopies, and passed me one. "Hopefully it'll work out."

I was touched by Joinee Whitby's efforts. Ian had been wrong about him. This was a genuinely nice man doing a genuinely nice thing. There was nothing scary about what he was doing at all. He wasn't my nemesis. I liked him. He was one of the good guys.

A homeless man walked by our table and asked us for money for a cup of tea. I know what it's like to be desperate for tea, and have often thought it's the one thing that could probably lead me to homelessness myself, and I think there was a definite moment when I felt our souls connecting. I'm pretty sure he did too, although he hid it well. I fished about in my pocket for some change. Matt did the same. Charity was just in the air today.

Moments later the landlord of the pub walked out to collect some glasses and we watched as he tore Matt's poster down and screwed it up. Matt silently and patiently fixed four more balls of Blu-tack to the back of another poster, stood up, and placed it carefully on the wall.

"There," he said, proudly, smoothing it out, and sat back down.

I considered the poster. It was another example of e-mail and the Internet making things that little bit easier for us. The Internet had been good to Matt for other reasons, too.

"I met my girlfriend on the Internet. She was downloading something, and I could see her doing it online, and there's a program where you can send messages to each other, so we started messaging, and that was that. I was lucky, really. They usually turn out be to be forty stone and living in Alabama. Mine was lovely and living in Yorkshire."

"People are always trying to get me to do that messaging thing."

"I use it to keep in touch with some of the joinees, actually," he said. "I have about forty-three I correspond with. I speak to lots of them throughout the day."

"That's nice," I said, but feeling somehow like I was the one who should have said that. Shouldn't *I* be the one checking up on them throughout the day to make sure they were okay? I was a bad Leader.

I was feeling deeply ashamed of myself for having even contemplated what Ian had said to me about Joinee Whitby. Sure, he'd known my address, but that's because he'd done what anyone who spends their day in front of a computer does. He finds his job boring, so he surfs the Internet. He looks stuff up. He clicks about a bit. So what?

"You have a lovely apartment, by the way."

The words hit me like a bullet. They'd come out of the blue, and they'd confused me. My mind raced. There must be a logical explanation for what he'd just said. Had he been there before? Had I invited him over? Did he know my neighbors? I didn't know how to take his statement.

"A lovely apartment?" I asked, slightly shocked. "Do I?"

"Yes. It's lovely."

"Er . . . how do you know I have a lovely apartment?"

"I'm not saying this in a stalker way, it's just . . . you know. You have a nice place."

"But how do you know? I don't understand . . ."

"They've got pictures."

"Who have?"

"Some of them are for sale, so . . ."

"What are?"

"The apartments. The owners of the building or the estate agents were selling some of them, so I took a look at a few pictures of properties similar to yours . . ."

"What, in the newspapers?"

Well—fair enough—maybe he'd recognized the name of the building I was in while house-hunting, or something.

"No, I wanted to see what your apartment was like, so I looked up the buildings on the website of an estate agent I found that was local to you, and tried to find a flat similar to yours . . ."

"You are a very scary man," I said, almost involuntarily.

"No, not at all. I have a thirst for information, that's all. Not about you in particular, but about *everything*."

I wanted him to prove it. I wanted to get a pack of Trivial Pursuit cards out and then test him. On *everything*.

"So long as you don't have a thirst for balaclavas and hunting knives, that's fine . . ."

I was slightly in shock at all this. But I put it down to the fact that we live in entirely different worlds. His, where every piece of information, public and private, is immediately to hand and technology rules the day, and mine, where if the toaster isn't working properly I hit it with a shoe.

I felt Matt was similarly shocked. Shocked that I'd reacted like this to what he saw as a perfectly normal, everyday procedure. I decided I'd overreacted. So he'd been interested in what my flat looked like. So what? I was interested in what *his* house looked like. And his village, for that matter. So I asked him. And he told me. And I felt we were more even.

I took him around the corner, to Regent Street, and the nearest McDonald's, where I bought him a burger and found us a table. But before I could sit down, he was up at the counter again. He'd spotted a homeless man outside, and had instinctively headed for the tills to buy him a cheeseburger and fries.

I was impressed by his actions in the name of Join Me. He was a truly sensitive soul.

"I'm prone to crying at soppy things," he said, when I mentioned this to him. "The running joke at home is that I cried at *Twins*."

"You've got twins?"

"No. Just one kid. Max. No, I cried at the film *Twins*."

I cast my mind back. "What . . . the Danny DeVito and Arnold Schwarzenegger vehicle? The one where it turns out they're twins? But that's a riotous '80s comedy . . ."

"I may have had a bit to drink."

Aha.

• • •

I bid Whitby good-bye outside Borders, and headed toward Carnaby Street to meet Ian.

Just before I got there I could feel my mobile vibrating in my pocket. Ian's number came up. He was probably ringing to tell me he'd be late.

"Hello?"

"Dan . . . guess where I am?"

"Somewhere that means you'll be late?"

"I'm nearer than you think."

Ian was being mysterious. It's not good when Ian's being mysterious.

"Where are you? And why are you being mysterious?"

I scanned the road, but couldn't see him anywhere.

"What's the most unlikely vehicle for me to be in right now?"

I re-scanned the road. Virtually opposite me was a huge, white stretch limousine. The type you see over and over again on a Saturday night cruising down Charing Cross Road, and despite knowing that it's either a debauched hen night or some kind of local radio winner, part of you always wonders whether Leo Sayer might pop his head out the door, or you might catch a glimpse of Gary Coleman on his way to some audition or other.

"You're not in the limo, are you?"

"Yep."

"Is Gary Coleman in there?"

"What?"

"What are you doing in the limo?"

"Waving at you!"

I couldn't believe it. I crossed the road, smiling, and stood next to the limousine, studying my own reflection in its blacked-out windows.

"I don't understand!" I said. And I didn't. This wasn't his car. I've been in his car lots of times. I would've remembered if this was it.

"I'm still waving at you, you rude bastard."

I stood there, an incredulous look on my face, and started to wave at the general area where I thought Ian would be sitting. I knocked on the glass, smiling.

"Peter the driver is waving at you now!"

I stepped back and started to wave at Peter the driver. His window wasn't blacked out, and I continued waving while he just stared at me, a rather worried smile on his face.

"Hello, Peter the driver!" I tried.

"Why don't you come in?" said Ian.

"Okay!" This was exciting. I'd never been in a stretch limo before. I reached for the door handle and tried to open the door. The limo started up and inched away from me slowly. I heard the central locking chunk-click.

"What are you doing?" I said.

"Just standing about."

"In a limo?"

"No, outside Starbucks."

I looked up. Ian was grinning at me, mobile in hand, while I, his supposed friend, was apparently attempting to break into a parked limousine, and waving at God knows who. Maybe one day I'd see Gary Coleman talking about that moment on some confessional chat show as one of the most frightening of his life.

"You tit," I said, as I sat down with my tea.

"I'm sorry. You should have seen your face. I'll pay for your tea by way of apology. So. How many joinees have you got?"

"Enough, thank you. Although I'd have one more if you'd join me."

"I'm not joining you. You're not getting that pint off me."

"I don't want a pint off you! Will you stop going on about that pint! It's not a bet! So just join me, will you?"

"No. So. Where've you been?"

"With a joinee."

"That's nice. How's the average joinee shaping up, statistically?"

"He's Belgian."

"Eh?"

"It's all I'm getting at the moment. Dozens of them. Every day."

"I see. And which joinee were you meeting today?"

"Joinee Whitby."

"Whitby? I didn't think you were actually going to go through with that! He's trying to get control of your Join Me thing, Dan!"

"He's *not* trying to get control of Join Me, actually. You're very wrong about him. He happens to be a kind and generous man, who gives money to tramps and buys meals for the homeless. He's even printed his own posters to help him do his good deeds."

"Can I see?"

I dug into my pocket and found the poster Matt had given me. I unfolded it, straightened it out, and gave it to Ian, who regarded it with some suspicion.

"I see."

"What do you mean?"

"Well, look at what he's doing. Read it, Dan."

I read it.

"Yes?"

"Do you see one mention, Dan, of Join Me on there? Of your website? Hmm? Of anything you or the others are doing? About the Karma Army?"

"But it's the spirit of the thing that matters."

"No, Dan. Whitby is quite clearly preparing to launch his own thing. I warned you about him. He's had enough of Join Me. He's launching . . ." He paused while he read it again. "He's launching the 'Can I Help?' Collective."

"He's *not* launching the 'Can I Help?' Collective. He just wants to help, and he's asking if he can. He's been having trouble doing good deeds."

"Doesn't sound like it. You said he gave someone some money. And bought someone else some food."

Ian was right. It had seemed to come awfully easily to Whitby. Almost like he'd been doing good deeds all his life. That bastard.

"Mark my words, Dan, he's up to something. I was right. He's definitely after your joinees."

"That's ridiculous," I said. "How could he even think . . ."

Hang on . . . He'd said he was chatting daily to forty-three joinees, hadn't he? Forty-three of *my* joinees. What was he talking to them about, exactly? What was he telling them? Was he poisoning their minds? Turning them against me?

"Who arranged the meeting?" said Ian urgently.

"We both did, kind of. I mean, *he* chose the time and place, but he only suggested meeting up in the first place because he wanted to say hello—"

"Uh-huh," said Ian. "I don't think he just wanted to say hello. I think that was a cover. I think he was information gathering. What did he ask you?"

"Nothing. Well, he just asked what some of the other joinees were doing."

"Interesting," said Ian. "That's interesting."

"He wouldn't need me to gather information from anyway. Not when he's got his computer and the Internet."

"What do you mean?"

"I just mean he's able to find out lots of things from the Internet. It's like a talent he's got. He'd be able to find out what other joinees were up to very easily without me. He's already found out loads of stuff."

"What sort of stuff?"

"Just the usual. My address, what the inside of my flat looks like."

"What? That's not the usual! What school you went to—*that's* the usual. Finding your address and what your flat looks like is *not* the usual! Dan, that's not normal!"

"Isn't it?"

"What else does he know?"

I was terrified as I realized the truth.

"I have no idea. Maybe nothing. Maybe everything."

• • •

I left Ian a little later and wandered back toward Oxford Street. I was meeting Hanne as agreed just after she finished her weekend shift, at 5 P.M. or so. I was looking forward to it. I knew it'd do me good to think about something else for a while, especially after my day with Whitby.

But whatever. I could forget about that now. Because I was going to meet Hanne. My girlfriend. The person I can always lean on. My rock.

• • •

"Danny, I think we shouldn't see each other for a while."

She may as well have punched me.

"What?" I said, a bit too loudly for the restaurant we were in.

"I think we shouldn't see each other for a while. I've been thinking it over. And I've been talking to Janne."

Janne. Hanne's flatmate. She's never liked me much.

"And what does Janne think?"

"She thinks you're odd. She thinks you're not giving enough time to me."

"Well, she's right. Not about the 'odd' bit, but about the 'time' bit. And now that you've told me that, I can—"

"Danny . . . all the excuses you've been making lately. Going to your parents. Working in the bath. Being with all these new friends who I've never met. It doesn't add up. I mean, I phone you up one day, and you're in Loch Ness with a vicar. And I've decided I don't believe you were ill the other night, either."

"You heard me cough a bit!" I tried.

Hanne didn't look impressed.

"Look, maybe I wasn't as ill as I made out," I said. "I'm sorry. I've had things on my mind. I'll make this up to you."

"You always say that. But there's always some excuse. And what have you had on your mind? Maybe I can help. I'm your girlfriend. I understand these things . . ."

Was this the moment I'd tell Hanne? Was this the moment I'd finally come clean and tell her everything I'd been doing?

Then she said, "So long as it's not another stupid boy-project . . ."

I stopped in my tracks. She'd said it as a joke. She'd smirked after she'd said it. She didn't have a clue that that was exactly what it was. My mind stalled. I'd been on the brink of telling her, but now auto-pilot took over and the part of my brain designed to maintain and preserve my relationship kicked in.

"No," I said, squeezing her hand. "And now that we've had this chat, it'll all change, I promise, Hanne."

And she smiled, and she squeezed my hand back, and I knew that I'd bought myself some more time.

But I also knew that if she ever found out, I'd be in it up to my neck.

E-mail

To: Dennis M. Hope, President of the Lunar Embassy and Galactic Government
From: Danny Wallace, Leader, Join Me & The Karma Army

Dear Dennis!

I have just taken a look at your website and I see that you are in London this week, visiting some of your Lunar Ambassadors in the UK. I've been doing the same as you and trying to meet as many of my joinees as possible. As Joinee Saunders told me, personal contact really is the key!

But if you're in London, do you fancy meeting up? We could swap notes and develop strategies, and perhaps even show each other some pictures of our people? Maybe we can find a way of involving our joinees in each others' projects.

It would be like if Jesus and Buddha met up for a coffee and a catch-up.

Hope to see you soon!

Danny

P.S. I think the amount of time I'm spending on this is taking its toll on my girlfriend. Any advice?

E-mail

To: Danny Wallace, Leader, Join Me & The Karma Army
From: Dennis Hope, President, Lunar Embassy and Galactic Government

Dear Danny:

Greetings from the Lunar Embassy and the Galactic Government.

Thanks for the invite. Unfortunately I have returned to the USA. I would have loved to be involved in your project and if you find a way to make it work I still would be. Thanks again for the invite.

With warm regards from the Galactic Government and the Lunar Embassy,

Dennis M. Hope
CEO/President—Galactic Government
AKA: "The Head Cheese"

P.S. As for your girlfriend, remember: in this life, we need to *cherish* those that we love . . .

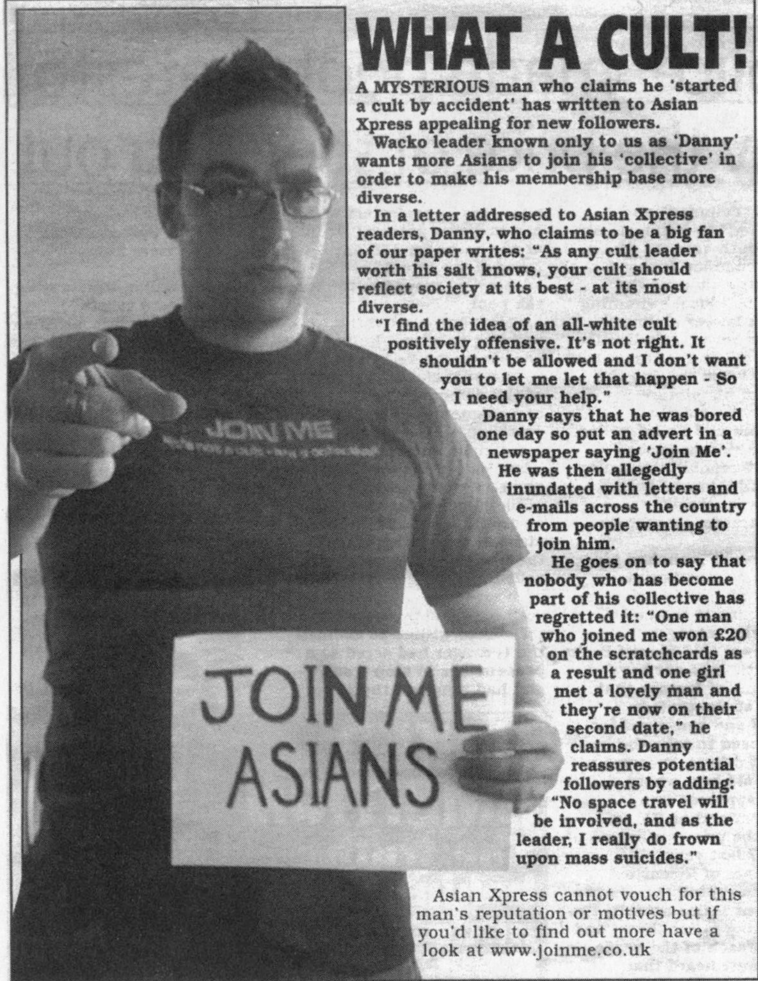

WHAT A CULT!

A MYSTERIOUS man who claims he 'started a cult by accident' has written to Asian Xpress appealing for new followers.

Wacko leader known only to us as 'Danny' wants more Asians to join his 'collective' in order to make his membership base more diverse.

In a letter addressed to Asian Xpress readers, Danny, who claims to be a big fan of our paper writes: "As any cult leader worth his salt knows, your cult should reflect society at its best - at its most diverse.

"I find the idea of an all-white cult positively offensive. It's not right. It shouldn't be allowed and I don't want you to let me let that happen - So I need your help."

Danny says that he was bored one day so put an advert in a newspaper saying 'Join Me'. He was then allegedly inundated with letters and e-mails across the country from people wanting to join him.

He goes on to say that nobody who has become part of his collective has regretted it: "One man who joined me won £20 on the scratchcards as a result and one girl met a lovely man and they're now on their second date," he claims. Danny reassures potential followers by adding: "No space travel will be involved, and as the leader, I really do frown upon mass suicides."

Asian Xpress cannot vouch for this man's reputation or motives but if you'd like to find out more have a look at www.joinme.co.uk

CHAPTER · 20

10. *And so the army of Daniel was swelled by folks of divers complexions, from every city and province.*

11. *So long as they were pale.*

For a week or so, I absolutely changed my ways.

Ladies—you may think your man is perfect, and if you don't wish to become disillusioned with what you've got, then I would look away now. Because for that week—yes, *all* of it—there was no boyfriend in the world more perfect than Mister Daniel Frederick Wallace.

I was attentive. Supportive. Thoughtful. Loving. I bought her a Chocolate Orange and ran her a bath. I listened to her talking about shawls without once interrupting. I started using my oven gloves and bought a stainless-steel peppermill for my flat. I found the Ikea catalogue and read to her from it. I told her I was considering learning Italian, and said wasn't feminism great? In short, I was the man of every girl's dreams. And Hanne seemed to be enjoying it—with some degree of reservation at first, with open arms later on.

"Let's go shopping!" she'd say, and I'd say yes, and off we'd go.

"Let's go to the park!" she'd say, and I'd say yes, and off we'd go.

"Let's go shopping!" she'd say, and I'd say "But we went yesterday," and she'd look at me like I was mad, so I'd say yes, and off we'd go.

I was still writing reviews for the magazines, and made sure Hanne could see all the work I was doing just to keep her in Chocolate Oranges. But my work was suffering. Suffering, because I was only really working when Hanne could see me. She assumed, of course, that I spent much of my day doing the same things. And I did nothing to imply otherwise.

But I *wasn't* spending my days doing that. I was spending my days doing secret, covert things. I'm not proud of misleading her. But I am proud of what I achieved. I just couldn't work out whether I was a bad man or not.

• • •

"Ian, am I a bad man or not?"

"What?"

"Am I a bad man or not, for keeping this from Hanne?"

"I don't know why you just didn't tell her in the first place."

"Because then there wouldn't have been a *second* place. I'd have been stopped."

"I dunno, Dan. It's tricky. I wouldn't have kept it a secret. But then, I wouldn't have started something like this. Anyway . . . let's see 'em, then . . ."

Ian had come round to the flat specifically to look at my collection of joinees. I opened the drawer and brought out the small box packed with passport photos.

"So this is them?" he said.

"No," I said. "That's someone *else's* box of passport photos. I don't know how it got here."

"How many are there?"

"Just under seven hundred. And before you ask, they're fifty-one percent male, forty-nine percent female, probably living on the ferry between England and Belgium, and they're very happy with their lot, thank you very much."

"Seven hundred, eh? Some way off then, Dan. Don't be expecting that pint too soon."

"It's not a bet, Ian. Stop making out it's a bet."

But he wasn't listening. He was studying my people.

"Look at this bloke," he said, picking up a photo of Joinee Garden. "He looks like a lot of fun. And this one—she's fit. Wouldn't mind joining her."

"Oh, so you'd join *her,* but you won't join *me,* eh?"

"I meant 'join' as in . . . you know . . . sex, and that."

"That doesn't even make sense. And anyway, that's Joinee Harfield, leave her alone, she's getting over a break-up. She's been on a few dates with someone, though, so I'll think she'll be okay. And she was on *The Weakest Link,* too."

"They're great," he said. "A top bunch. One thing, though . . ."

"What's that?"

"Well, it's a little bit . . . *unrepresentative,* isn't it?"

"How do you mean?"

"It's hardly society-at-large. Not a very broad range of people."

I didn't get what he meant. There were men, women, kids, pensioners. There were long-haired people, short-haired people, people with glasses, people with piercings, people who looked friendly, people who looked scary . . . You couldn't get a more diverse bunch.

"Thing is, Danny . . . they're all white."

Ah. Fair point. My God.

I scattered the photos over the carpet and studied them. He was right, to a certain degree. I'd never really noticed it before, but I had nowhere near enough non-white people in my collective. And that was a very shocking thing indeed. Maybe I was being too politically correct with this, but I couldn't help but feel concerned. It just wasn't right. Why was I basically only appealing to white people? What was I doing wrong?

"Are you a racist, Dan?" said Ian.

"What? No! I'm going out with a Norwegian! And don't ask *me* why no one from an ethnic minority has joined me—they could've done if they'd wanted to."

"So you're saying it's because they're lazy?"

"No! Stop trying to make me into a racist! I'm not a racist!"

I studied the pile again.

Salvation!

"Look! This is Joinee Wong!" I half-shouted. "I'd forgotten about him! He's Chinese! See? I'm not racist!"

"Whatever you say, Dan. I just think it's a little sinister. You can't expect me to join you and this band of white people you've collected together for this cult of yours."

"They're not all white! And it's *not* a *cult*—it's a collective. I wish people would remember that."

I remained puzzled, until that evening, when I was absentmindedly flicking through cable TV. I found *Sky News*. I left it on in the background while I fixed a broken pen and looked up just long enough to see a man on my screen. He was confident, and smart, and talking extremely smoothly about something which had affected the Asian community. But I'd stopped listening now, because I was reading, and trying to commit what I was reading to memory. His name and job title were on the screen. "Amar Singh, Editor, *Asian Xpress*."

Of course! An Asian newspaper! An appeal in one of those would be *sure* to bring 'em in. It was surely a sign.

I dashed to my computer and found the website of the *Asian Xpress*. And there I found deep encouragement. Underneath the title of the newspaper, was its slogan: *The Voice of British Asians*. If I wanted to talk to British Asians, I should surely do it using their own Voice. And the man I'd seen on TV, Amar Singh, was in charge of that Voice. He was the boss. The man at the top. The man who could claim, above all others, to *be* the Voice of British Asians. I decided I should try and meet Mr Singh face-to-face, to convince him to publish an appeal.

I looked for where the paper was based. And I discovered something I couldn't quite believe straight away. Something which startled me.

Their office was at the end of my road. I could see it from my window. Fair enough, it's a small world. But you're not supposed to be able to see it all from your window.

• • •

That evening, I went to that address. Mr Singh and I arranged to meet at the pub right opposite his building. At first I was amazed at the scene. Here we were—the Voice of British Asians and the Voice of Polish Butter—in many ways two classic cultural icons, sitting together for probably the first time in the history of the world. But there was something about Amar's expression and manner that made me feel like a junior scriptwriter having to pitch his big idea to a Hollywood fat cat. I could afford no mistakes. I only had one shot at this.

"I need some Asians," I said, in as straightforward manner as I could muster. "Or some black people if you've got them."

"I see. And what do you 'need' these Asians for?" he said.

"For the past few months I've been asking people to join me. I'm collecting them together, and we do good deeds and stuff. I've got lots of them. But then when a friend came round my flat yesterday to have a look at them . . ."

"You keep these people in your flat?"

"No, no. In a box."

Amar look stunned.

"Photos of them, I mean. Not the actual people."

I laughed nervously. Amar didn't.

"Anyway, my friend came round and pointed something disturbing out—that basically everyone in my collective was white. And that's not the way it should be. So I would like some of your readers to put that right."

"What you are basically telling me is that you are a cult leader and you want to capture some Asians."

"No! It's not a cult—it's a collective. And I wouldn't be capturing them—I'd just be asking them to do good deeds."

"You think Asian people don't do enough good deeds?"

This wasn't going too well.

"I'm sure they do!"

"Why do you want them, then? Because we make good workers?"

"Eh?"

"Do you not think Asian people have suffered enough under brutal white regimes without having to follow your every whim as well?"

"I'm not brutal! And I'm sorry about all that stuff! Listen—"

"Have you heard of the Raj, Mr. Wallace?"

"It's nothing like the Raj! Please don't think it's like the Raj!"

This man hated me. His expression was unwavering. Maybe I'd been stupid being so conscious of the race thing. But just when I was about to plead with Amar for his understanding and then leg it when that too somehow backfired, a smile cracked on his face.

"I was messing with you!" he laughed. "Look at your face!"

I exhaled for what seemed like the first time ever.

"Sorry," he said. "I couldn't help it. Buy me a beer and tell me more about it . . ."

And I did. And we got on brilliantly. Amar had seemed to forget he was on deadline, stayed for another beer, and confessed he was getting quite into the idea of Join Me.

"I might even join you myself," he said. "Just to set a good example to other British Asians."

"Well, you're the *Voice* of British Asians. What you say must be heard."

"I think we can definitely put something in the paper about this. We might have to brush it up a bit. Make it more intriguing to the Asian people. We'll say you wrote a mysterious letter."

"Whatever you think," I said.

"Can you get me an appropriate picture? Ideally, one of you."

"I don't really put pictures of myself around," I said. "I don't want the publicity for myself. Just for Join Me. And my girlfriend doesn't know I'm doing this, so it's tricky."

"Does she read the ethnic media?"

"No. She reads *People*."

"You'll be fine, then. I think it would really help the readers to know who they're joining. You've got a trustworthy face. They're far more likely to get in touch if they can look into your eyes."

And Amar stayed true to his word. The article and photo appeared in that Friday's *Asian Xpress,* and read as follows:

WHAT A CULT!

A mysterious man who claims to have "started a cult by accident" is appealing for Asian followers.

Wacko leader known only to us as "Danny" wants more Asians to join his "collective" in order to make his membership base more diverse.

Danny, who claims to be a big fan of our paper, says: "As any cult leader worth his salt knows, your cult should reflect society at its best—at its most diverse. I find the idea of an all-white cult positively offensive. It's not right. It shouldn't be allowed. So I need your help."

The article continued, giving details of how people could contact me, before finishing with a strict warning: *"Asian Xpress cannot vouch for this man's reputation or motives."*

Blimey. They weren't taking any chances. And I now understood what Amar saw as "making it more intriguing." Not only was I now seemingly referring to Join Me as a cult, but according to the headline I was now a complete and utter cult myself. Oh, and a "wacko leader." I just hoped people wouldn't misread that as "Waco leader," and mistake me for David Koresh.

I was happy with the article, though. And a couple of days later I received, in the post, a passport photo from my first Asian joinee. Amar Singh. The editor of the *Asian Xpress*. The Voice of British Asians. Even if not one more Asian person joined me, I'd have the official spokesman of an entire ethnic minority on my side.

But more Asian people *did* join. Joinees Banarjee, Bhogall, Khan and Sarmah dutifully did as the *Xpress* had asked, and sent their photos to me. Joinee Sarmah even wrote: "I am pleased you have appealed for more Asian people to join you. Things which are exclusively white, black or Asian are not right. Especially if they are all-white."

I also received an e-mail from a man called Gubs Hayer. He was a producer with the BBC Asian Network, had read all about me, and wanted me to be interviewed on that night's *Late Show,* broadcast to Asian people throughout the world. He said it would be a great chance for me to add more Asians to my collective. I agreed with him. I did the interview; more people joined me as a result. And the *Asian Xpress* appeal was still working a few days later, when I received a brown, A4 envelope, containing the following anonymous message . . .

> *Hello. I saw your picture in the* Asian Xpress *and read about what you had to say. For both of these reasons I enclose this book as I think you need it more than I do.*

I took the book out of the envelope and read its title. *How to Succeed with Girls,* by Steve Marshall. Well, really. There was no need for that.

I chose to take it not as an insult, but as a kind and generous gesture which was aimed at helping me get more women to join me. I flicked through the book, subtitled, *The Complete Guide to Success with Girls,* just to see if there was anything I could pick up and utilize in my ongoing quest to reach a thousand. There wasn't.

I shoved the book in my drawer and got on with my day. Now satisfied that my collective represented humanity at its most diverse—and that I was up to a rather pleasant and impressive 713 joinees—I was free to continue as before. I called Ian first, though.

"Right," I said, "it's much more ethnically diverse now. So will you join me?"

"No. And can I have that blonde joinee's phone number?"

"No," I said. "But I've got a book you can have instead."

• • •

It was a Tuesday, about threeish, and we were in a taxi on our way into town. It was a red one, if that helps you build your mental picture, and the driver had a hook nose.

"I'm going to Dublin," said Hanne, out of the blue.

"I thought we were going shopping," I said.

"No, not now. This weekend. I only just found out today. There was a deal on the Internet and Claire bought four tickets for a quid each. So we're flying there Saturday morning and coming back in the evening. Bit of shopping, nice meal, that sort of thing."

I tried to reply, but "It'll do you good to get . . ." was as far as I got. Because, unless my ears were playing tricks on me, I'd just heard something a little odd on the radio.

"Can you turn that up?" I asked the driver.

"What're you doing?" asked Hanne.

It was BBC Radio 2, and the nation's favorite daytime show, *Steve Wright in the Afternoon.*

"Nothing," I said. "So what made you choose Dublin?"

And as Hanne began to speak, and I began to nod as if I were paying her the utmost attention, a man named Miles Mendoza began to talk in some detail about Join Me and the Karma Army . . . and I was stunned.

"So this is the website of the week, Miles?" asked a man whose voice I recognized as that of Mark Goodier, standing in for Steve Wright, and Miles said yes, and my heart leapt. I started to smile the biggest smile in the world and strained to keep control of it so as not to alert Hanne to what I was hearing. But imagine it! Several million people listening to a man talking about Join Me! And me unable to say a thing about it!

"You know how I like a website with a story," said Miles. *"Well, this is a website with a story. It all started a few months ago, when a man named Danny placed a small ad in a local London paper . . ."*

My eyes were about as wide as they could get at this point. I tried subtly to cover my mouth to stop my smile from showing.

"What's the matter with you?" said Hanne.

"Nothing. Tell me more things about stuff."

She looked at me oddly, but that really didn't matter, because Miles had started to go on and on at great length about my very important work.

". . . so initially people didn't know what they were joining, but the weird thing is that that didn't actually stop them from joining . . ."

Mark Goodier laughed. Join Me had made Mark Goodier laugh! And that made *me* laugh!

"What are you laughing at?" said Hanne, and I stopped instantly.

". . . with joinees going out every Friday and spreading good . . . buying coffees, befriending the elderly, that sort of thing . . ."

"That sounds amazing!" said Mark Goodier.

Mark Goodier said it sounded amazing! Amazing! Mark Goodier! I laughed again.

"What *is* it?" said Hanne.

"Nothing," I said, trying to look very serious. "Go on."

". . . and so the Karma Army was born . . ."

"The Karma Army?" said Hanne, clearly realizing I'd been listening to the radio. "Wasn't that a film, or something?"

"No," I said, struggling to look like I wasn't all that bothered by what Mr. Mendoza was saying. "So anyway. When are you going to Dublin again?"

". . . and their brief when they met up was to find an old man and make him very happy . . ."

Mark Goodier laughed again! Very loudly, this time! So did the cab driver! I struggled not to squeal like a lady.

"The flight's on Saturday morning," continued Hanne, oblivious. "I'll come straight round to yours afterward. We can cook dinner. Or you could always get a ticket too, you know . . ."

"Er . . . well . . . I think I'm . . ."

"Working?" she said. "You're always working now . . ."

" . . . and one of the things they did concerns a bloke who calls himself Raymond Price . . . "

"Always working now," I blindly repeated, using a clever tactic girls don't know about to hide the fact that I wasn't really taking it in.

"Well, you *are,*" she said.

"Are," I said. It's amazing how well that works.

". . . same scam for over fifty years . . ."

"You're not even listening to me, are you?" said Hanne. Well, I assume she did, because I wasn't even listening to her. I've no idea what she said. All I know is, the whole of the UK was suddenly being told about Raymond Price. About how he'd been conning innocent members of the public out of money by feeding them the same lie year after year, and about how, instead of finding him and shouting at him, they could support The Raymond Price Fund For Keeping Raymond Price Out Of Trouble!

Blimey! The fund I started—and which currently stood at around £18—had just been given official backing by the BBC! I was now more or less as established and worthy as Children In Need or Comic Relief!

And, as our cab pulled up in the middle of Soho and Hanne grumpily got her things together, I giggled. And giggled. And giggled.

And Hanne said, "I don't know what you're bloody laughing at," and that made me giggle even more, and eventually I was just one big, red-faced giggling mess.

And I think that's when Hanne realized for the first time that life with me was never going to be all Chocolate Oranges and stainless-steel peppermills.

And that's a moment I would come to regret.

• • •

The response from the Radio 2 listeners was astonishing.

They had visited the site in their thousands, and I had over a hundred messages to wade through when I got home.

And there were also e-mails and letters from people who wanted to tell me all about—yes—Raymond Price. Sightings were sent to me from all across the land. Intrigued, I checked the Raymond Price Fund to see whether anyone had donated any money to keeping the old fella out of trouble . . .

And they had.

All of a sudden, TRPFFKRPOOT was worth £61!

I was thrilled by the amount of people continuing to join me on a daily basis. And by the strange little events that were starting to take over my days.

For instance, someone from *The Ruby Wax Show* phoned me up and said Ruby had been handed a Join Me leaflet and wanted me to go on her BBC1 TV show to talk about it. I didn't know what to say. Would a morning chat show be the right way to come out to Hanne about being, effectively, a cult leader? I told the producer that I had something I had to do first, and would call them back. But there were *lots* of things I had to do first . . . because lots of things were happening.

Joinees had started creating their own Karma Army websites, giving details of what they'd been up to and how. Six joinees set up a small stall in Covent Garden and handed out leaflets and stickers. Joinees Woollven and Douglas plastered a Northampton monument with Join Me posters and handed out free, gift-wrapped presents to strangers. A games designer called Joinee Wilkins broke the rules at his place of work and managed to slip dozens of Join Me signs and even a picture of me into the Las Vegas level of *Destruction Derby Online* on the PlayStation 2, in order to secure that vital teenage market. His bosses found out and were annoyed—until he explained the concept of the Karma Army and they decided to leave them all in. In addition, Join Me was infiltrating local newspapers and just about every local radio phone-in show you could imagine.

I made an hour-long appearance on Ian's radio show in which he played the official Join Me song to the nation, but took great delight in still not joining me—despite taunting me and saying I'd never reach a thousand. The official Join Me song was also downloaded from the Internet and played on a national radio station in Germany one morning, but I am yet to find out how or why. Still, it got me my first German joinee.

Join Me continued to spread across the globe. I was now receiving photos from countries like Poland, Italy, Hungary and the Czech Republic. A law student in Norway joined me. He told me his personal motto was: *"Everything goes, said the old lady, she was frying a frog in the toaster,"* which either means some things just don't translate, or Norwegian law students are psychos. And I was also starting to get a significant number of photos from Australia, as well as from more far-flung places, like Singapore, Hong Kong and Mumbai. A joinee on holiday in Addis Ababa also got in touch to tell me that he'd been upstairs in an Ethiopian Internet café waiting for something to print out when, just for the sake of it, he decided to have a look at the computer's history bar. And he was shocked to see that the third link down led to the Join Me homepage. Word really was spreading right across the Earth.

I needed to create the maximum impact so that I could get my thousand joinees before I could admit my actions to Hanne. Which is why I knew automatically where my next trip would be, and when.

Hanne would fly to Dublin on Saturday. And I would fly to Amsterdam.

I had been contacted by a man named Martijn Flatland. He had a friend who'd accidentally recorded my appearance on that Belgian chatshow. He and Martijn liked it. They liked Join Me. They wanted their other friends to like Join Me too. But they'd only do that if I'd come and visit them in order to give a short speech on the benefits of joining the Karma Army. Meeting ten potential joinees would be roughly ten times better than meeting just one. I had to be back in the flat before

Hanne, but that was fine—Amsterdam is only a forty-minute flight away.

So I found a ticket for a tenner.

I packed a marker pen, and a small flipchart.

And I set my alarm clock, and went to bed.

Wereldverbeteraar beweegt tot het doen van goede daden

DANNY ZOEKT 'MAATJES'

door DENISE HOOGLAND

SCHIPHOL — Ook na tekst en uitleg blijft het een gek verhaal. Wie verzint zoiets, vraag je je af. Maar dat is aan de 26-jarige Britse schrijver Danny Wallace wel toevertrouwd. Zijn avontuur begint zoals altijd na een avondje hangen op de bank. Verveeld vraagt de jongen zich af wat er zou gebeuren als hij een advertentie in de krant zou plaatsen met alleen de tekst JOIN ME, zoiets als DOE MEE. Zouden mensen reageren? Zonder dus te weten waaraan ze meedoen? Nou en of, is gebleken. Dat dóen mensen. Danny bewoog al meer dan 800 jongeren in Europa. Samen vormen ze 'the Karma Army' en verrichten elke vrijdag duizenden goede daden.

We ontmoeten Danny Wallace op Schiphol, waar hij net aankomt met een vlucht vanaf Londen Luton. Eigenlijk een heel gewone jongen. Dolce en Gabanna-bril, zijn haar speels overeind en onder zijn warme winterjas draagt hij een shirt met het opschrift 'The Leader'. „Dat is ontstaan uit een grapje hoor. Dat jullie niet denken aan een soort enge sekte of zo", reageert hij verontschuldigend op onze gefronste blikken.

„Nee zeg, integendeel. We proberen de wereld gewoon een klein beetje zonniger te maken door in ieder geval op vrijdag iets goeds voor een ander te doen; iemands auto wassen of boodschappen doen of zo. Natuurlijk zou ik als een echte leader voor dat doel zoveel mogelijk zieltjes willen

na de eerste advertentie al zo'n 100 reacties had verzameld, raakte hij er van overtuigd dat hij iets moest doen met al die

iets moois aan de contacten te verbinden. Danny bekent eerst nog stiekem gedacht te hebben om gekke activiteiten

we bij op onze website *www.joinme.info* We hebben onszelf ook gekscherend the Karma Army genoemd", zegt Danny, ofwel het Karmaleger.

met zijn allen zo'n 50.000 goede daden per jaar zouden kunnen verrichten."

The Karma Army strekt zich inmiddels uit tot Noorwegen, België, Frankrijk, Griekenland en Zwitserland. „Vooral in België werd ik bij-

'Ik verzamel mensen als postzegels'

dat the Karma Army een prachtig initiatief is waar iedereen aan zou moeten meedoen. „Ik ben ervan overtuigd dat mensen diep van binnen allemaal goed zijn en goed willen doen. In verenigingsvorm is dat nu eenmaal makkelijker", zegt hij, terwijl we

■ Danny Wallace verzamelde al 800 aanhangers om zich heen die net als hij iedere vrijdag een goede daad verrichten voor hun medemens.

FOTO: THEO TERWIEL

ILLUSTRATIE'S: DILYS DE JONG

"Danny Searches for Mates" in De Telegraaf.
Accompanied by the haunting artwork of Dilys de Jong

CHAPTER · 21

1. *In those days Daniel entered into a winged chariot, and journeyed to the land of Holl.*
2. *There he made smooth the hairs upon his lip.*
3. *When he had done this he departed thence.*
4. *But Happy is the man that locketh his drawers; for he shall prolong his days.*

Hanne had decided that as my flat was marginally closer to the airport than hers, she'd stay at mine before her trip to Dublin. She reckoned this meant she could leave nearly an hour later than she would if she were staying at hers, thus giving her nearly enough time to decide on what shoes to wear.

As soon as I'd heard her taxi beep-beep outside at whatever ungodly hour it was, followed by the sound of Hanne softly clicking my front door shut, I hurriedly got up myself. Because *my* taxi would be arriving in just ten minutes.

I knew my trip to Amsterdam would have to be an incredibly short one. But I knew I could make it count. In far less than a single day, I'd be spreading the word throughout the people of Holland, as well as notching up another ten joinees and returning to London with more passport photos for the collection. The citizens of The Netherlands, I reasoned, would be up for joining me, if they were anything like their neighbours to the north, the Belgians. That lot had taken me under their wing quickly enough. I was sure that by the end of the day I'd be feeling like a Dutchman through and through.

Just as I was about to jump into my taxi, though, I remembered the nature of the day's meeting—I'd be trying to convince some people to join up, and, furthermore, to spread the word around Holland so I could complete my quest. So I ran back upstairs, dashed to my Join Me drawer, flung it open and, while the taxi driver impatiently and insistently sounded his horn downstairs, grabbed a handful of leaflets and passport photos to show to my potential joinees. I slammed the drawer shut and legged it downstairs before the driver decided that his horn wasn't really waking up enough of my neighbors for his liking, and he'd have to get his tamborines out.

• • •

I arrived at Amsterdam Schiphol airport to be greeted by Denise, a journalist from the national newspaper *De Telegraaf*. Denise had turned up because the night before I'd called *De Telegraaf* out of the blue and told them I was a world-renowned philanthropist with something important to announce. Well, it wasn't strictly lying. I was a "philanthropist" in the sense that I was encouraging acts of kindness, and I was "world-renowned" in the sense that if they believed me, I might well be in *De Telegraaf* next week, and thus renowned in Holland, which is in the world.

Denise, however, had been very suspicous of me—and extremely blunt during her ruthless telephone interrogation. When I met her, she was a far less fearsome character, just as any woman becomes when you notice she's six months pregnant and struggling to walk instead of waddle.

"At first I thought you were maybe a hoaxer, or a British media joker, or something to do with playing jokes on journalists," she said. "But now I see you are just . . ."

She was struggling for the right word.

". . . a special," she said.

"Oh," I said. She'd clearly meant it as a compliment, but round my neck of the woods, being called "a special" won't really win you any girls.

So I turned my mobile phone off, and Denise—calm, quiet and professional—and me—a special—sat ourselves down at the Burger King in the airport and talked the whole thing through.

"I need to appeal to the Dutch," I said, pointing my finger in the air.

"I'm meeting some people later on who I think will join me, but I need to make the most of my short time here. I have around eight hundred joinees. I'd like a thousand. I know that the Dutch people will not disappoint me. I know that they will come to my collective and do their best for me. I know that . . ."

Denise had stopped writing and was just looking at me, slightly concerned, but I continued anyway.

". . . I know that the people of this fine nation will take to the spirit of the Karma Army like their neighbors, the Belgians. I know that the people of the Netherlands will join me."

It was a rousing speech, I thought, and Denise seemed happy enough with what she was getting. We talked for a further half an hour or so, I had my picture taken looking all serious and worthy in the arrivals lounge, and then I said good-bye and caught the train into town. Denise's article would be coming out the following week, she told me, and she was going to urge her readers to do the right thing and send me their passport photos forthwith. She said she'd text me later in the day to see how my meeting with the Dutch went.

It was nearly one o'clock and I had only four hours before I had to catch my plane home, if I was to be back in my flat by seven that evening. Hanne would be back soon after that, and she'd be popping straight round to let me cook her dinner and maybe watch a film.

But now . . . now I had Amsterdam to conquer. So, I hopped on a tram to the Leidseplein, the square where I'd be meeting Martijn Flatland and his group of potential joinees. They were to congregate in a bar called Palladium at two o'clock for an hour, while I talked them through the scheme for the duration of their various lunch breaks. I walked in, found a quiet corner with enough room for eleven people, and got my flipchart out. I knew that with such a large group of people, I'd need to go some way to hold their attention while talking them through what would be expected of them if they signed up to the Karma Army . . . but I didn't really know what to say. Just bringing a small flipchart had been enough to make me feel in control of the situation, but now that it was just me and some blank pieces of paper . . . well . . . suddenly I didn't feel quite so confident.

Nevertheless, I knew I had to make an impact on these people, and so endeavoured to scribble some things down, and at one minute past two I was delighted to look up and see a man I'd come to know as the Dutchman, Martijn Flatland.

"Hello, Danny!" he said, extending his hand. By which I mean he held his hand out for me to shake, not that he had some kind of crazy extendable hand. "It's nice to meet you! The others will be here . . . *momentarily*."

I noticed the great pride with which Martijn had used the word "momentarily" and smiled.

'So who's coming down?'

"Oh, just some friends of mine. Two from work, a neighbor, an old university friend, things like that. We have all seen the video of *De Laatste Show* when you were on. And one of my friends is the one who taped it. We get Belgian shows here a lot from satellite. Although I would warn you, this friend is not normal. He watches a *lot* of Belgian TV shows. A *lot* of them. So he is considered . . . well . . ."

"A special?"

"Yes, exactly," said Martijn, laughing at his apparently loopy friend. "He is very much a special. Oh, here comes some peoples now . . ."

I watched as a man and a woman walked into the Palladium and started to remove their jackets as they approached.

"This is Tanya and Anders," said Martijn.

I said hello and asked them to take a seat, and soon enough more people were upon us.

"Maybe we should order some food," said Martijn. "Would you mind us eating while you talked?"

"Not at all," I said, grateful that they'd have something to distract themselves with while I embarrassed myself in front of them. So club sandwiches and halves of beer were ordered, and by the time they arrived, my ten promised potential joinees had all arrived and were each sitting in front of me, eagerly awaiting the beginning of my flipchart-based presentation. And it's usually at moments like this that I pause to ask myself exactly what I was doing. I was sitting in a bar in Amsterdam about to deliver a short speech to ten strangers on the merits of joining a scheme I'd thought up, only because I'd accidentally forced hundreds of other strangers to join something they'd known nothing about. And that's not normal for me. Not on a Saturday.

"So . . ." I said, standing in front of the Dutch audience, and clapping my hands together. "Join Me, then . . ."

I'd said that as an easy way of introducing the subject, but apparently someone had misunderstood.

"Okay!" said a man at the table to my left. "I join you then!"

"No, hang on, not yet . . ."

"I will then join you, too!" said the lady with him, now holding out a passport photo in front of her.

"No, no, I was just saying 'Join Me, then' as a way of gearing up to the talk, I wasn't demanding that you join me!"

"But that is why we came!" said Martijn, looking confused.

He had a point. And I'd managed to lose control, only one sentence in. Each person was now fishing around in pockets, or wallets, or handbags, trying to be the next one to hold a photo proudly in the air.

"Well . . . that's great," I said, happy but slightly deflated. "But don't you want to see my presentation?"

Everyone just sort of looked at each other.

"I've brought a flipchart," I said timidly.

Martijn took the lead.

"Yes. Yes, of course we do. Even though you said it all on *De Laatste Show,* which we all have now seen on video, you go ahead and say it again. Do your presentation, and *then* we will join you then."

"I have to be back at work at three," said Anders.

"Me also," said someone else.

"Well, I'll make it quick."

I turned the first page of the flipchart over. To be honest, I'd kind of lost my enthusiasm for the whole thing now.

The page read DO NICE THINGS.

"Do Nice Things" I said, pointing at the writing, rather vaguely.

I turned the page. It now read EVERY FRIDAY.

"And . . . do them . . . every Friday," I said. "Er . . . I suppose that'll do, on the presentation side of things."

There was a murmur of approval from all concerned and everyone agreed that it all sounded like a fabulous idea, and had I done a lot of public speaking before, because I was very good at it. And then they all started tucking back into their sandwiches and drinking their beers and there was really very little else to be said.

My new friends, the Dutch, talked cheerily and openly about Join Me. One in particular—a girl now named Joinee D'Huyvetter—was rather inquisitive.

"So these good deeds that we're all going to be making," she said. "What good deeds do *you* make every Friday?"

"Er . . . well . . . good question," I said, "I suppose my good deeds are . . . you know. Organizing stuff. And public speaking. And trying to further the movement."

"So you do no good deeds yourself?"

"Well, I organized some peanuts for an old man," I said. "Once."

"Ah," she said. "So you are pressing your moustache."

I nodded when she said this. I have *no idea* why I nodded when she said this. I suppose I'd assumed I'd misheard and hadn't wanted to challenge her. But then the words kicked in and I had to say . . .

"I'm doing what?'"

"You are pressing your moustache."

"Right," I said. "Am I?"

"*Je Snor Drukken*. You're letting others do all the work. You're pressing your moustache."

Again, I nodded, as if I bloody understood a word the woman was saying. She was doing a little mime now, as she showed me what it would look like if someone were to press their moustache.

"I see," I said. "Okay then."

I think I'd met a fellow special.

• • •

Just before three, my brand new Dutch joinees were getting ready to leave to go back to work. I'd learned, in the last twenty minutes, that two of them were teachers, one a musician, one a programmer for a Polish satellite sports station, two were students and the rest working in various shops and restaurants in and around Amsterdam.

I still needed a couple of hundred more joinees before I'd finished my quest, but this was good. I was making sure the joinees I was collecting together were dedicated, and kind of heart. I know that gaining ten brand-new joinees may only be inching one percent toward my final goal, but I think I'd managed to drill into them just how important it was for them to spread the word and get me more joinees. One percent would soon be two percent and before long five percent. Maybe, given enough time and effort, my collective would one day even be *ninety percent* Dutch, like prostitutes, or clogs.

"I think my friend Wim may like to join," said Tanya. "I will tell him all about it this afternoon."

"Here," I said, giving her the flipchart. "Maybe this will help."

And that was that. I had given my brief presentation—which had ended up far briefer than I'd thought it would—to ten Dutch people in a bar. And soon it was time to get back on the train which would take me to the plane which would take me home.

I'd done well in Amsterdam. At least twenty new Dutch joinees would spread kindness—the potential for good Dutch deeds was limitless. As I walked through Stansted airport, I was happy. I'd be home in good time for Hanne, and the day had been a quiet success. Especially when I remembered the interview for *De Telegraaf.* That'd spread the word, all right. Actually, Denise had said she'd text me to see how the day went, hadn't she? I took my phone out. It was still turned off. So I turned it on, and within a minute or so it bleeped to let me know I had a message. Three messages, in fact.

But they weren't from Denise the journalist.

They were from Hanne. She'd sent the first at 10 A.M. that morning. I hadn't seen it because I'd been too busy being interviewed.

YOU AWAKE? MY FLIGHT WAS DELAYED. NOT WORTH GOING JUST FOR FEW HOURS. ON WAY HOME.

Oh, shit.

The next message had been sent an hour later.

WHERE ARE YOU? AM IN YOUR FLAT.

Uh-oh.

How was I going to explain where I'd been and why I hadn't

answered her text messages? Should I come clean? Maybe it was time. Maybe it was finally time I told her what I'd been up to.

But as it turned out, I wouldn't have to.

The next message I read told me that much.

YOU SAD WANKER.

Hanne had found out about Join Me.

• • •

She wasn't in the flat when I got back. I hadn't expected her to be. But she'd left me a note. One which made my heart all but stop.

Danny
There is something very wrong with you.
Hanne

It had been left where I would find it, and in a place which would make its context clear.

Hanne had found my secret Join Me drawer. A drawer I'd forgotten, in my haste to leave that morning, to lock. A drawer packed with passport photos of complete and utter strangers. A drawer which also had newspaper clippings from odd newspapers, with pictures of me holding up small signs and being greeted by foreigners. A drawer which, to be honest, could look a little confusing to someone from the outside. Someone who should never have been on the outside in the first place.

I read the note again. There was nothing about it which gave any clues as to Hanne's mood. How had she reacted? There were no block capitals, no exclamation marks, no signs of annoyance. But, equally, there was no little kiss at the end of her name, no little smiley face, no playful doodle. Just our names, and those seven calm, cold, emotionless words. *There is something very wrong with you.*

How did she feel? Was she amused? Was she being dry? Or was she so angry that that was all she could think of to say? I re-read her text message. YOU SAD WANKER. Could that have been written in a jokey way?

I picked up my mobile to dial her number but couldn't quite face it yet. Jesus, I felt so stupid. I should have told her ages ago. I should have come clean, and admitted it all to her. She loved me, after all. She'd understand, if anyone could. Would she really have been angry, or thought I was odd? Well . . . yes. But possibly only for a little while. It suddenly became clear—I'd taken a big risk in not telling her, when I should have taken a smaller risk and done the opposite. Somehow it had felt the other way round before. When had that changed?

I dialed her number. Her answerphone was on. What should I say? How should I react to finding her note? Should I treat it as a joke? Did I take it very seriously? Do I apologize? I panicked and said nothing, just hung up, leaving a few seconds of silence for her to listen to at her own convenience.

My stomach churned. I looked again at the drawer. What had she seen that could possibly annoy her? Well . . . we've established that. Hundreds of passport photos. Letters from joinees. Those newspaper clippings. A CD of the official Join Me song. A death threat. A photo of me with the Magnificent Seven. And . . . shit. A book called *How to Succeed with Girls.*

I was in a lot of bloody trouble.

• • •

"Janne, is Hanne in?"

Hanne wasn't answering her mobile. She wasn't answering her work phone. She wasn't responding to my e-mails. So I'd hopped on a bus bound for Islington and turned up on her doorstep. And now here I was, standing, hopeful, in front of her flatmate, Janne. I'd put my best shirt on and combed my hair a bit.

"No, Danny, she's not in."

"Can I come in and wait for her? Please? I think she's angry with me. Possibly *very* angry. But she might not be. She might be impressed with me. It's very hard to tell."

"She's angry with you," said Janne flatly, dashing my hopes in an instant.

"Are you sure?" I said desperately, "because the two emotions are very easy to confuse."

"She called you a useless twat who keeps pointless secrets and wastes his life on stupid boy-projects."

"But did she sound impressed when she said it?"

Janne just looked at me.

"Danny, what have you been doing?"

"Nothing bad, I promise! The exact opposite, in fact! I've been improving people's lives!"

"Not Hanne's life."

"Well . . . no. But not mine either. I didn't *want* to keep all this a secret from Hanne, please believe me."

"You shouldn't have. She's your girlfriend. *She* should be your priority. You should be improving *her* life, not other people's. She told me some of what you've done. What if she'd done all that to you? All these new 'friends' all the time? And what if you'd needed her to be with you and then found out she was on the other side of the world when you thought she was tucked up in bed?"

"Belgium's not the other side of the world! And I'd have been happy for her! I'd *love* to go out with a minor Belgian celebrity!"

"So Hanne's not good enough for you now? You're after Belgians now?"

"Of course she's good enough! Look, Janne, let me in. Let me sit and wait for her. I'll explain everything to her."

"She said you'd say that. And she said not to let you in. She'll call you. Don't call her. She's leaving you."

And she closed the door softly, and put the chain on.

I walked my way back to the bus stop, never once looking up from the ground.

• • •

Hanne didn't return any of my messages that day. Or the next. A more paranoid man might have thought she didn't want to talk to me. I knew what she'd seen, and I wanted to set things straight. After all, there was nothing *evil* about what I'd done. Nothing *bad.* Plenty of boyfriends do far worse things. I explained this in about half a dozen e-mails over three days, hoping she'd read even one of them. My week became one of depressing isolation. Whereas once I'd rejoiced in communicating with my joinees, now their e-mails and letters became a sad and constant reminder of what I was close to losing.

There was only one person I wanted to speak to. And she didn't want to speak to me.

• • •

I awoke in my flat, a few hours later, to the sound of my phone ringing. I stumbled out of bed, knocked a glass of water over, whacked my shoulder on the doorframe and limped for the phone. I should always remember to put my glasses on before getting out of bed.

I picked the receiver up, slightly breathless.

"Danny? It's Ian."

"Hello, mate . . ."

"Sorry, did I wake you?"

"No, no, no . . ." I said, which I always do, as if being asleep in my own home is the most shameful thing I could have been doing. "I was just a bit . . . asleep."

"Cool. So . . . you and Hanne . . ."

"Yeah. It's bad. She found out about Join Me. But she won't let me explain it from my side."

"Let's meet up."

• • •

It was nearly 9 P.M., and I was at the Royal Inn.

Ian was waiting for me on the corner.

"Good day?" he said, which was stupid.

"Not really," I replied. "Bit of a bad one."

"I've been there, mate," said Ian, nodding. "But I'm still not joining you."

"I don't care about any of that, Ian. I care about Hanne."

"Talk me through it."

And I did. I talked about how Join Me had got out of hand, and how I should have stopped when I had my first hundred joinees, and about how that would have been the best time to have come clean to Hanne. I talked about how guilty I felt, about what a bad boyfriend I'd been, about all the dinners and films and happy times I'd missed out on and denied her because I'd . . . well . . . got carried away. And Ian listened patiently, and said "right" in all the right places, and at one point even softly mock-punched me on the arm, which I thought only really happened in father-and-son scenes in made-for-TV movies.

"I don't think all's lost," said Ian. "I think Hanne's teaching you a lesson. Showing you what it's like to be without the person you love for a while. She'll be back. But you can't blame her for feeling confused. You'd hidden all that stuff from her. It must have been like finding out you had a bit on the side. Only in this case your bit on the side was . . . well . . . a cult."

"It's not a cult. It's a collective."

"You take my point."

I sighed. He was right. I did understand it from Hanne's side. I just wished she could understand it from mine. But she didn't seem to want to hear my side of the story. If only I could reach her. Ian put his pint down on the table and looked at me, seriously.

"Thing is, Dan," he said, "I know where Hanne is."

"Where?" I said.

Ian avoided my eye.

"She's gone back to Norway for a while."

And I nearly dropped my pint.

Fagernes

CHAPTER · 22

3. *A cold north wind did blow, and the water was congealed into ice, and Daniel trembled in his nakedness.*
4. *And Daniel was almost lost.*
5. *But Hanne the Norwegian had pity upon Daniel, and did fashion for him a coat of many colors from the hairs of her beard.*

It was snowing and all I had on was a flimsy leather jacket with no buttons down the front and a dodgy cotton T-shirt. Well, and trousers and socks and stuff, but you get my point.

I was *freezing*.

Freezing, as I walked out of the airport and onto the train. Freezing, as I tried to find my way from the train station to the bus station. And freezing, as I wondered what on Earth to do with myself for the one freezing hour and twenty freezing minutes I'd have to stand around in a freezing Oslo waiting for the bus to leave.

I jogged into the Europa shopping center and, when my hands were warm enough to work again, sent Hanne a text message. I AM IN NORWAY. If at any point she decided to turn her phone on, that was a message I was sure she couldn't let lie. I'd just have to wait for her response.

I ambled around the shopping center for a little while, looking at this and that, and watching crowds of Norwegians brace themselves as they prepared to leave the warmth of the shops for the bone-chilling cold and sharp winds of the outside. I knew it'd be my turn next. It's usually at times like this that I start to wish I still lived with my mum and dad. There's no way my mum would have let me go to Norway that day wearing what I was wearing. She'd have laid my warmest socks out on the bed that morning, and demanded I wear the mittens my grandma insists on making and sending every Christmas, and she'd probably even have made me wear some of my dad's thermal underwear from the '70s. And it's usually at times like *this* that I start to realize I'm glad I *don't* still live with my mum and dad.

But the time came to leave that shopping center, and with a cup of coffee clenched between my fists like a hot water bottle, I made a break for the station.

On the bus, a few minutes later, my phone beep-beeped to tell me a text message had arrived.

WHAT? PLEASE SAY YOU ARE JOKING. YOU ARE NOT IN NORWAY.

It was too late. I *was* in Norway. And what's more, I was on my way to her house.

AM ON THE BUS. WILL BE IN FAGERNES IN THREE HOURS. I rested my head against the window, watching the wide streets of Oslo narrow as we made our way out of town. And then I closed my eyes, and tried to think about what the hell I was going to say to Hanne when I got to Fagernes.

And then I fell asleep.

• • •

I stepped off the bus with six or seven other people, and onto the icy concrete below. It was cold. Incredibly cold. So cold that Hanne was wearing just about every item of clothing I'd ever seen her wear, including some I'm glad I never did. Snowtrousers, huge boots, furry hat, oversize gloves, odd blue scarf obscuring her face. She had the family dog, Emily, a massive black poodle, with her. And Emily—to be honest—is how I recognized her.

"I've missed you," I said, giving her a hug.

Hanne, not Emily. I haven't missed *her* since she peed on my shoes last New Year's Eve. Emily, not Hanne.

"Hi," said Hanne. "Jesus . . . what are you wearing?"

"A T-shirt," I said. "And a jacket."

"So typically British!" said Hanne. "It's minus *eleven* here! Why aren't you wearing anything warmer?"

"I didn't think there *was* a minus eleven."

"Come on," said Hanne, taking me by the hand. "Let's get inside . . ."

We walked, with Emily, to the Fagernes Tavern, facing a frozen fjord. In the distance, one man was walking steadily across it with two bags of shopping in his hands. I bravely took my jacket off and Hanne removed two or three layers of waterproofing, and we sat in the bar and ordered hot chocolate.

And before she could say anything, I apologized. Profusely. And I explained. Desperately. I held her hand as I talked, and though I knew it all sounded odd, I also knew Hanne was taking it all in.

And Hanne had a lot to say. She scolded me for not acting the way I should have. For all the missed evenings, and parties, and for all the excuses she'd had to make on my behalf.

And so I made promises. Promises I knew I would have to keep. Promises I *wanted* to keep. I promised to pay more attention to her, and spend more time with her, and be just like I was again. I told her I loved her, that I'd got carried away, that I'd tone it down. And she nodded, and stayed silent, and squeezed my hand once or twice, and nodded some more.

"This is all so stupid, Danny," she said, at one point. "Why didn't you just tell me what you were doing?"

"I thought you'd make me stop," I said. "And I'm so close to the end, now—"

"Of *course* I would have made you stop," she said. "Anyone would! It's *ridiculous*. Making people join you for no reason, and then having to *come up* with a reason. It's another stupid boy-project, that's all. I warned you what would happen if you did this again! Why couldn't you have just stopped it?"

"I didn't have the heart. And I was enjoying myself. And these people were relying on me. They *wanted* to do good . . . they just never had enough of an excuse before."

"They shouldn't have *needed* an excuse," said Hanne sternly.

"But we all do sometimes. It's easier to do something good if you feel it's for a reason. Rightly or wrongly, that's the case."

"They were just showing off, these people. They thought, 'What's the point in doing anything good for anyone if there's no one there to see it?' Did they think you were God? Did they think that as long as they knew someone was watching them that made them better people?"

"No! The bottom line is, they've done a lot of good, my joinees. Just in little ways, maybe. But little ways can be important. I only need 138 more, Hanne, and then I'll stop, I promise. I'll have done it for Gallus. We've improved some people's lives through this . . . it's made a difference, somehow . . ."

Hanne squeezed my hand.

"Danny," she said. "You sound like a bloody nutter."

The words hung in the air.

Did I really? Did I really sound like a bloody nutter? I don't know. I didn't think so. But maybe I did.

A thought struck me. It had been there for a while—certainly since I'd arrived in Norway—but it suddenly made more sense.

Normality seemed really attractive right now. Maybe it really was time to go back to real life.

I stared at my hot chocolate.

"Danny," said Hanne, and I knew what was coming next. "If you and me are going to get back together, then you have to make some serious decisions."

She was right.

I really would.

• • •

It was snowing outside and Hanne had decided to take Emily back to the house. We had more to talk about, though, and I didn't really feel up to saying hello to her family, so it was agreed that I'd wait for her at the tavern and she'd return as soon as she could. She left me a oversized green ELKS jumper she'd been wearing under one of her other layers, I put it on, ordered another hot chocolate, and considered what Hanne was proposing.

A total and utter ban on any form of spontaneity.

Well, that was how *I* chose to word it.

She'd chosen her words more carefully. "Stop acting like a fucking nutjob."

Believe me, I saw Hanne's point. But how did she think I could just stop doing the things I enjoy doing? Yes, I might be a better boyfriend if I did . . . but how would it affect me as a person? What would this ban on spontaneity do to me?

I enjoyed the freedom of my life. The rules I chose to obey were governed by basic morality, but apart from that, my rules were my own. That's how Join Me started. That's how all this took place. And yes, that's what led me here, to face up to what I might very well lose . . . but it's like Joinee Saunders had shown me . . . because of him, I'd set myself another rule in life: that I'd be happy to travel and meet those who have joined me. Without that way of thinking, I probably never would have got out of bed in the mornings. I wouldn't have met the people I'd met. Seen the places I'd seen. Done the things I'd done. And now I was being asked—told?—to give all that up.

I thought about how to break the news to my joinees. They'd known something was up, I wasn't answering my e-mails as much. Never looking at the website. Never paying attention to my duties as Leader. I'd been too preoccupied with thinking about my girlfriend, about what I might lose. Perhaps I could just do what I'd very rarely done thus far, and come clean. I could just tell them about the mess I'd found myself in. About how this grand collective of freelance philanthropists had come together not through any great need to do good, but because I needed a bloody reason for having got them all together in the first place. I was no do-gooder. My heart wasn't pure. I'd acted under desperation and pressure and the attraction of power.

I knew that that would be all I'd have to do to break their little hearts, and have them leave me. They'd wander off, in their own directions, disappointed and angry at the Leader they'd once held in some esteem.

And what about Gallus? What would he think of it all? Well, he wouldn't be able to talk. He'd given up after one week and three joinees.

He's the last person who could judge my behavior. He'd probably even *approve* of my disbanding the collective. After all, *his* spontaneity had been crushed, and *he* was happy enough.

But what would Gallus have achieved if he *hadn't* given up? Did he *want* to give up his idea, and then his shop, and become a farmer? Maybe. Did he want to spend his whole life in the same place, with the same thousand people, doing the same everyday things, every single day? Again—maybe.

But what if he hadn't?

What if that one moment when fate or disappointment or his bossy old wife had finally killed his ambitions had never happened? What if Gallus's "stupid boy-project" had grown? Worked? Spread? How would his life have been, if he'd made another choice? Who would he have become? What could he have achieved? Would we, those few months ago, have erected a *statue* at his funeral rather than a simple gravestone? Who can say?

Hanne would be on her way back now, and I had to make my decision. Could I really promise that nothing like this would ever happen again?

I couldn't.

So when she arrived, I breathed deeply, told her, and prayed that she'd been bluffing.

She hadn't.

"Then I suppose it's over," she said, and we hugged. "I'm so sorry."

I felt as if I'd been hollowed out, and hugged her again, hard.

• • •

Sitting in the cold at that bus stop in Fagernes, waiting for the late bus back to Oslo, I had plenty of time to think about what I'd done. What Hanne had done. In my mind, I suppose I must have looked like a brave romantic hero, sitting in the snow, catching a bus to an unknown destiny. In reality, I was wearing a big green ELKS jumper and I looked like a knob.

And the thing is, you're probably now thinking that it'll be okay; that Hanne and me will get back together. Maybe you're even hoping it. And if this was a made-up story, I'm sure we would. I'm sure that just as the bus was leaving she'd turn up with tears streaming down her face, and I'd jump off the bus and kiss her, and we'd go back to hers and drink mulled wine and laugh. Or maybe she'd already *be* on the bus, and I'd sit down next to someone in a hat, and they'd take it off, and it'd be Hanne, all packed and ready to come back to London with me and start again.

But as I sat there, cramped and pushed up against the window by the fat lad next to me, I started to realize something. No one was going to stop the bus as we pulled out of the station. No one was going to show up out of the blue and take me away.

Because this, I am sad to report, is a very true story indeed, and sometimes, much to my regret, life just doesn't work like it does in those other books.

Vil du være med?

SIMEN TVEITEREID
TONE GEORGSEN (foto)

– Neinei, det er ikke politikk, det er ikke religion, jeg ber ikke om penger, bare join me.

En engelskmann har reist fra London for å stå på Karl Johan med en plakat over hodet, han fryser, han roper at han vil ha nordmenn.

– Men hva er dette for noe? Hva gjør du? (En mann med pelslue spør.)

– Det er ikke en kult. Don't worry.

I skuffen hjemme hos Danny Wallace ligger nå flere hundre passfoto av fremmede engelske kvinner og menn, samt noen belgiere og en skotsk sogneprest. Resultatet av Dannys annonse i en engelsk avis der det sto «Join Me. Send ditt passfoto til denne adressen».

Ikke noe hva, ikke noe hvorfor. Bare Join Me. Og noen hundre mennesker joinet. Ikke til å unngå at noen spurte hva de hadde joinet, hva de skulle gjøre.

Danny grublet. Det var jo bare et påfunn. En fiks idé. Men folk sendte mailer og brev, kalte Danny Wallace sin «leder». Leder av hva? Han måtte finne på noe.

OK, JEG KALLER DET «KARMA ARMY», tenkte Danny. Han laget en Internettside og erklærte at alle som har sendt inn sitt passfoto nå har sluttet seg til «The Karma Army», og at blant forpliktelsene i denne armèen er å gjøre en god gjerning hver fredag. Den må være «tilfeldig, uventet og snill».

Blant rapportene hittil:

Absurd. *Danny Wallace har vært journalist og tekniker i BBC. Nå*

CHAPTER · 23

10. *Then Daniel consorted with Paal, son of Peder, a soothsayer and a mighty man of wealth.*

Oslo was dark and frosty and *I* wasn't exactly in the sunniest of moods, either.

I didn't really know what to do with myself, to be honest. I suppose I'd been hoping to stay over in Fagernes, once Hanne had seen the light and accepted the ways of Join Me into her life. But that hadn't gone quite to plan.

But I have friends in Oslo, and so I decided to phone one of them. Erik would doubtless provide me with food and shelter me from the elements. And it would be good to see a friendly face. One that'd cheer me up.

So I called him, surprised the life out of him, and we agreed to meet at the Scotsman pub on Karl Johans Gate. Mainly because it was the one place I could be sure of not mispronouncing.

I sat at the front of the pub. But I had forgotten quite how expensive Norway is, a fact which was rammed home when I had to part with £6.60 for my pint.

£6.60! Kick a man when he's down, why don't you?

"Danny, hello!" said a cheerful voice to my right. It was Erik. It had started to snow outside again. Either that, or Erik has a hell of a dandruff problem for a man who shaves his head every morning.

"Hi, Erik," I said, hugging him. "I've had a bit of a dodgy day . . ."

• • •

Erik took me back to his flat in the East End of Oslo. It used to be an old frame-maker's shop, and the beige antique sign still hangs above the windows outside. He looked after me that night. He cooked a dinner of elk meat and fresh vegetables, made me milky tea, and played soothing music. By which I mean he put a nice CD on, not that he got a harp out. Everything was designed to cheer me up, and it was almost working. But Erik had some questions about Join Me.

"I can see why she thought all this was a bit odd. Especially if she feels you were ignoring her, too," he said.

"But I wasn't. Ignoring implies I did it on purpose. I didn't. Not at all. I was just distracted. I still love her. I'd still do anything for her."

"But not give this up? Not ditch your joinees?"

I sighed.

"I can't. I can't ditch them. And it's not just because of Join Me. It's also because of what it represents. Hanne wanted me to promise that I'd never do anything like this again. But this is a *good* way to live. My whole reason for giving up my job was because I wanted more freedom . . . and she wanted me to give that freedom up. Forever. And besides, I'm almost finished. I can't give up now."

Erik nodded. He understood.

"Do you have any joinees in Norway?"

"One," I said. "His name's Per. A law student in a place called Averøy; or somewhere. His personal motto is: *'Everything goes, said the old lady, she was frying a frog in the toaster.'* Does that translate to you?"

"No. He sounds a little psychotic," said Erik. "So you have just him in Norway? But you have them elsewhere?"

"Yeah. I'm pretty big in Belgium."

"Well, if you only have one . . . then tomorrow we should work on that," he said. "You have to use your remaining time in Norway positively. It seems only right, if you've made your decision. Maybe you can get the rest of your joinees tomorrow!"

Erik's idea stuck in my mind for the rest of the evening. I had thought I'd be going to bed that night a wrecked and desolate man. And while I was genuinely deeply sad, I was also optimistic. Maybe it was because the full effects of Hanne's decision hadn't hit me yet, but I was excited by what I could do the next day in Oslo. A whole day in Norway. A day to spread the word.

I decided Erik was right: I had to get back into the spirit of Join Me. I had to finish what I'd started.

And so I vowed I would, and then crashed out on his sofa.

• • •

It was 8 A.M. the next morning, and I was already on the phone.

"Hello, is that Simen from the *Aftenposten?*"

"Simen speaking."

"Hi, Simen . . . my name's Danny Wallace . . . I don't know if you remember me, but a couple of years ago you came to interview me and my old flatmate Dave, because we were traveling through Norway to meet one of his namesakes for a bet. And I had to make up with my girlfriend, too, who had left me at the time, because I was spending all my time traveling about meeting strangers."

"Yes! How are you? What are you up to these days?"

"Oh, same old, same old."

"Did you make up with your girlfriend in the end?"

"Yes. But we've split up again."

"Oh. Why?"

"Much the same reasons as before. Listen, I've a story you might be interested in . . . I'm in Norway to spread the word of the Karma Army and try to get some Norwegians to join me . . ."

"Don't get me wrong, Danny," said Simen, when I'd finally explained my plans for the day. "I like the story a lot. But space in the newspaper is tight this week, because of this and that, and . . ."

"Simen," I said. "I have a Join Me T-shirt."

I let the words sink in.

"You have a Join Me T-shirt?" he said, his interest in my story suddenly raised. "What does it say, this Join Me T-shirt you have?"

"It says . . . *Join Me.*"

Norwegian journalists love novelty T-shirts. It's a fact of life.

"Right. I will make more space in the newspaper. We need to meet very soon. Are you free at one o'clock?"

I told him I was, and we agreed to meet outside the parliament building, in the middle of town, at 1 P.M. precisely.

Erik got up about half an hour later and put some coffee on. I sat at the breakfast table and explained my plans for the day.

"I'd like to help," said Erik. "What do you need me to do?"

"I'll need a big piece of cardboard. A thick marker pen. And a photocopier."

Erik smiled.

"Come with me . . ."

• • •

Ninety minutes later and I was sitting in a café in the middle of one of Norway's biggest shopping streets with three hundred photocopied leaflets and a big yellow piece of cardboard, on which I'd inevitably written, "JOIN ME, NORWEGIANS."

I found the number for the TV2 newsroom and dialed it. I asked to be put through to Paal Pedersen's extension, and he picked up immediately.

"Pedersen."

"Paal, this is Danny Wallace."

I was taking a risk. I'd only met this man once before, for about ten minutes, at a friend's barbecue in Brighton.

"Er . . . Danny . . . Yes . . . How are you?"

"I'm fine, thanks . . . listen, do you remember telling me that if I ever needed a favor, I should call you?"

He hadn't actually said that, but then, why would he?

"Er . . . yes . . .?"

• • •

I informed Erik that at four o'clock that afternoon a reporter and camera crew from TV2 would be meeting me in town in order to talk to me about Join Me for an upcoming news bulletin.

"Great," he said. "You see? You are using your time positively. How could Hanne not be impressed by this?"

I hadn't thought about that until now, but yes—Hanne *should* be impressed. While some men would crumble after being dumped by their girlfriends, others, like myself, tend to try and dominate the Norwegian media. The next day, when I featured on a news bulletin and in the biggest newspaper in the land, how could she fail to see that she had made a mistake and that I was the man for her? Well, clearly, if I was wearing an oversize ELKS jumper. So I took it off, and, as we wandered toward the center of town, I handed it to a tramp. To be honest, he didn't look all that impressed with it, but sod him—it was warm, and sometimes you have to be cruel to be kind.

Erik and I walked past the grand Domkirke and on toward the parliament building. I'd be meeting Simen the journalist here a little later on, and noticed that I already had competition in the leafletting stakes. Two middle-aged women were handing out green photocopied fliers. As I approached, I was handed one. *"Jesus vil löse alle dine problemer!"* it said, and, being reasonably intelligent, I worked out that this was probably a Christian message. So I took their leaflet, but said, "You'll have to take one of *my* leaflets in return."

I tried to hand one of the ladies a photocopied Join Me flier, but she was having nonc of it. She waggled her finger in the air, and tried to walk away, but I followed.

"Here," I said. "Take my leaflet."

She didn't like that, and quickened her pace, hurriedly walking off.

"An eye for an eye!" I called out. "It applies to leaflets as well!"

Still, I suppose that at least this proves that Christians prefer to give than to receive.

And so I set about leafletting. Erik lent a hand, and together the two of us tried to stop whoever we could, with our big sign and two even bigger grins. But it was tough going. We were eyed with more suspicion than I dare say any two men who've ever stood in the middle of Oslo holding a sign saying "JOIN ME, NORWEGIANS" had ever been eyed with before. Maybe you've done this yourself. As you'll know, then, the Norwegians are not the easiest people to strike up a conversation with under these type of circumstances.

I decided to opt for the direct approach.

"Excuse me, are you Norwegian?" I said to a clearly Norwegian passer-by who'd apparently decided that eye contact with me would be tantamount to suicide.

"No," he replied, in his very Norwegian accent.

"Well, it doesn't really matter if you're not, because . . ."

"No," he said again, and he was off.

This happened again and again until I was under the impression that not one single person in Oslo was actually from Norway. It was incredible. There are five million Norwegians in the world, and not one of them was home.

I sat down next to two girls on a bench. They seemed to be talking about something a little personal and upsetting, so I left it for a few minutes until I realized time was of the essence, and this might be just the sort of thing that would cheer them up. So I reached over and tapped one of them on the shoulder.

"Excuse me," I said. "Would you like to join me?"

"No," said the girl, before turning away and mumbling something in Norwegian.

"It's not working, Erik," I said. "What's the matter with you people?"

"I'm sorry, Danny," he said. "I really am."

But I persisted. For another forty minutes I relentlessly tried to stop every single person who walked by. And I received odd look after odd look. But no one seemed at all interested in what I was doing. It was all too much, especially after the night I'd just had.

"I only need another 138," I said. "Just another 138! Don't they understand?"

"Maybe it's the wording," said Erik. "We don't really know what joining means."

I looked at the sign. Maybe Erik was right. Maybe it was a bit left-field. So I flipped the piece of card over, got my pen out, and wrote:

WANTED: NORWEGIANS

Incredibly, this seemed to do the trick. All of a sudden, we were raising smiles. People were pointing. And they started to approach me.

"Excuse me," said one elderly chap in a hat, "what do you want Norwegians for?"

"I collect people," I explained. "Like stamps. I already have lots of Belgians and French and Greek and so on . . . but Norwegians are rarer."

"What a nice idea," he said. "People as if they are stamps. Okay, you can collect me."

The man and his wife both took a leaflet and after I'd explained the proper purpose of things, they promised to send me their passport photos and start doing their good deeds each and every Good Friday.

Erik left soon after—I suspect out of embarrassment—but that was okay, because I was now never alone for more than a minute. The words "Wanted: Norwegians" had struck a chord with the Scandinavians, and I was now chatting happily with scores of them, each taking leaflets and promising to sign up. It was looking good. Maybe I would get my 138 joinees out of this after all. I was certainly attracting enough interest. At one point, two drunk men leaned out the back of a van. One had a moustache, ponytail and an American accent and wanted to know if I was casting for a porn film. I told him if I was, he'd got the part. His friend, a Norwegian, stumbled out of the van—which, for no apparent reason, was marked "The Karaoke Van"—and told me that if I was asking people to do good deeds, I was ten years too late for Oslo.

"It's all drug addicts now, man," he said. "Look around you."

I had a look around. It looked quite nice. There was a lady selling chestnuts and a boy with a balloon.

"The place is a mess. Destroyed. Drugs and gangs. You're too late."

I told him it's never too late. I told him that for his first good deed, he should run for office somewhere in Oslo, as a random act of kindness toward his fellow citizens. His face lit up, like I'd just told him he was Superman. He promised he would run for office next chance he got. If he did, and he was elected, then the people of Oslo have my most sincere apologies.

Next, I talked to a lady from Sweden who told me she already undertakes random acts of kindness, by taking flowers to old people's homes, and giving pet food away to stray dogs. I asked her if she'd ever got the two confused, and she said no, why would she give pet food to old people, and I said I was just joking, and she got all offended and walked off.

"You seem to be doing very well!" said a voice behind me, all of a sudden. It was Simen. He'd brought a photographer with him, who, without my knowing, had been taking various pictures from a distance for quite some time.

And so I sat down with Simen and explained exactly what I was doing, gave him the averages so far (thirty-one years of age, fifty-three percent male, ninety-eight percent straight, most popular personal motto: "Shit happens!") and he told me that to really get a feel for Join Me, he wanted to see me in action. So back to the streets we went, and I campaigned hard, while Simen stood slightly to my right, scribbling into a notepad.

Outside the parliament building I met a lovely couple, Steinar and Johanne, who decided that Join Me was just what they'd been missing all their lives.

"We will join you," said Steinar. "And we promise we will do our good deeds."

"It's something we should always do anyway," said Johanne. "Like, maybe we could invite a homeless man into our house for a night."

Simen looked shocked at what Johanne had said. Not as shocked as her boyfriend Steinar, but very shocked nevertheless.

"It's amazing," said Simen, "that people would be considering acts of such a grand scale after only reading a . . . well . . ."

"A slightly tatty leaflet?" I said.

"Well, yes."

"Those two there are essentially very kind people. They just need an excuse to do something kind."

And on and on I went.

"Okay, Danny," said Simen, half an hour later. "I think we have enough there. The article will be out in the next couple of days. I got enough for a whole page here, so I hope that more Norwegians join you as a result. Oh, and here . . ."

He handed me one of the two coffees that had appeared in his hands in the last few minutes.

". . . my first random act of kindness. Have a coffee on me. You look very cold."

• • •

That night, on the plane home, I was a strange little mess of emotions.

It had been a good day, despite all the odds. I'd spread the word in Norway, secured a few joinees, been interviewed by their biggest newspaper and even made an appearance on that night's TV news . . . and all when, by rights, I should have been sitting in a darkened room, deeply depressed, drinking cups of tea and listening to sad songs.

Four hours later, back in London, I was doing just that.

But I knew one thing.

I had to complete my journey. This had to be worth it. I had to make it to a thousand. I couldn't quit now. Not now I'd come so far. If I did, I'd be setting a precedent for my life that maybe I'd never come out of—that maybe Gallus had never come out of. This had started out as something for him. Now it was something for me.

I had to start the final push.

JOIN US

CHAPTER · 24

4. *And Sophie of Bruges offered Daniel a cup filled with tea.*
5. *And Daniel took up the tea and was thankful, saying, Thanks.*

In the days after my return from Norway I was like a man possessed. The very moment I'd returned home I'd ripped open what post I had and totted up my new joinees. The fact that I'd been away for a few days, and had been avoiding my duties for the few days before that, meant that I'd amassed quite a few . . . and the sight of all these new faces, all at once, gave me great encouragement.

I only needed ninety-nine joinees. Ninety-nine! I was so, so close to the end. My collection was nearly complete and I could almost smell my return to some semblance of normality. I'd given up a lot to make this happen, and I knew I had to get it over with. I was getting desperate for joinees, and being dumped by my girlfriend had, in a weird way, only spurred me on to do even better.

I made a cup of tea and sat down at my computer. There were the usual several dozen e-mails from people asking me how they could join up (to which I replied instantly, virtually *begging* them to do so), a few claims of Raymond Price sightings and the odd piece of abuse (apparently, the word "tosser" is also used in Canada . . .). But right at the bottom, I found an e-mail from someone or something called "Preventie" . . . and it was marked highest priority . . .

> ***To:*** *Join Me*
> ***From:*** *Preventie*
> ***Subject:*** *Help?*

Stedelijke Preventiedienst Stad Brugge
Blinde Ezelstraat, 8000 Brugge

Hello,

I found your website by co-insidence and it's so amazing gooooood. How did you start such an initiative, because we're interested to do something simular in Bruges. Can you send me some information and good tips, please. We want to make our plans a little more concrete . . .

Looking forward for your information.

Greetings, Sophie

Well, that was nice. At first glance, it seemed as if someone wanted to set up their own branch of the Karma Army in Bruges. Ah, the Belgians. They never fail me. And they'd be more than welcome to set up a spin-off organization. All they'd have to do is post me their passport photo and then gather up a few joinees of their own. Sophie had put her phone number at the end of the e-mail, so I thought rather than send her a long-winded e-mail with tips on how to do her good deeds, I'd give her a quick call instead.

It wasn't her who answered, though.

"Stedelijke Preventiedienst," said a man.

"Oh . . . hello . . . is Sophie there, please?"

"No, she is not in the office right now."

"Oh, I didn't realize I was calling her at work, sorry."

"Is this . . . the Join Me man?"

Blimey.

"Er . . . yes . . . how did you—"

"Sophie said she had sent you an e-mail. We are all very interested in what you are doing."

"Oh. That's nice."

"Yes. And Sophie has been thinking for a while of starting something a bit like it here in Bruges, through this office."

"What . . . like a work club, or something?"

That sounded great. I started to wonder how many people worked with Sophie, how many potential joinees the company employed. Maybe they'd be all I needed to finish this quest off.

"Well, not exactly. We want to do a similar thing, but we have to run the idea past the Mayor first."

"The mayor? What mayor?"

"The mayor of Bruges."

I was stunned. What on Earth did the mayor of Bruges have to do with any of this? What number had I called? What was going on here?

"Who are you people?" I asked.

"This is the . . . what would you call it . . . the town hall. Like the council. So I will tell Sophie to call you to talk more about your Karma Army."

And, slightly shocked, I put the phone down and said good-bye. Yes. In that order.

I made another cup of tea and tried to think about what was going on. Could it really be that someone from the office of the mayor of Bruges had found out about the Karma Army and now wanted to instigate a similar scheme over there? Someone certainly seemed to be interested in what I was doing. Someone from the city council! And they wanted me to advise them. *Me!*

And then the phone rang.

It was Sophie.

• • •

"So . . . what line of work are you in?" said the man in the seat next to mine, who'd managed to begin a conversation with me by belting me in the face with his rucksack.

"I'm an international goodwill adviser, with special responsibility to Bruges," I said. "Yeah, I'm just on my way there now, actually. I'm going to give a brief presentation to some of their top people. I would've brought a flipchart, but I gave it to a Dutch woman recently. How about you?"

"Telesales."

"Right."

It was the next day and I was on a packed train leaving Brussels central station on my way to Bruges. I was thrilled. This was quite a big thing. The event, I mean, not the train.

Sophie and I had decided to meet at her offices, just off the Grand Place in the beautiful city center, where I would talk her through how I'd started Join Me, how the Karma Army had come about, who my joinees were, and what they did each and every Good Friday. And she was going to listen. And take me seriously. And maybe even take some notes.

I, Danny Wallace, would be responsible for someone *taking some notes.*

And not just that—I would, for the first time in my life, be *directly affecting Belgian social policy!* And which of us can ever forget the first time we did *that?* I'm sure you have some pretty fond memories yourself.

"Danny, come in, let's get a coffee," said Sophie, when I finally arrived. She was an impish lady, dressed head-to-toe in black, and had a kind face. "Or a tea if you would prefer."

I tried to look like it didn't matter, and I'd be happy with whatever. But I couldn't do it.

"Tea, please."

"Okay, come through here . . ."

We sat at a table in a fine and grand room, tucked away at the bottom of the ancient building where Sophie had her offices.

"Do you like Bruges?" she asked. And yes, I did. Cobbled, winding streets with elegant buildings, hugged by narrow canals . . . it takes someone who lives in Bow to fully appreciate somewhere like Bruges.

"Now, Danny," said Sophie matter-of-factly, "like you, we think it is important to do good, and to have a social responsibility. We have been trying to encourage people to be nice to one another by giving them sweets."

"Sounds good," I said. She was talking my language. "A kindergarten approach."

"We handed out thousands of them, attached to paper cards like these."

She handed me a brightly colored card. It was in Flemish. I couldn't read it. I didn't know how long I should pretend to be reading it before putting it down without seeming rude. I gave it five seconds.

"We made many of them," said Sophie.

I stared at it some more, and nodded. Nope, I still couldn't understand it. But I liked it. A lot.

"You can keep that," she said.

"Thanks."

"Read it later."

"I will certainly look at it some more, yes."

This was great. It was like coming home. Here I was, sitting with someone who was taking a "stupid boy-project" as seriously as I was. And *she'd* managed to get council funding!

"Now," said Sophie, pouring my tea, "we want to do something special. I saw the movie *Pay It Forward,* and I thought to myself, now *there's* a good idea. I thought to myself, maybe *we* can be kind of like that."

Bloody Haley Joel Osment. Always stealing my thunder. Still. Where was he now? Not in Bruges talking to someone who knows the mayor, that's for sure.

"And I also saw what you are doing, and it is similar to what we want to do. And so I would like your advice . . ."

"No problem," I said, giving her two thumbs up.

It turned out that Sophie and her colleagues had decided that they wanted to start something called the Ambassadors scheme. Anyone interested in joining them would get a special badge which they would wear at all times. They'd also be given three other badges, and once they'd done a good deed for someone, they'd hand over one of those badges. Then that person could apply for some extra badges of their own, and start doing good deeds themselves. Sophie hoped that eventually everyone in the city would be wearing an Ambassadors badge.

I had to hand it to Sophie—this was a sophisticated scheme. But before I could give my expert opinion, there were a few important details I needed to go over.

"What's the badge like?" I asked.

"Well, we don't have the design yet. But it has to be something grown-up," she said. "Something serious and mature."

"Oh," I said, sensing that her approach was probably going to be quite different from my own. "I see. So it's quite a grown-up thing, is it?"

"Well, yes. But these Ambassadors are all very middle-aged people. They wouldn't wear a childish badge. There are already fifty-one of them."

Fifty-one, eh? I made a sympathetic face. Fifty-one wasn't really all that impressive. How intimidated Sophie must have been by my presence, a man in command of nearly a thousand dedicated joinees. A man who . . . hang on . . . fifty-one people? What if those fifty-one people joined me, *as well as* the Ambassadors scheme? That would more than *halve* my workload in one easy moment!

"Do you think . . ." I said, "that maybe these fifty-one people might join *me,* as well . . . ?"

I had hope in my eyes, but the look on Sophie's face told me she was about to dash it. I suddenly realized . . . I had crossed a line. I had come here offering help, and now it looked like I was here to steal her joinees. I was becoming the Joinee Whitby of Bruges.

"Er . . . I don't . . . it's . . ." Sophie was struggling to work out how she should react, and I became instantly and deeply ashamed. I mean, I was now an experienced collective leader. I should've known better. What if I'd asked a fellow collective leader for advice in the early stages of Join Me, and he or she had then tried to nick what few joinees *I'd* had?

"I'm sorry . . . I didn't mean for—"

"Let's just talk about what you did," said Sophie, waving the thought away and moving the conversation along. I felt so cheap. Like a parasite. I resolved to make it up to her by giving her the very best tips I could, for as long as she could stand hearing them. Because the important thing here, today, in the city of Bruges, wasn't completing my quest, or nicking her joinees, or spreading the word of the Karma Army. Sophie's Ambassadors and my joinees would be working together whether they liked it or not, toward a common goal: being nice. That was the important thing . . . spreading the good for absolutely no personal gain whatsoever.

And if that last line doesn't get me at least a mention in the New Year's Honors List, then I don't know what bloody will.

We talked for maybe an hour before I realized I had started to repeat myself, and Sophie looked like she was about to nod off.

"Well, Danny, thank you for coming over," she said.

"Not at all," I said. "Thank you for the tea. And good luck with your Ambassadors. I hope your badge turns out to be lovely. And suitably mature."

I was happy, as I walked through Bruges, trying to find a bus that would take me to the train station. I'd enjoyed my meeting with Sophie. Especially on my way out, when I discovered that her department, *Stedelijke Preventiedienst,* would be known in English as "Crime Prevention."

How brilliant did that make me feel?

Now not only was I some kind of freelance international goodwill adviser . . . now, at long last, I was also a *crimefighter!*

• • •

In the morning, I made a cup of tea and, after trying to come up with a dozen other ways to put it off, finally took a look at my mail.

I was pleasantly, yet regretfully, surprised. The article in *De Telegraaf* had obviously been published that week as promised, and people from all around Holland had sprung into action. Denise must have done an amazing job of selling the Karma Army . . . the Dutch weren't just keen to join, but positively *demanding* that they be let in. Fifteen of them sent their pictures that day. Twelve the next. At the same time, the TV appeal and the article in the *Aftenposten* had also apparently started to make waves in Norway. My joinees had heeded my pleas and asked friends and families once again to sign up, and a night of radio phone-in show assaults had paid off, too, with passport photos arriving from all around the UK as a result.

I was up to 972 joinees. And yet I wasn't as happy about it as I would have been just a month or so earlier.

The day after, more arrived. I opened the envelopes, calmly and quietly.

Joinee 973. Joinee Michaels. A zoologist from Lancaster.

Joinee 974. Joinee Rosenberg. A student at Cardiff University.

Joinees 975 and 976. The Holter-Andersens. A young husband and wife from Norway.

Joinee 977. Joinee Berens. A systems analyst from Chichester.

The next morning, when a similar amount arrived, I just sat on the floor of my living room and stared at my huge pile of passport photos. Whether I liked it or not, this was it. The end was just around the corner.

Two days later, I was up to 990. The day after that, when I'd made no effort to do anything whatsoever and had stayed in bed until nearly 2 P.M., I received another three envelopes in the post. I didn't open them. The next day, I received three more. I didn't open them either. I couldn't. I didn't want to look. I didn't want to *be* at 996 joinees. The following day I received another four. That would take me to a thousand. If I opened them.

But what if I *didn't* open them? What if I never opened another envelope? What if I moved house and didn't tell anybody? I could stop the collective from ever growing past 990. I could keep this going forever. I could be the *Leader* forever.

I walked around my flat with those ten envelopes in my hands for what seemed like an hour. Should I open them? Should I achieve my last ten joinees, here and now, and have done with it? Or should I hide them, deny all knowledge, live to Lead another day?

I picked up the phone and dialed. It rang, and was answered.

"Hello?"

"Ian, it's Danny."

"Hello, mate! How's it going?"

"Very well," I said flatly. "Very, very well."

"Doesn't sound it. Got your thousand yet?" he laughed.

I didn't laugh.

"The pub, Ian. Today. Be there."

And I slammed my phone down, dramatically.

And then I realized what I'd done and rang him back and told him which pub and at what time, and he said could we make it a bit later, and I said okay, and he said bye and so did I.

It was just like in a film.

HORSE & GROOM

CHAPTER · 25

18. *Then those over whom Daniel had dominion, who were called Join-ees, did each divide their first-born into four parts.*

19. *And three parts they cast away.*

I walked into the Horse & Groom to find Ian waiting for me in the corner.

"Well, I finally did it," I said, sitting down.

"You don't seem very happy about it," said Ian.

"I am. Honestly. This is what I've been working toward, after all."

I sullenly placed my ten still unopened envelopes on the table in front of me.

"You haven't opened them!" said Ian.

"It's a historic moment," I said. "It didn't seem right doing it on my own."

"This is exciting!" said Ian.

"Well, prepare to buy me that pint," I said.

"Oh. So all of a sudden it's a bet, is it? Now you've done it?"

"For the last time, Ian, it's *not* a bet. But if it was, I won. So . . ."

I picked the envelopes up.

"My final ten joinees. The last ones I need to complete my collective of a thousand. This is it."

Ian sat forward in his seat, evidently far more keen to see who'd joined me than I was. I felt like making a short speech, about how far we'd come, about what we'd achieved, but I'd probably have embarrassed myself, so I picked up the first one and just got on with it.

"Hang on, hang on," said Ian. "So you're nearly there. You don't seem happy. When you've opened these envelopes, you've done it! That's it! It's over!"

"And maybe that's the problem. I don't want it to be over. Hey . . ." I said, having an idea. "How about we have a little wager? How about you bet me I can't get . . . say . . . two thousand joinees?"

"Eh? I thought you were too old for bets? I thought you'd moved on?"

"I'm not going out with Hanne any more. I've moved so far on I'm back where I started."

"Forget it. You wanted a thousand. You've *got* a thousand. I'm excited! I want to see who's joined!"

"Okay," I sighed, and picked up the first envelope.

"Hang on!" said Ian. "A reminder of the averages, please. I need to know who's ended up joining you."

I smiled, took out my wallet, found a tatty piece of paper, and looked at my joinee stats.

"Well," I said, "remember that the next ten envelopes could change everything by almost a tenth of a percent each, so don't go thinking that these are definitive."

"Fine."

"Right. My collective is . . . approximately fifty-four percent male, forty-six percent female. The average joinee is about 5 feet 9 inches tall, thirty years of age, and has probably spent around two years of that time in Belgium. They have nearly a quarter of a child. And—but this is just a personal viewpoint—they are very nice indeed."

"You may proceed."

I opened the first envelope.

A photo fell out.

Joinee 991. A man. A man who would now be known as Joinee Long. A technician from Marlborough.

I smiled a bittersweet smile, and opened the next one.

Joinee 992. Another man. Joinee Hopkins. A Scottish plumber. Welcome.

Joinee 993. A woman. Joinee Jennings. Works in marketing, in London. Writes with glittery ink.

Joinee 994. Joinee Jack. A nine-year-old boy who wrote "I made a

CD of the Join Me song from the Internet and I listen to it every day in the car with my dad." I'm willing to bet that his dad goes insane within the year. For some reason, that fact made me oddly proud. People were getting a kick out of Join Me in so many different ways. It was fun for all the family. And this moment here, in the Horse & Groom on Great Portland Street . . . this was the climax. I could feel the enjoyment creeping up on me again. And as I started to open the envelope of Joinee 995, I had to stop . . .

I suddenly found myself getting very, very excited. The sight of these new joinees, spread over this pub table, and the sight of an even more excited Ian, made me realize . . . we were getting there. We were really *getting* there. Within a few seconds, I'd have my 995th joinee . . . and then my 996th . . . and just a few minutes after that I would legitimately be able to claim that I had a thousand joinees. A thousand!

"Get on with it," said Ian.

And I did.

Joinee 995. A woman in her thirties. Joinee Simms. She'd found a Join Me leaflet in her local library in Bristol. Hello!

Joinee 996. A Dutchman! Joinee Bos lives in Hilversum and read about me in *De Telegraaf.* "I am happy to be with you!" he wrote. Not as happy as I now was, Joinee Bos.

I picked up the next envelope and opened it with a smile.

Which is to say I smiled while I was opening it, not that I have some kind of magic smile which can open envelopes.

But disaster!

"No!" shouted Ian, before laughing. "Well, it serves you right for getting so cocky!"

Gah! There was no picture with this one! It was a mere letter, from someone calling themselves Laura Fulford, requesting more information about joining . . . *Curses!*

"There's still hope," I said, a desperate tone in my voice. "Sometimes people send me two at once. A boyfriend and girlfriend deal, that sort of thing. Or a mother and child—that's happened a couple of times. It could still work out!"

Ian just smiled and sat back in his chair.

"So close . . ." he laughed.

I tore the next one open. There was only one picture, but thank God there was a picture at all. Joinee 997. Another Joinee Smith. My tenth. I quickly put him to one side and tore the next one open.

Joinee 998. Still only one picture. Joinee Allison. Shit. Why didn't she have a twin? Why are some people so inconsiderate? Come on. Please . . . the next envelope *has* to have two pictures . . . don't tease me like this . . . don't make me *fight* for a thousand, then *not want* a thousand, then *want* a thousand, then *not have* a thousand . . . this *has* to be over . . .

I opened the envelope.

I took out a piece of paper.

I unfolded it.

And I found just one, single, solitary passport photo.

Joinee Selby. Joinee 999. A man who looked, in his photo, like I felt. Deflated. Beaten. And largely disappointed with life.

"Christ . . ." I said. "I thought that'd be it. I thought I'd be *done* today."

"I think it'd be quite funny if you gave up at 999 joinees," said Ian, a little unhelpfully.

"This isn't a joke, mate. I know I have to make it to a thousand. If I stop, or if I fail, it sets a disturbing precedent for the rest of my life. If I give up, it might mean I'll always give up. It'll make me a quitter. It'll mean I started something I couldn't finish."

"You'll get another joinee," said Ian. "You can't help it. You'll be up to a thousand in no time."

"But I'm exhausted. I genuinely thought that would be it. I was getting all excited. But there's always tomorrow's post, I suppose. See if anyone else joins up."

"So you've still not won the bet."

"It's not a bloody bet!"

"No, I know . . . thing is, though, there's still one envelope left . . ." Ian was pointing to an envelope tucked behind the pub menu. I'd apparently overlooked it.

"Eh? How did I miss that?"

It was white, slightly creased, and marked "Join Me, P.O. Box

33561, London E3 2YW," but interestingly, there was no stamp on it. How did it get here? Maybe it had fallen out of one of the others? I held it up to the light, and yes—there was what looked like a passport photo inside. I realized just how badly I wanted this to be it.

"This could be the final one!" I said, not quite believing my luck. "Oh, thank God! My thousandth joinee!"

I tore it open. I took the picture out. I studied it. And I couldn't quite take it in.

It was Ian.

"Well . . ." he said, smiling. "I'd been waiting for the right moment . . ."

I shook his hand, more firmly and with more manly meaning than I think I've ever shaken anyone's hand with before. There was high emotion in the air. But I just didn't know what to say.

"Now," said Ian, standing up, "I reckon I owe you a pint."

Well . . . a bet's a bet, I suppose.

• • •

When it sank in, a few moments later, I felt *brilliant.* Brilliant, as Ian and I drank our celebratory pint. Brilliant, as we phoned some friends and told them where we were and got them to celebrate with us. Brilliant, at midnight, in a curryhouse in Soho, sharing six bowls of Chicken Dansak and ten nan breads between the lot of us. And brilliant, as I awoke the next morning with a hangover that I felt, for once, I had well and truly earned.

I was shattered by the strange mix of emotions: delighted that I'd done it, disappointed that it was over. But today wasn't a day for sitting in bed watching *Oprah* and regretting the drinks of the night before. So I sprang into action. I made a few phone calls and got dressed. I found a color photocopier in the print shop down the street. I scattered handfuls of passport photos across it, and took dozens of photocopies, until I had a duplicate of each and every joinee. And then I went home and put the originals into a small box, I put the small box into a small bag, I caught the tube to Paddington, I clambered aboard the Heathrow Express, I checked in at the airport, and I caught a plane to Switzerland.

There was now just one thing left to do.

JOIN ME
JOIN ME

CHAPTER · 26

5. *And Daniel cried, Hearest thou not, Swiss?*

I was tens of thousands of feet in the air, somewhere over France or Germany, with my small box of joinees on the tiny tray table in front of me, marveling at their cheeky, grinning faces.

I had my thousand joinees. I'd achieved my goal. I'd achieved Gallus's goal. I'd managed to get a thousand people to Join Me.

And it felt good. In fact, the night before, with my friends, in the pub, it had all seemed like such an *achievement*. A pointless quest which, somewhere along the line, had managed to take on a vital point and a real meaning—not just to me, but to a thousand other people, and to the thousands more people whose lives *they* were touching through unexpected good deeds and random acts of kindness.

I'm not saying we changed the world. I'm just saying we changed *some* people's worlds. Maybe in the tiniest ways possible, but . . . you know . . . maybe not. Maybe, now, they'd be more inclined to do the same for someone else. Maybe that person would do the same for yet another someone else. Maybe one day we'd *all* be doing it. Maybe one day we'd *all* be able to claim that we'd made hundreds of old men very happy, affected Belgian social policy, really been *part* of something.

But I'd taken it as far as I could, for now. I had to move on, and put a stop to this obsession with my joinees. I had to go back to normality—the normality Hanne had so craved. I missed her, and I missed what we had. But at least I'd seen this through. I'd proved to myself that even the smallest ideas can grow into something . . . well . . . rather wonderful.

But would this really be the end of the Karma Army? Well, no.

I didn't think so. An e-mail from Joinee Reverend Gareth Saunders that morning had proved that much to me. "Join Me," he wrote, "has just become a part of everyday life. If it's Friday: right! I've got to do some random act of kindness. Even if Join Me stopped today, I would probably continue doing random acts of kindness, because I've seen the difference that it makes to people. It cheers them up, and for a moment makes them feel special and noticed and important."

That summed it up, for me. I hoped that maybe my other 999 joinees thought the same. I flicked through my box of photos. Hundreds of happy, smiling faces. So many people I'd met, or at the very least corresponded with. So many I now counted as genuine friends.

There's Joinee Jones, the first joinee. Right behind him, Joinee Cobbett. There's Gaz, and Whitby, and Saskia. There's Joinee Jenni. The Newcastle boys. Joinee Jade of Durham. Estelle. Dr. Spacetoad. That nutjob Joinee Benjamin.

A thousand people I would never ordinarily have met. A thousand people who wanted noth—

Hang on.

Joinee Jade of Durham?

What was it about Joinee Jade of Durham again? What was it about that face? That name? What was it she'd done?

Oh . . . Oh, fuck.

• • •

"Please . . . please!" I begged. "You have to join me! Please!"

The woman was wide-eyed and startled. She shielded her child's ears and tried to walk around me. I turned and gabbled at her as she did so.

"I thought I had a thousand joinees but then I realized that one of them had left Join Me ages ago because she didn't know what it was all about and I forgot to take her picture out of the pile and she's been there the whole time and now I know I've only got 999 joinees and now I need another one really quickly!"

I was in the middle of Zurich, standing on Bahnhof Strasse, holding a big white sign that read JOIN ME SWISS, and I was now responsible for reducing a small child to tears. I still couldn't believe my own idiocy. Joinee Jade! *Why* had I kept her picture in the pile? Why hadn't

I thrown her away? She'd found it easy enough to ditch *me* . . . and what must the person sitting in the seat next to mine on the plane have thought of me? A red-faced, swearing man counting and recounting and re-recounting a huge pile of passport photos and always coming up with and spitting out the same *infuriating* number: 999! Gah! *999!*

I still needed *one joinee!* Success and glory had been unfairly batted out of my hands. I had come to Switzerland to finish this, to bring Gallus his joinees, to end the quest, and just when I'd been on the brink of success, I'd been pushed to the brink of insanity.

"Please!" I yelled at a man in a hat. "Just stop! Just stop for a second!"

"No time," said the man.

"Please! I'm on a flight home tonight . . . I need someone to join me before I can go home! I can't go home without having done this!"

The man said nothing and walked straight by. It was awful.

Five minutes later and things had got so desperate that I was standing by the side of the road, pleading with the motorists stopped by a red light. I tapped on someone's window. They didn't roll it down. They didn't even look at me. This was all getting too much. I'd bought a ticket home for that night. My plan had been to get to Switzerland to deliver my joinees to Gallus and then fly home and fall asleep. I couldn't face the stress and strain of Join Me any more. I needed rest. Recuperation. And most of all, I needed another bloody joinee.

I scoured the street for potential joinees . . . the place was packed with shoppers . . . surely, *surely* one of them would have time for a chat?

"Please, madam, stop . . ."

"I don't speak English," said the lady.

"You quite clearly *do!*" I wailed, my hands in the air, but she was gone.

"Excuse me . . ." I said, to a teenager who walked straight past me.

"Excuse me . . ." I said, to a man who did the same.

"Please . . ." I said, to someone else. "Just give me a second . . ."

Can you imagine the sheer, bloody frustration? No one was listening to my very important message. I was becoming angry. I had to calm down. I had to play this cool. And maybe I had to ditch the sign.

I started to fold it up, but as I did, I heard the voice of an angel, directly behind me . . .

"What does this mean? This 'Join Me Swiss'?"

I froze. Oh my God. Someone was interested. I couldn't blow this. What should I do? Should I play it straight? Or should I wrestle them to the ground and go through their wallet for passport photos.

"Hello . . ." I said, turning round to face a youngish man, in a large brown coat. Did he look like a joiner? It was too early to tell.

"Hello," he said back. "I was just wondering what your sign meant."

"You'll think this sounds odd," I said, in as moderate and casual way as I could. "But I need a Swiss person."

The man smiled.

"What for . . . ?" he said.

• • •

Have you ever been so happy that you went out and bought a man you've only just met a fondue? I have.

I'd thought, a day or two previously, that the moment I got my final joinee would be something of a sad one . . . but it was now utterly joyous. I was so incredibly grateful to Christof for agreeing to join me that now here we were, myself and my thousandth joinee, in Adlers on Hirschen Platz, sharing a big yellow fondue and two cold beers. I don't think I've ever felt so incredibly comfortable, relaxed and rested as I did just then. This time I'd done it. Beyond a shadow of a doubt (though I kept going through the math in my head . . . 999 + 1 . . . yes, that's definitely 1,000), I had achieved my goal.

"Do you understand what this means?" I said, beaming. "Do you have any concept of what you've done?"

"Not really," said Christof. "But I'm glad I've done it!"

What a brilliant joinee. If I'd thought to bring a party popper, believe me, I'd have popped it there and then. And before you ask, Joinee 1000 is an opera singer. He attends Zurich University. He enjoys tennis. Each of these facts I adored, not because I adore opera, or university, or tennis, but because this man, this brown-eyed, brown-haired, brown-coated man, was my savior. His photo was in the box with the others. And, at the end of the meal, he walked me up Bahnhof Strasse, to the station, and helped me to find a train that would take me near Mosnang, and the end of my journey.

• • •

Sixty minutes later, after I'd watched the fields and villages and toy towns of rural Switzerland chug happily by, I was standing in my great-uncle Gallus's village. It was late afternoon, and cold.

I had the box in my hands. There was no way I was losing sight of it.

I started the walk to the old farmhouse, and suddenly remembered Hanne. I wanted her to know I'd done it. That, despite everything, at least I'd done *this*. I got my phone out and texted her.

I HAVE NEARLY FINISHED! TEN MORE MINUTES! ANY CHANCE OF GETTING BACK TOGETHER AFTER THAT?

As I made my way down my great-uncle's road, her reply arrived.

NICE TRY. X.

Oh well. Hanne had always said that if things got bad between us, she'd dump me somewhere neutral. I just hadn't thought she'd meant Switzerland.

I passed a sleeping cat and found the house. Still unkempt. Still wooden. Still silent. No one had moved in yet, so I felt fine about walking into the rickety wooden toolshed, and finding myself a small shovel.

From there, I climbed over a fence and walked on, into one of my great-uncle's now neglected fields.

This, I suppose, is where he'd have put his hundred joinees. The hundred people he'd wanted to live on his land. The hundred people he'd never got.

I walked, for a couple of hundred yards or so, and found a suitable spot. I dug a hole.

I wrapped my box of passport photos in a plastic bag, and I laid it carefully in the ground.

I covered it up, patted the earth down, and smiled.

"There you go, Gallus," I said. "All of them. One joinee for every man, woman and child in your village. They've all joined you."

I stood up.

"We did it."

I looked around for someone to be proud in front of, but I was alone.

There was a perfect silence.

JOIN US
JOIN us

CHAPTER · 27

KARMAGEDDON

> ***11.*** *And Daniel said, Peradventure shall Join Me be called instead Join Him.*

Four weeks later, on a cold December afternoon, I was standing at the bottom of Oxford Street, in a light rain, awaiting my joinees.

I had called a meeting.

Our first.

A Join Me-et, if you will.

Or "Karmageddon 1," if you won't.

At 2 P.M. precisely, I raised a sign above my head. I wonder if you can guess what it said.

I had no real idea of who would turn up that day, of who would brave the weather just to come along and say hello to some bloke most of them had never met—the bloke they'd called their Leader.

I soon would.

"Hello Danny," said a voice to my right. I turned around. All seven of the Newcastle boys had turned up. Each wore a "Join Us" T-shirt, and a smile. Their Greek tans had faded somewhat, and they were soaked through, but here they were! After a seven-hour journey! I was touched.

"Hey!" I said, delighted. "You came!"

"Wouldn't have missed it, mate," said Patrick, and I wanted to hug him, but I didn't get the chance. Joinees Jonesy and Cobbett were suddenly there. Then Joinee Gaz arrived, fresh off the coach from Oxford.

Joinee Glanville followed moments after, with his mum, who'd brought a passport photo and wanted to join too. Then Joinee Whitby turned up, with Joinees Jess and Jenni. The Vis à Vis boys jumped off a bus to be there, and soon I was utterly surrounded by joinees, new and old.

I was tap-tapped on the shoulder and turned around.

"Hello, Danny," said a man with a goatee beard and an accent. "I'm Wilfried. I got the e-mail you sent out. I came from Belgium to be here."

My God. A man I'd never met before—a perfect stranger—had travelled *all the way from Belgium* just to say hello to his fellow joinees.

"And you said in your invite that you would buy everyone a beer, too," he said.

Bloody Belgians.

Soon more joinees were upon us. Joinees from Devon. Two from Scotland. Three from Manchester. Dozens of others.

Thrilled, I led my people on a march up Oxford Street, spreading good karma, handing out fliers, and doing random good deeds for complete strangers, until Great Portland Street, where we found the Horse & Groom, in many ways the spiritual home of Join Me. I'd booked the function room, put some money behind the bar, and within an hour there were fifty of us, laughing, joking, making new friends.

"Someone's just told me this is some kind of cult thing," said the worried-looking woman responsible for hiring me the room. I'd grown weary of calling Join Me a collective by now. I reasoned it was time to call a cult a cult.

"Yes, it is," I said. "In fact, it's a suicide cult. This will be our first and, indeed, our last meeting."

At 4 P.M., the Vis à Vis boys, wearing two "Official Join Me Band" T-shirts I'd had made for them, got their instruments out, and I sang, quite badly, the official Join Me song. The barman, Mark, looked very confused by what he was now witnessing. I cleared my throat, welcomed my joinees . . . and then prepared to tell them the news. The news I'd spent the last few weeks deliberating over.

"My joinees . . ." I said. "My people. My proud and noble warriors of goodness."

I looked around the room. Happy faces, crowded around pub tables.

"I . . . have something to tell you. It's not an easy thing for me to say, and I wish I didn't feel I had to say it, but believe me . . . I feel I do. It concerns the future of Join Me . . . and . . . well . . . my place in it . . ."

A few of the happy faces had slowly turned into strangely serious ones. I noticed Joinee Jones swap a concerned glance with one of the Newcastle lads, but I continued . . .

"The Karma Army has exceeded my expectations in so many ways. It took over my life for a while, and that was a wonderful thing, but on this day, the day of our first-ever meeting, well . . . I . . ."

There was total silence. I took a deep breath, looked to the ceiling, and said it . . .

"I am resigning as Leader of Join Me."

Gasps. A shocked, shouted whisper of *"What?"* Even Mark the barman looked surprised.

"The thing is," I said, "I never asked to be Leader. It was never a title I *earned*. You lot just started calling me that. And I suppose I got carried away with the power. I let it take over my world. But think about it . . . this has been a dictatorship all along. I was never *elected* Leader. I never *deserved* to be Leader. And you know what? There's someone here today who *does* deserve it. He deserves to be Leader far more than I do . . ."

The joinees looked around. They looked confused. Who was I talking about?

"I'm talking about Joinee Whitby."

Joinee Whitby—once my most feared nemesis—was shocked and pale. All eyes were suddenly upon him. He didn't know what to say. But I did.

"Joinee Whitby is a good man. A man willing to put the effort in. When I feared he was out to take Join Me away from me, I was spurred on to greater things. Without my having to ask him, he made badges, and posters, and he even tried to paint a small child's face with the words 'Join Me.' All while I faffed around, not really knowing what I was doing or where I was headed. I want to give Join Me to him. I want *him* to lead you. But I also understand that by doing that, this will still be a dictatorship of sorts. So . . . I've prepared ballot papers . . ."

As I said this, ballot papers and pens were handed out among my still stunned joinees.

". . . I want you to think very carefully, joinees, and vote for who you think should be the Leader . . . I know you know less about him than you do me, but seriously. Joinee Whitby is a good person. You're *all* good people. You put your trust in something that most of you knew nothing about. You took pleasure in doing your random acts of kindness. There are now just over a thousand of us . . . that's a thousand random good deeds each and every week that would probably never have happened . . . fifty-two thousand of them a year, and growing, and just because of *us!*"

It was precisely what they needed to hear. They let out a huge cheer, and broke into applause, and glasses were clinked, and a few people slapped each other on the back. The warmth in the room was now amazing. Maybe it was because I was standing right in front of the fireplace. Or maybe it was because these people—my people—exuded it. As the applause died down, I spoke, quietly . . .

"The one thing I've learned from this whole adventure is that people in general are essentially good. They're nice. It's not like it seems in the papers. Everyone talks about improving the world, and how we could make it a better place. But really . . . this is a *good* world, and maybe all we've got to do to make it a better place is realize that."

Maybe I'd pushed it too far with that last bit, because one or two faces in the crowd had started to turn green, so I decided to ditch the *Dawson's Creek*-isms and get on with the real business of the day . . .

"Anyway, that's all I wanted to say. Think about this carefully. The Karma Army lives on, all around the world. But it's up to *you* how it does that."

I looked in as many eyes as I could.

"Cast your votes now . . ."

On cue, the band started to play the theme tune from *Countdown,* and I sat down on one of the large leather sofas next to the fireplace, slightly nervous. I looked up to see Joinee Whitby, leaning against the wall, looking just as nervous. We smiled at each other, and I gave him a little thumbs-up.

In my last official act as Leader that afternoon, I had asked Joinee Bond to be the official ballot security, as he had once been a security guard at a Tesco supermarket in Preston, and was thus the closest thing we had to a policeman.

I had given my joinees the chance to vote me out and start afresh. To begin again, with a new, exciting Leader—one who actually looked like he knew what he was doing. It would give Join Me a new direction. A new sense of momentum. And it would give me a little time, to recall Hanne's words, to "Stop acting like a fucking nutjob." It was a chance I thought my joinees deserved. I hadn't made the decision lightly. After I'd returned from Switzerland, people had continued to join me, and I realized I had to make a choice. Continue with Join Me, or continue with the rest of my life.

"Good luck," said Joinee Jonesy. "I voted for you."

"Thanks," I said.

I looked into my pint. Part of me still really wanted to be involved in all this, no matter how much work it'd be. Part of me still really wanted to be able to make decisions. To lead the people who'd joined me. To always be the Leader. But in my heart I knew I had to do this. Ten minutes later, Joinee Bond was back with the results.

"The votes have been counted," he announced, with incredible Mancunian gravitas. "It has been a very close-run election."

Close-run. Jeez. I felt a pang of emotion. Was this right? What was I doing? Did I really want to give this away? This is mine . . . this *was* mine . . .

"I have counted the votes myself, and they have also been counted by an independent body—Mark, the barman."

I looked over at Mark the barman. His eyes were giving nothing away. He wasn't even looking at me. Had I lost? Had I given my collective away? Had I made what I would come to see as a terrible mistake? Had I worked to get a thousand joinees just so I could take my place among them? Was this *really* for the best . . . ?

"With the largest share of the vote . . ."

Uh-oh . . .

"I am proud to say . . ."

Deep breath.

"Your Leader is . . ."

CHAPTER · 28

Dear Danny,

Please find enclosed my passport-sized photograph. I suppose if I can't beat you, the least I can do is join you . . .

Love,
Hanne

P.S. I heard you won the election. Well done. I still think there's something very wrong with you, though. xx

ST. JAMES'S PALACE
LONDON SW1A 1BS

From: The Office of HRH The Prince of Wales

4th February, 2003

Dear Mr. Wallace,

His Royal Highness applauds the initiative taken to establish 'Join Me' and is thrilled that so many good deeds have been done as a result. The Prince of Wales believes very strongly that the world in which we live can only become a safer and more united place if we all make the effort to tolerate, accept and understand each other. His Royal Highness is, therefore, not surprised that the world is a better place because of the work of Joinees.

The Prince of Wales congratulates all Joinees for their good deeds so far and has asked me to send his very best wishes for future acts of kindness.

Yours sincerely,

Mrs. Claudia Holloway

Danny Wallace, Esq.

EPILOGUE

28. *And here shall be an end.*

29. *Or shall there be?*

Well.

There we have it.

And here I am.

In the arrivals lounge of John F. Kennedy International airport, in New York, in a café, sipping a coffee.

And in five minutes or so, once I've caught my breath and worked out where I am and wiped the coffee off my laptop, I will find myself a taxi, get in it, and ask to be taken to Manhattan.

I hope my first American joinee will be pleased to see me.

I hope he'll be proud to be the very first member of what the world will come to know as the American Karma Army (aka AKA).

And most of all, I hope he keeps proper tea bags in his kitchen, because it's been the best part of a day, and I'm bloody *dying* for a cup.

Whatever happens in the next day or so, I think together, my American joinee and I will be able to make a difference over here.

Whether it's the smallest difference to a stranger's afternoon, or the biggest difference to a stranger's entire *life* . . . we'll do *something.*

And you know what? I can't wait.

I've already made some notes, in fact.

I have noticed, for example, that you lot tend to have a fascination with that whole "Zero Tolerance" thing.

My message to you?

Maximum Tolerance.

I think that together we can do it. Together, we can tidy up the Americas, just like I wrote in my ad.

I hope to use my time here productively. I hope that, when I leave, the word of Join Me will be spreading far and wide. I hope I will find joinees in every town and city across the States, from Vicarkicker, Arkansas, to Tupperware, Alaska.

And most of all, I hope that by the time you finish reading this sentence, you will have already decided that you—yes, you—want to Join Me.

You may have reached the end of this book, but you haven't reached the end of this story. This is just the beginning of the adventure. And I'd like you to be a part of it from now on.

But I should get going.

Before I wave JFK good-bye and find myself that cab, though, there are a few things I thought you might like to know . . .

As you may have worked out from Hanne's letter, I was indeed officially elected the Leader of Join Me, that day in the pub. I was delighted. A majority of approximately ninety-eight percent sealed my victory, and the first thing I did was promote Joinee Whitby to Gold Joinee. Partly in recognition of his sterling efforts in the name of the Cause, and partly because he only got two percent of the vote and I felt guilty.

But since part one of my adventure ended, I am pleased to report that people have continued to Join Me in their droves. The current number of joinees stands at 3,314. Nearly two hundred thousand random acts of kindness have so far been undertaken in the name of the Karma Army.

And you have no idea how much that makes me smile.

The World Kindness Organization (WKO), based in Singapore, is currently considering an application to make the Karma Army the official kindness movement for the UK and Europe.

I'm rather frightened by that, mainly because if it happened, they'd make me wear a tie and speak at important functions in Japan in front of "proper" people.

Joinee Spacetoad's arm made a full recovery, and he is now back to busking on the streets of Paris.

The Bruges Ambassadors scheme is now up and running, and is a huge success.

The money raised in 2002–03 and 2003–04 for The Raymond Price Fund For Keeping Raymond Price Out Of Trouble was donated to Help the Aged.

We are currently accepting donations for 2004–05.

The bet between Joinees Jonesy and Cobbett as to whether or not Cobbett could visit a pub next to every tube station in zones one and two of the London Underground was eventually won by Joinee Cobbett. He was photographed with a pint in hand in no less than 134 pubs.

What a night that must've been.

The marvelous Dennis M. Hope wrote to me to congratulate me on the completion of my quest.

Dennis continues to gather his own collective together with the aim of travelling to the Moon and setting up a human colony based on equality and fair play. If you would like to join him—and I urge you to do so—then visit *www.lunarembassy.org*.

It is thought that such an initiative will eliminate all human indecency and create a sociological event that will be talked of for millennia.

Copycat.

• • •

In late January 2003, I received, completely out of the blue, a letter from 10 Downing Street. A lady called Melissa Chowdhury was writing on behalf of Prime Minister Tony Blair.

"Mr. Blair has asked me," it said simply, "to send his good wishes to all those involved with 'Join Me.' "

I have absolutely *no idea* how Tony Blair heard about Join Me, or what prompted him to write. But I thought it was lovely.

More shockingly, a few days after that, I received another letter in the post . . . this one from none other than Prince Charles himself!

Charles had dictated a letter saying that he applauds the world of Join Me, and wanted to extend his warmest wishes to all joinees.

He said: "The world is a better place because of the work of Joinees."

The only possible explanation for this is that at some fancy do or other, Tony Blair took Prince Charles to one side and told him all about the Karma Army.

Nice one, Tony!

• • •

An executive from the BBC has asked me if I want to make a TV documentary series about my joinees.

Someone from film legend Jerry Bruckheimer's office requested a meeting, with a view to creating some kind of Hollywood blockbuster out of the Join Me adventure.

I am slightly annoyed, therefore, that I didn't embroil myself in more explosions along the way, and am regretful that I never thought to employ a streetwise, comical black sidekick, who could have accompanied me on my travels, and made smart comments whenever I looked a bit grumpy.

Oh well. You live and learn.

The Vis à Vis boys—Christopher and Wayne—are currently composing a rock musical based on the Join Me story. A concept album is currently underway, with tracks including "The Ballad of Danny & Hanne," "Song of the Happy Old Man" and "Shit! I Forgot My Dog Collar!"

Sales of butter in Poland are up eleven percent.

The word of Join Me has continued to spread far and wide.

The work of the Karma Army has been featured in every major British newspaper and radio station, and in my duties as Leader I have been invited onto nearly every major British TV chat show, where I have done my best to confuse and bewilder a series of concerned-looking hosts with my tales of accidental international goodwill.

And it *has* become truly international, with journalists phoning me from Hungary, Spain, the Czech Republic, Italy, Germany, France, Denmark, Sweden, Australia, China, Malaysia, Singapore and even Colombia. As a result, small collectives of joinees have started to spring up all over the world, from Provence to Puerto Rico . . . and that makes me very happy indeed. But then, that's the Joy of Sects, I suppose.

I have been back to my great-uncle Gallus's grave, in Switzerland, to update him on all the gossip and goings-on from Join Me HQ.

I don't know whether he can hear me, but I like to think he can.

And, since you're probably wondering . . . no, Hanne and me never did get back together.

We do, however, remain the very best of friends.

Oh, and one last thing . . . Raymond Price is still at large.

If you meet the old devil, say hello from me.

Anyway. I've got a taxi to catch. Wish me luck.

And remember: make every Friday a Good Friday . . .

Danny Wallace

AND · FINALLY . . .

If you would like to join the American Karma Army and sign the Good Fridays Agreement in order to undertake random acts of kindness each and every Friday, send one passport-sized photograph to:

Join Me
P.O. Box 33561
London, E3 2YW
UK

Or check out the website, at *www.joinmeusa.com*—I'll see you in there!

And I'll be back in the USA soon, for my very own Second Coming! Bye!

Danny would like to thank . . .

Ryan Harbage and everyone at Plume, Jake Lingwood and the lovely people at Ebury (especially Stine Smemo), Simon Trewin, Claire Scott, Sarah Ballard, Sophie Laurimore, Jago Irwin, and all at PFD, Daniel Greenberg, Hanne Knudsen for her patience, Greta McMahon for reading it first, the very nice Dennis M. Hope, Bob Glanville, Banks & Wag, Jon Primrose, Dave Gorman, Ian Collins, Belgium, my mum and dad, Gallus Breitenmoser, and everyone who joined me . . . my first thousand joinees especially. You're all great.